# Origami Symphony No. 6

*Striped Snakes Changing Scales*

Books by John Montroll
www.johnmontroll.com
Instagram: @montrollorigami

## Origami Symphonies

*Origami Symphony No. 1: The Elephant's Trumpet Call*
*Origami Symphony No. 2: Trio of Sharks & Playful Prehistoric Mammals*
*Origami Symphony No. 3: Duet of Majestic Dragons & Dinosaurs*
*Origami Symphony No. 4: Capturing Vibrant Coral Reef Fish*
*Origami Symphony No. 5: Woodwinds, Horns, and a Moose*
*Origami Symphony No. 6: Striped Snakes Changing Scales*

## General Origami

*Origami Fold-by-Fold*
*DC Super Heroes Origami*
*Origami Worldwide*
*Teach Yourself Origami: Second Revised Edition*
*Christmas Origami: Second Edition*
*Storytime Origami*
*Origami Inside-Out: Third Edition*

## Animal Origami

*Dogs in Origami*
*Perfect Pets Origami*
*Dragons and Other Fantastic Creatures in Origami*
*Bugs in Origami*
*Horses in Origami*
*Origami Birds*
*Origami Gone Wild*
*Dinosaur Origami*
*Origami Dinosaurs for Beginners*
*Prehistoric Origami: Dinosaurs and other Creatures: Third Edition*
*Mythological Creatures and the Chinese Zodiac Origami*
*Origami Under the Sea*
*Sea Creatures in Origami*
*Origami Sea Life: Third Edition*
*Bringing Origami to Life: Second Edition*
*Bugs and Birds in Origami*
*Origami Sculptures: Fourth Edition*
*African Animals in Origami: Third Edition*
*North American Animals in Origami: Third Edition*

## Geometric Origami

*Origami Stars*
*Galaxy of Origami Stars: Second Edition*
*Origami and Math: Simple to Complex: Second Edition*
*Origami & Geometry*
*3D Origami Platonic Solids & More: Second Edition*
*3D Origami Diamonds*
*3D Origami Antidiamonds*
*3D Origami Pyramids*
*A Plethora of Polyhedra in Origami: Third Edition*
*Classic Polyhedra Origami*
*A Constellation of Origami Polyhedra*
*Origami Polyhedra Design*

## Dollar Bill Origami

*Dollar Origami Treasures: Second Edition*
*Dollar Bill Animals in Origami: Second Revised Edition*
*Dollar Bill Origami*
*Easy Dollar Bill Origami*

## Simple Origami

*Fun and Simple Origami: 101 Easy-to-Fold Projects: Second Edition*
*Super Simple Origami*
*Easy Dollar Bill Origami*
*Easy Origami Animals*
*Easy Origami Polar Animals*
*Easy Origami Ocean Animals*
*Easy Origami Woodland Animals*
*Easy Origami Jungle Animals*
*Meditative Origami*

# Origami Symphony No. 6

## Striped Snakes Changing Scales

Antroll Publishing Company

John Montroll

*To Kimmy*

Origami Symphony No. 6: *Striped Snakes Changing Scales*

ISBN-10: 1-877656-56-9
ISBN-13: 978-1-877656-56-9

Antroll Publishing Company

# Introduction

Welcome to the premier of the Sixth Origami Symphony! Striped snakes with color-change tetrahedra and pyramids combine with jungle and desert scenes to show the variety of origami. The snakes unify the symphony, as they would fit well in the jungle, desert or scenes with pyramids.

The symphony begins with theme and variation on snakes, and plenty of striped snakes with varied patterns abound. The second movement of favorite jungle animals includes an Oxpecker to take rides on a Rhino and other large mammals. Great care is taken to keep these models on the easier side. The minuet of eight color-change tetrahedra with a trio of pyramids adds interesting ideas with three-dimensional shapes. The desert models of the fourth movement include a Roadrunner, Chameleon and Iguana, Dromedary and Camel and end with a complex Scorpion.

The 38 models of this symphony can each be folded from one square sheet of standard origami paper. The models are designed to be able to hold well without spreading or unfolding. By curling the striped snakes, their layers stay together, and the tetrahedra and pyramids use locking techniques.

The diagrams are drawn in the internationally approved Randlett-Yoshizawa style. You can use any kind of square paper for these models, but the best results will be achieved with standard origami paper, which is colored on one side and white on the other (in the diagrams in this book, the shading represents the colored side). Large sheets, such as nine square inches,†are easier to use than small ones.

Origami supplies can be found in arts and craft shops, or at Dover Publications online: www.doverpublications.com. You can also visit OrigamiUSA at www.origamiusa.org for origami supplies and other related information including an extensive list of local, national, and international origami groups.

Please follow me on Instagram @montrollorigami to see posts of my origami.

I thank my editor, Charley Montroll. I also thank the many folders who continued to encourage me to develop the presentation of origami through an origami symphony.

I hope you enjoy Origami Symphony No. 6.

John Montroll
www.johnmontroll.com

# Contents

★ Simple
★★ Intermediate
★★★ Complex
★★★★ Very Complex

## First Movement
## Allegro: Theme and Variation on Snakes

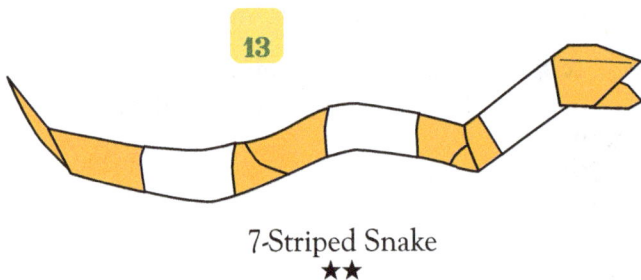

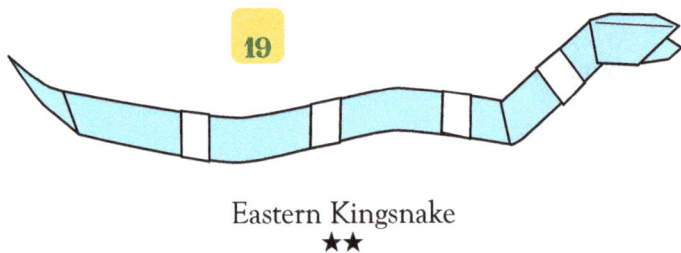

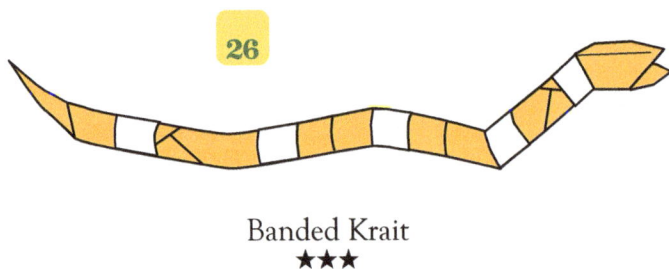

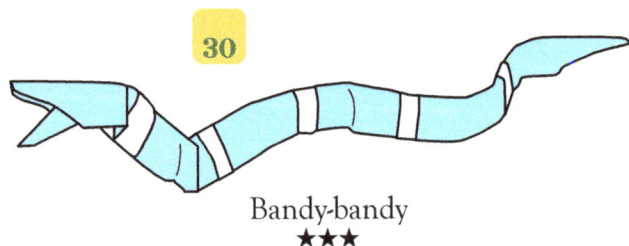

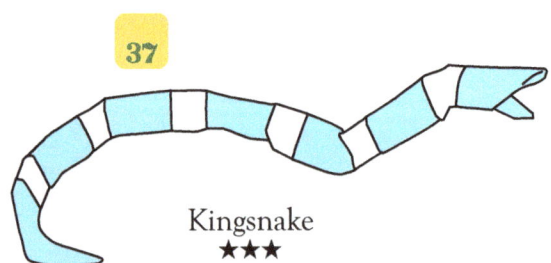

**11**

Simple Snake
★★

**13**

7-Striped Snake
★★

**16**

9-Striped Snake
★★

**19**

Eastern Kingsnake
★★

**22**

11-Striped Snake
★★★

**26**

Banded Krait
★★★

**30**

Bandy-bandy
★★★

**34**

13-Striped Snake
★★★

**37**

Kingsnake
★★★

## Second Movement
## Andante: Frolicking in the Jungle

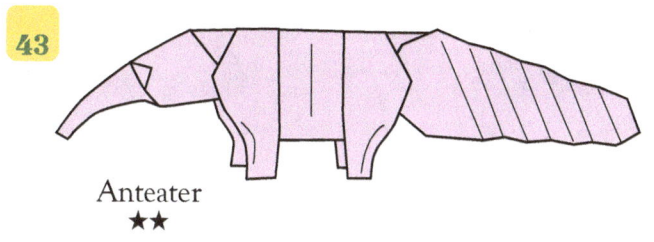

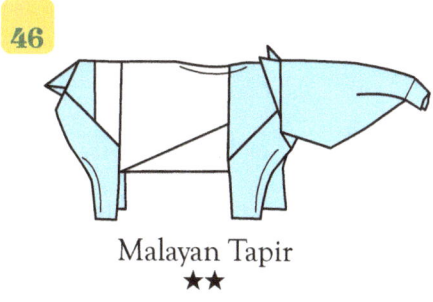

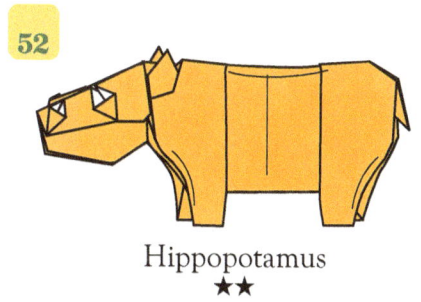

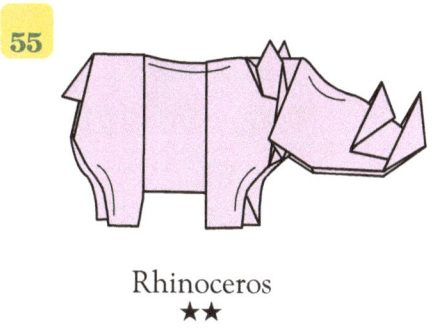

**40**

Lion
★★

**43**

Anteater
★★

**46**

Malayan Tapir
★★

**49**

Hippo with Mouth
★★

**52**

Hippopotamus
★★

**55**

Rhinoceros
★★

**58**

Oxpecker
★★

**61**

Elephant
★★

**64**

Giraffe
★★

**67**

Okapi
★★

## Third Movement
## Minuet: An Octet of Colorful
##         Tetrahedra with a
##         Trio of Grand Pyramids

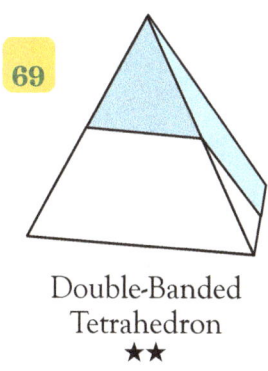

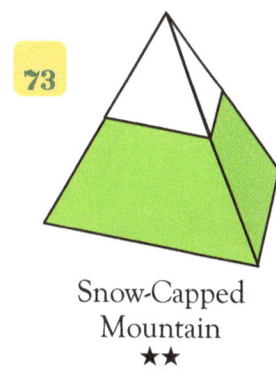

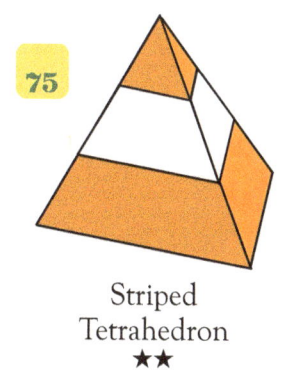

**69**

Double-Banded
Tetrahedron
★★

**71**

Triple-Banded
Tetrahedron
★★

**73**

Snow-Capped
Mountain
★★

**75**

Striped
Tetrahedron
★★

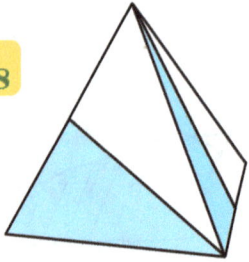

**78**

Radiant
Tetrahedron
★★

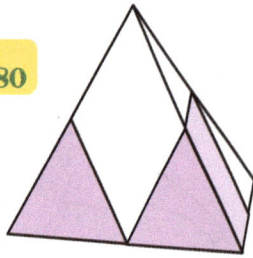

**80**

Tetrahedron
of Diamonds
★★

**82**

Tetrahedron
of Triangles
★★

**85**

Capped
Tetrahedron
★★★

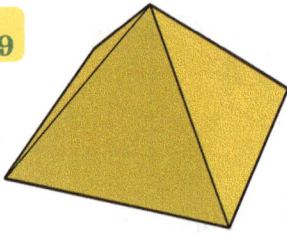

**89**

Great
Pyramid
★★

**92**

Golden
Pentagonal
Pyramid
★★

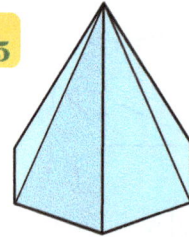

**95**

Hexagonal
Pyramid
★★★

## Fourth Movement
## Allegro: Deep in the Desert

**99**

Saguaro
Cactus
★★

**101**

Roadrunner
★★

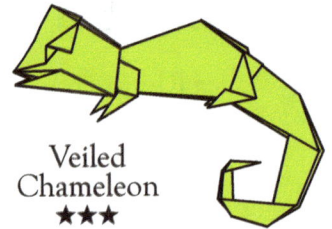

**104**

Veiled
Chameleon
★★★

**108**

Green
Iguana
★★★

**111**

Armadillo
★★

**114**

Dromedary
★★

**118**

Camel
★★

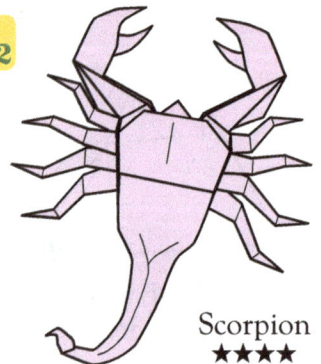

**122**

Scorpion
★★★★

# Symbols

## Lines

- - - - - - - -

Valley fold,
fold in front.

- -- - -- - --

Mountain fold,
fold behind.

————————

Crease line.

· · · · · · · · · · · ·

X-ray or guide line.

## Arrows

Fold in this direction.

Fold behind.

Unfold.

Fold and unfold.

Turn over.

Sink or three dimensional folding.

Place your finger between these layers.

# Origami Design and Math

Origami design is a fascinating topic and it is a personal experience that involves endless possibilities. While math is not essential for design, it can be necessary for certain models.

When working on Origami Symphony No. 5, I thought a striped snake would fit well in the second movement with intermediate models of woodland animals.

As I worked on the striped snakes, I noticed a method by which the stripes could vary while:
1. All the snakes would be the same length.
2. Once the stripes were established, the last few folds would be the same for all.
3. The number of white stripes could vary.
4. The stripes would be equally spaced.
5. The ratio of the white to colored stripes could vary, so the white stripes could be as thin as I wish.

To help with the designs, I wrote a math formula that showed how to divide the square paper, given the number of white stripes and ratio of white to colored stripes. This formula was used to design many snakes, one for Origami Symphony No. 5 and several for this origami symphony.

Math was used for many of the patterned tetrahedra and pyramids. This allowed the models to be folded in a simpler and more elegant manner. Math was also used for some of the animal designs.

Again, while math is not essential for design, there are some pieces that depend on it and the use of math gives more creative control to the designer.

# Origami Symphony No. 6

Origami Symphony No. 6 combines colorful patterns of striped snakes and colorful tetrahedra, along with jungle and desert projects. Great care is taken in the designs for efficiency to offer simplicity in folding complex structures.

Wake up, there's a snake! There are more snakes everywhere! The first movement with Theme and variation on snakes offers plenty of striped snakes and the number of stripes increase while the white stripes vary in thickness, yet all the striped snakes are built on a unified structure so the stripes are of equal thickness, equally spaced, and the snakes are all of the same length. With their open mouths, the snakes come alive.

The second movement, Andante, finds us frolicking in the jungle. Even a first movement snake would fit well in this jungle scene. These models were designed on unified structures. Two Hippo designs are presented, a Rhino with an Oxpecker greet a Lion and Anteater and a colorful Malayan Tapir is spotted by an Elephant. With most of the models under two dozen steps, even the Giraffe at 27 steps shows a simplicity in its complexity. Despite all the steps for the Okapi, it is really only one fold different than the Giraffe design.

The Minuet of colorful tetrahedra take us to a new dimension. Eight tetrahedra with various color-change patterns dazzle us. As one of the easiest of the polyhedron, I challenge you to design your own tetrahedra with interesting patterns. The trio of grand pyramids add complexity and boldness to structures and leads to the fourth movement.

Deep in the Desert, the fourth movement opens with a Saguaro Cactus. The cactus and pyramids add interesting backgrounds to desert scenes, which can, again, also include snakes. A Veiled Chameleon and Green Iguana scamper around while a Roadrunner keeps its distance from the Armadillo. A Dromedary and Camel pair, both under 30 steps, offer another glimpse into related structures. The symphony closes on a high note with a complex Scorpion.

A wealth of styles, structures, and color-change patterns unite the symphony. The theme of simplicity in complexity allows for there to be an underlying life-force to the folded models. I hope you enjoy these origami techniques and discoveries for a long time to come.

# First Movement

## Allegro: Theme and Variation on Snakes

Wake up, snakes abound! From gardens and woodlands to jungles and deserts, striped snakes bring mystery and charm. Adding multiple stripes on snakes creates a magical effect. The stripes are equally-spaced and vary in number and thickness, yet all the striped snakes are the same length when folded from paper of the same size. Fold carefully and be cautious of their hungry mouths.

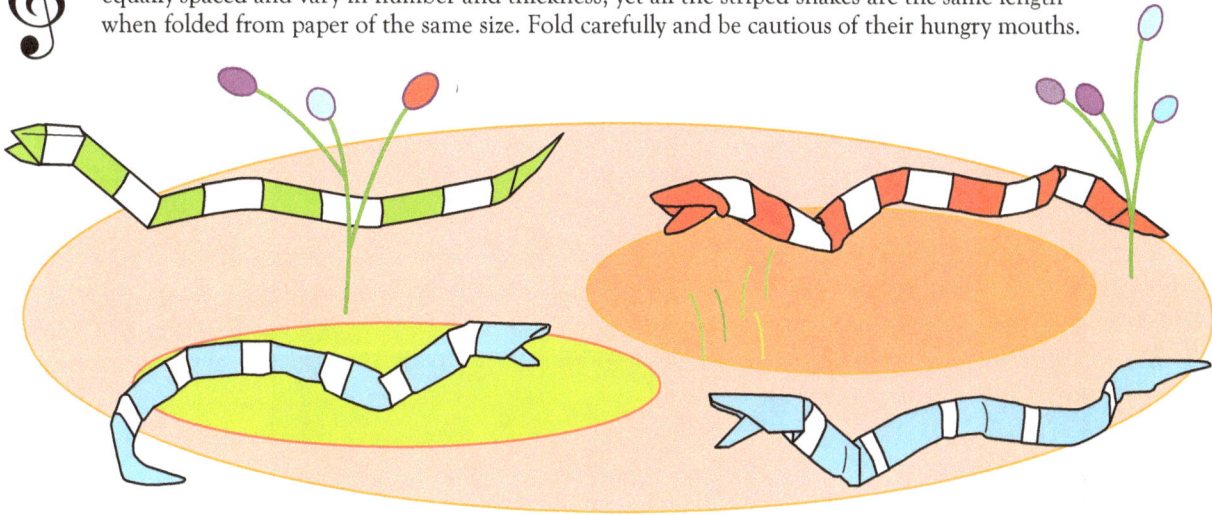

## Simple Snake

These amazing creatures come in all shapes, sizes, colors and attitudes. Some rely on deadly poison for protection, while others make themselves resemble other poisonous varieties while they themselves are harmless. Snakes have always been a source of wonder since the beginning of man and still hold a special place in many cultures, religions, art forms, and stories.

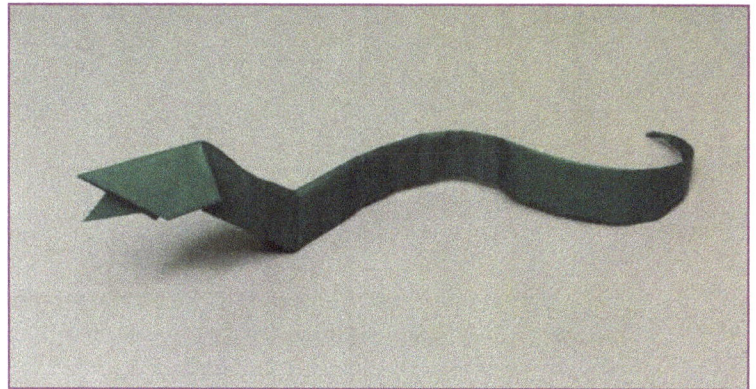

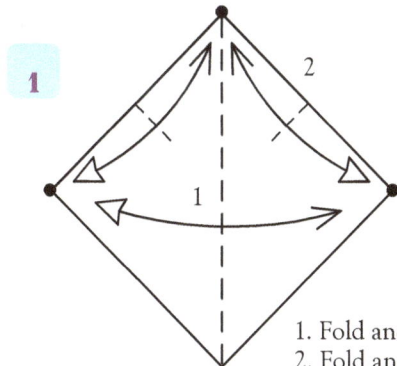

**1**

1. Fold and unfold.
2. Fold and unfold on the edge.

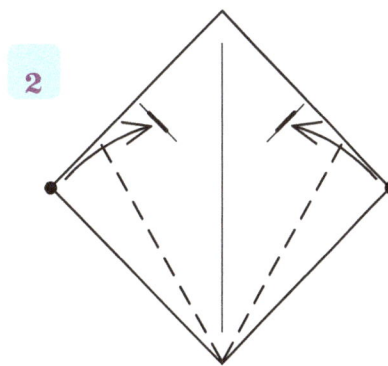

**2**

Bring the dots to the lines.

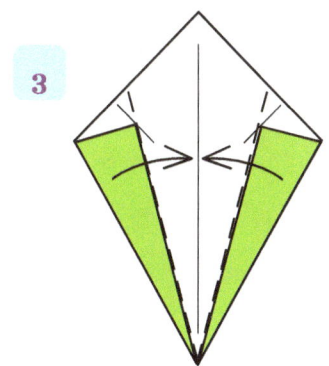

**3**

Fold to the center.

**4**

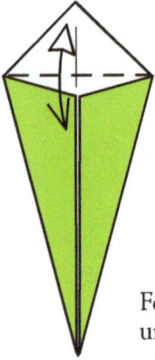

Fold and
unfold.

**5**

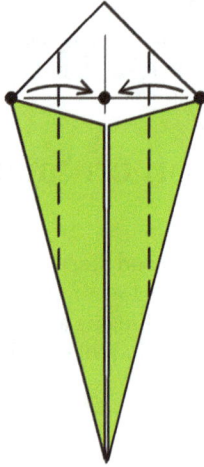

Fold and
unfold.

**6**

Fold and
unfold.

**7**

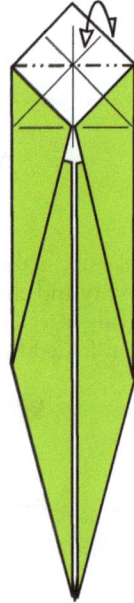

Fold and
unfold.

**8**

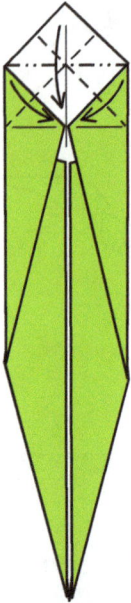

Fold along
the creases.

**9**

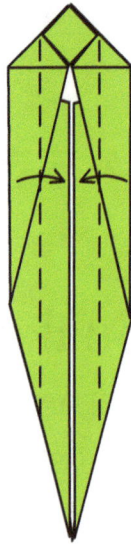

Fold to the
center.

**10**

Fold in half and
rotate 90°.

**11**

Make crimp folds.

**12**

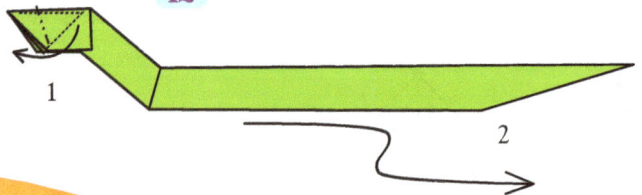

1. Reverse-fold the mouth.
2. Curl the snake.

**13**

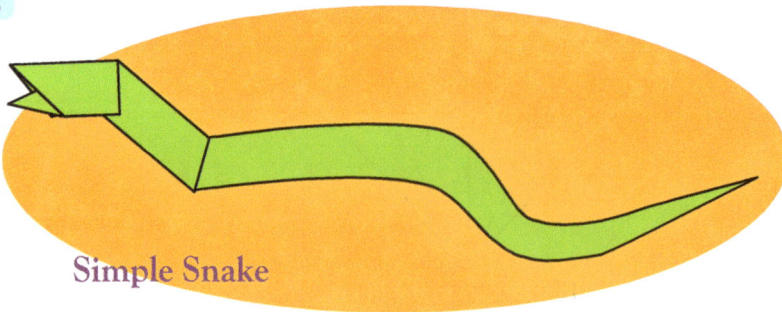

**Simple Snake**

# 7-Striped Snake

For the first striped snake, all the bands are the same length except at the head and tail. The method is similar for the rest of the snakes and the last few steps are the same for all. Using this method, snakes with varied number of stripes are still the same length from paper of the same size.

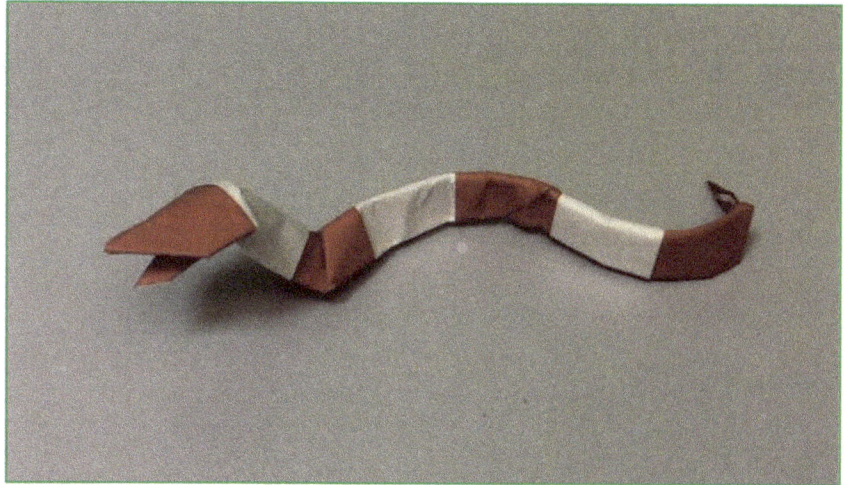

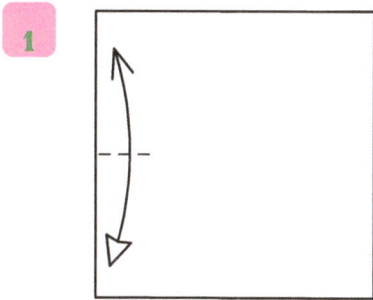

**1**

Fold and unfold on the left.

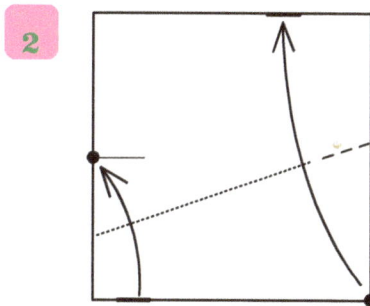

**2**

Bring the lower right corner to the top edge and the bottom edge to the left center. Crease on the right.

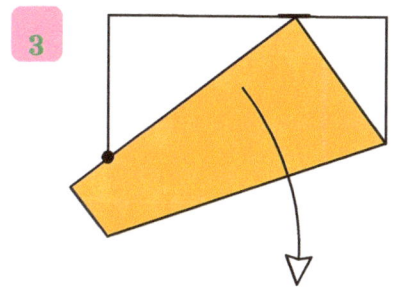

**3**

Unfold and rotate 180°.

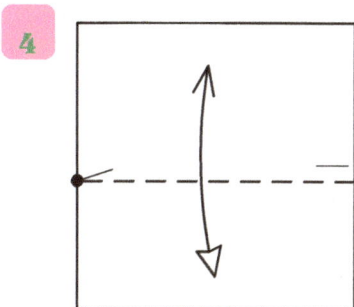

**4**

Fold and unfold.

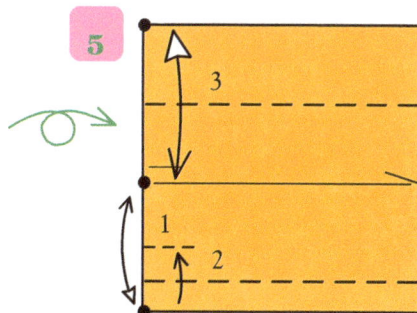

**5**

1. Fold and unfold on the left.
2. Fold up to the mark.
3. Fold and unfold.

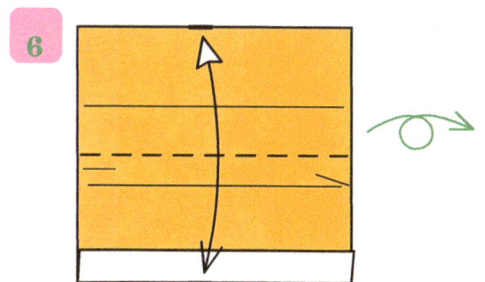

**6**

Fold in half and unfold.

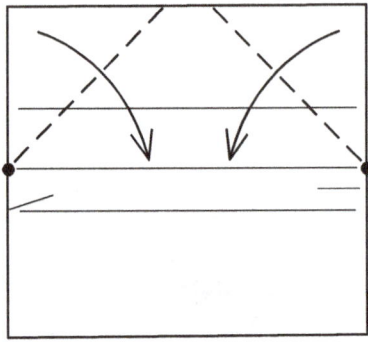

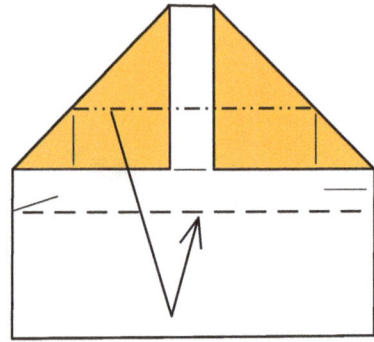

Pleat-fold along the creases.
Mountain-fold along a
partially hidden crease.

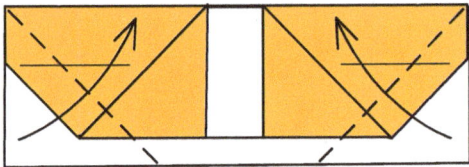

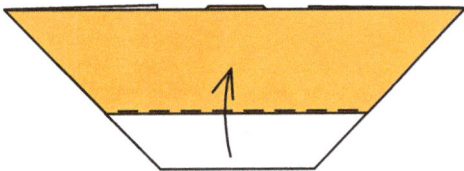

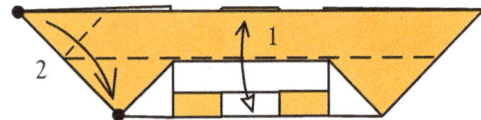

1. Fold and unfold.
2. Valley-fold.

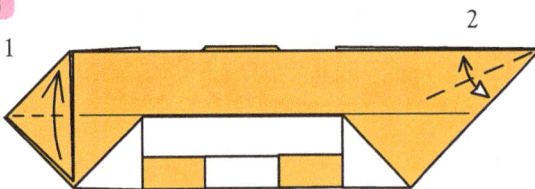

1. Fold up.
2. Fold and unfold.

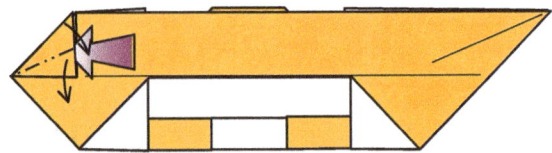

Squash-fold.

**15**

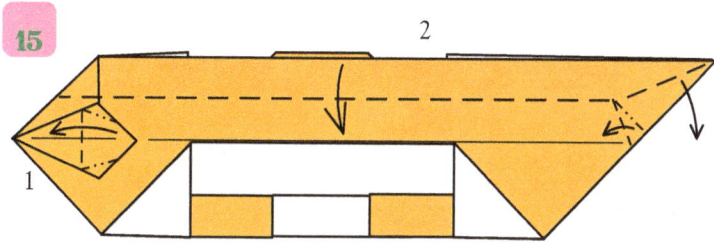

1. Petal-fold.
2. Fold to the center and
   rabbit-ear on the right.

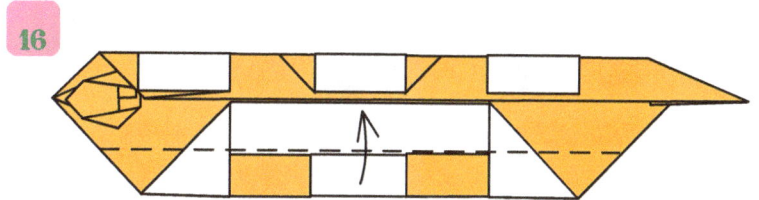

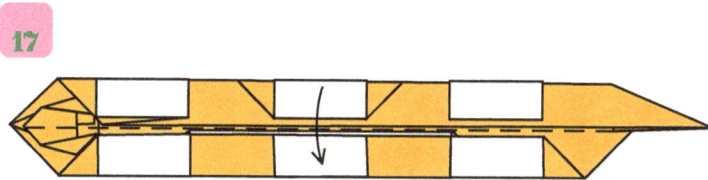

**16**

**17**

Fold in half.

**18**

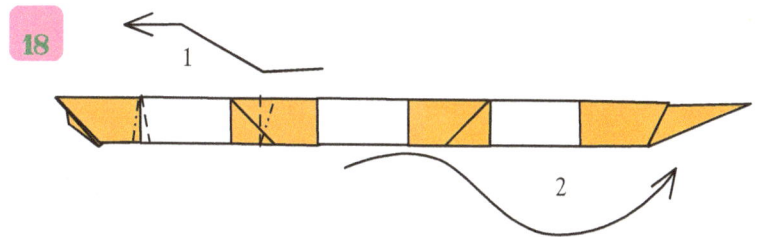

1. Make crimp folds and open the mouth.
2. Curl and shape the snake.
You can shape the snake in many ways.

**19**

7-Striped Snake

# 9-Striped Snake

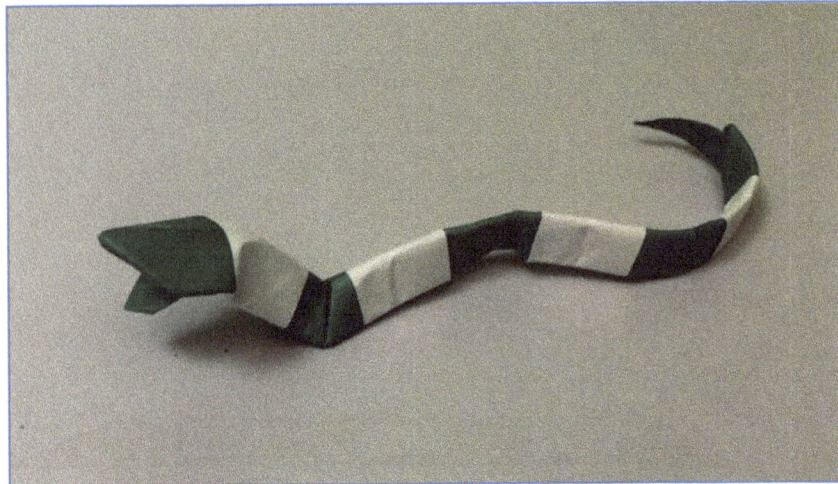

Many striped animals are poisonous or spray toxic chemicals. Creatures know to avoid those with stripes. Even sharks have been known to avoid striped animals. As a universal language, Nature has created stripes to communicate "poison". Some harmless animals have stripes to protect them by scaring their predators.

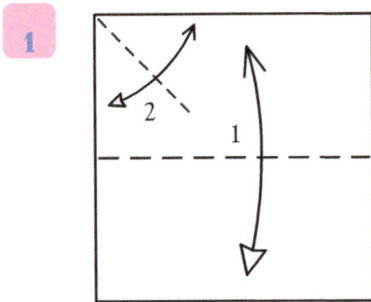

**1**

Fold and unfold
at 1 and 2.

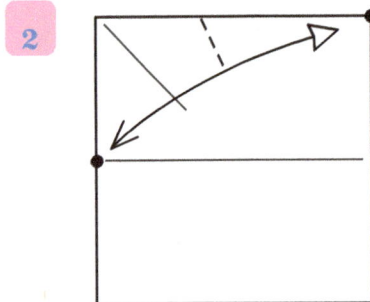

**2**

Fold and unfold on top.

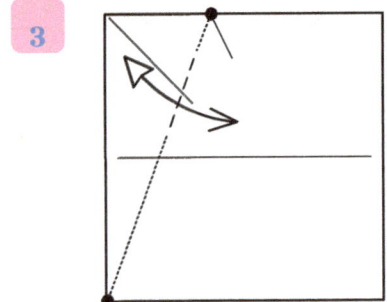

**3**

Fold and unfold along
the intersection.

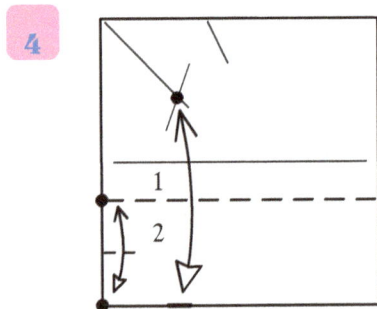

**4**

Fold and unfold twice.

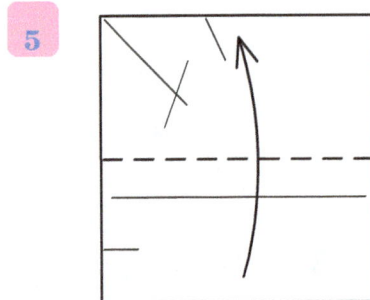

**5**

Fold in half along
the crease.

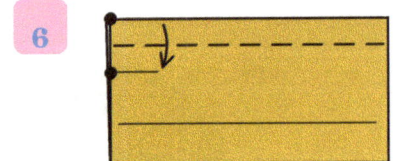

**6**

Repeat behind.

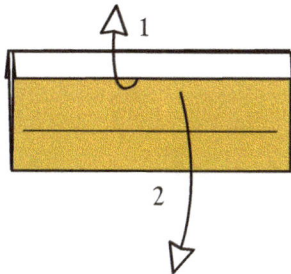

1. Unfold the strip.
2. Unfold from the center.

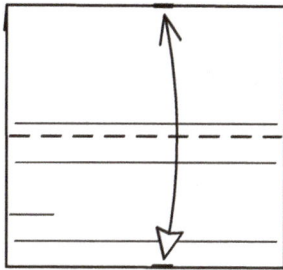

Fold and unfold.

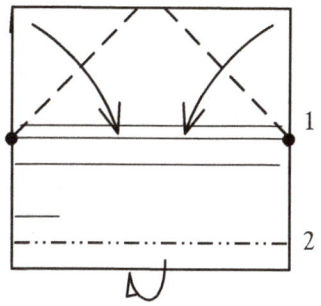

1. Fold to the line.
2. Fold along the crease.

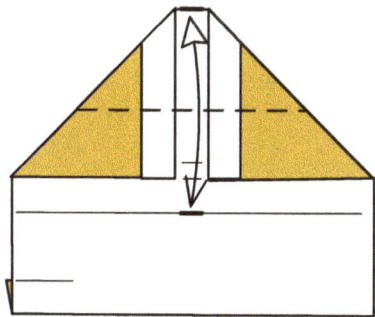

Fold and unfold.

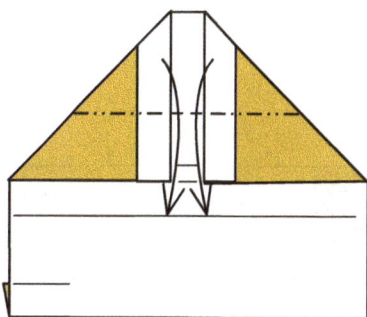

Make reverse folds
along the crease.

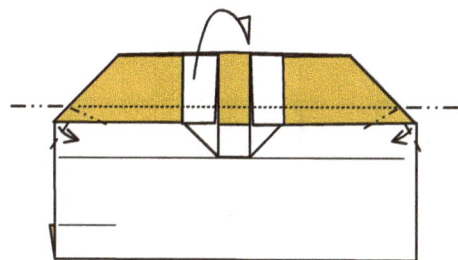

Mountain-fold along a hidden
crease. Make small squash
folds on the left and right.

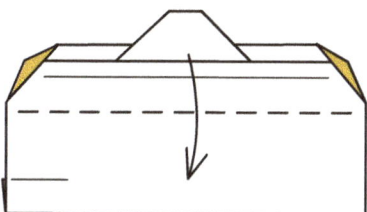

Fold along the crease.

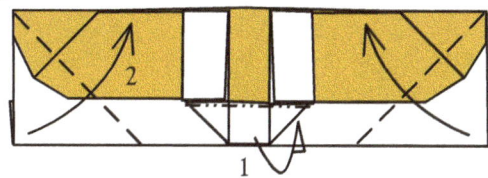

1. Tuck inside.
2. Fold up on the left and right.

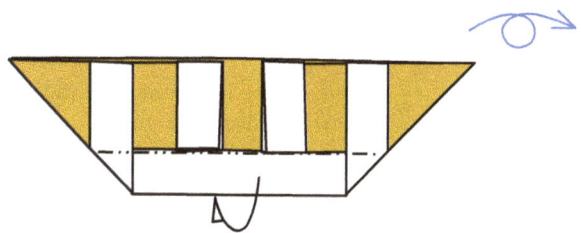

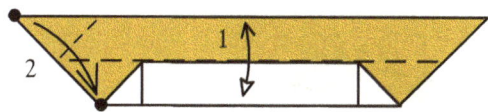

1. Fold and unfold.
2. Valley-fold.

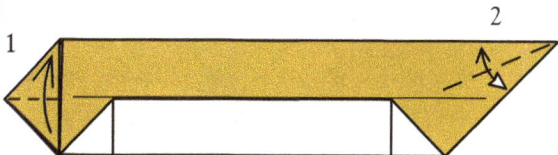

1. Fold up.
2. Fold and unfold.

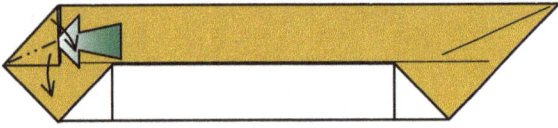

**18**

Squash-fold.

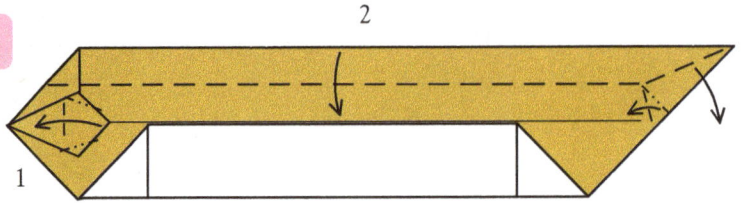

**19**

2

1

1. Petal-fold.
2. Fold to the center and
   rabbit-ear on the right.

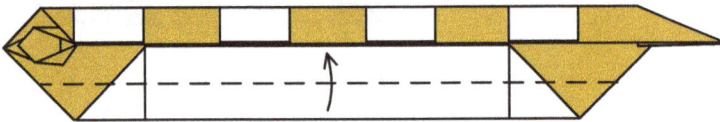

**20**

**21**

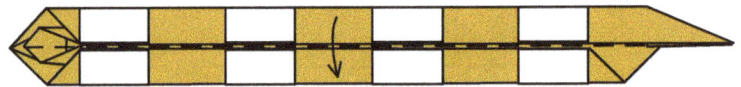

Fold in half.

**22**

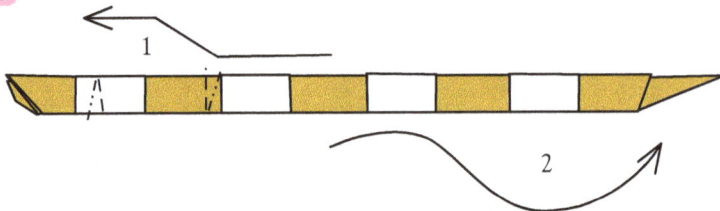

1

2

1. Make crimp folds and open the mouth.
2. Curl and shape the snake.
You can shape the snake in many ways.

**23**

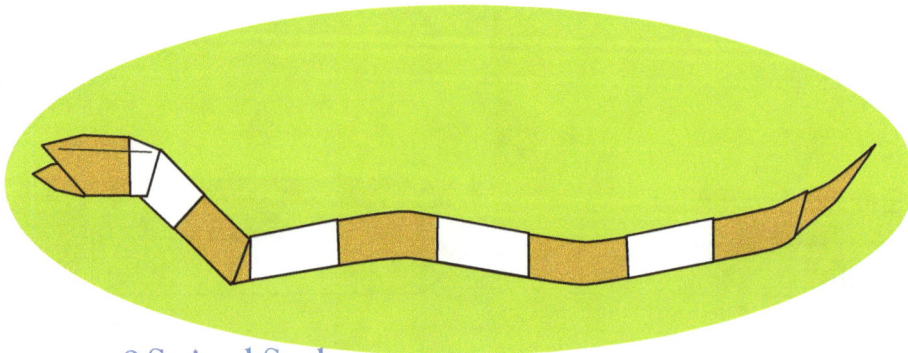

9-Striped Snake

# Eastern Kingnake

These snakes make their habitats in forests, swamps and even suburban areas in the Eastern United States. They are constrictors and are sometimes kept as pets.

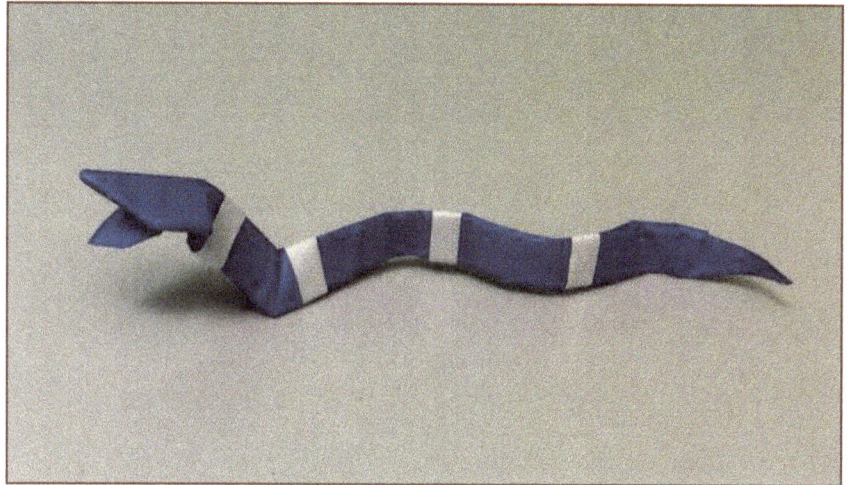

**1**

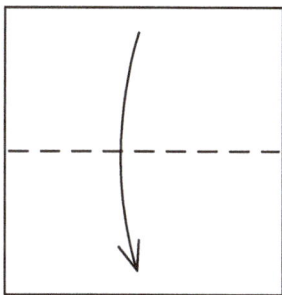

Fold in half.

**2**

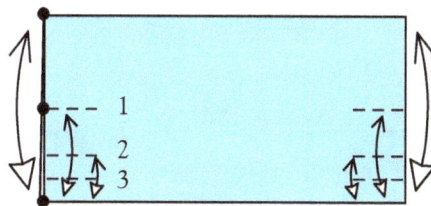

Fold and unfold the top layer three times on the left and right.

**3**

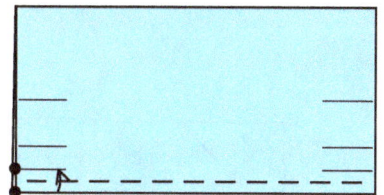

Repeat behind.

**4**

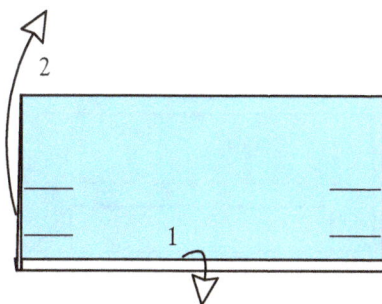

1. Unfold the strip.
2. Unfold from the center.

**5**

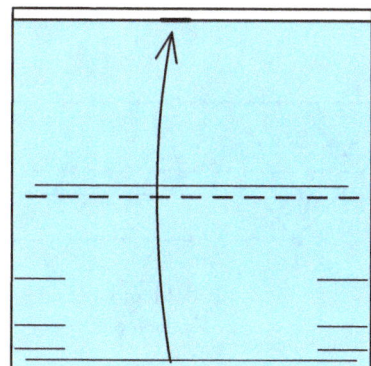

**6**

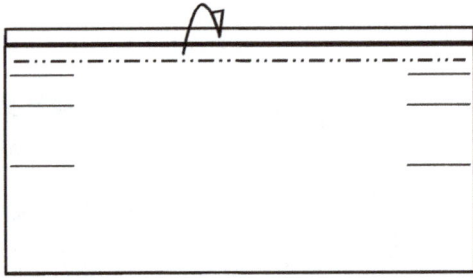

Fold behind along the crease.

**7**

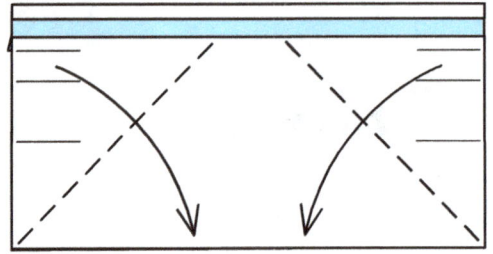

**8**

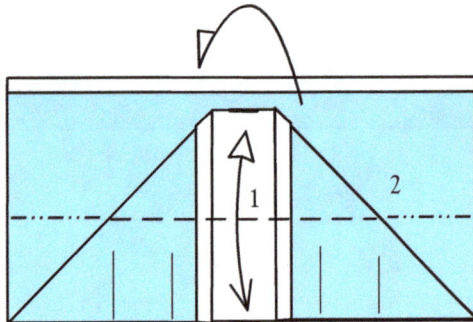

1. Fold and unfold.
2. Fold behind on the same line.

**9**

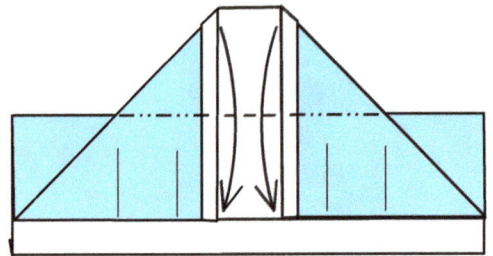

Make reverse folds.

**10**

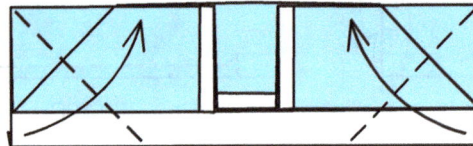

**11**

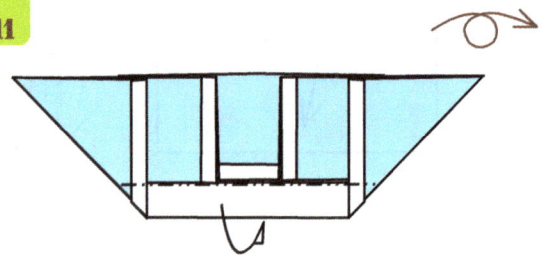

**12**

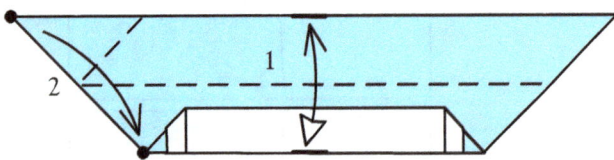

1. Fold and unfold.
2. Valley-fold.

**13**

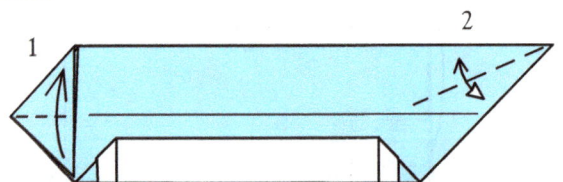

1. Fold up.
2. Fold and unfold.

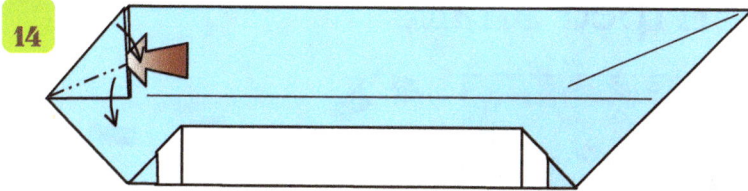

Squash-fold.

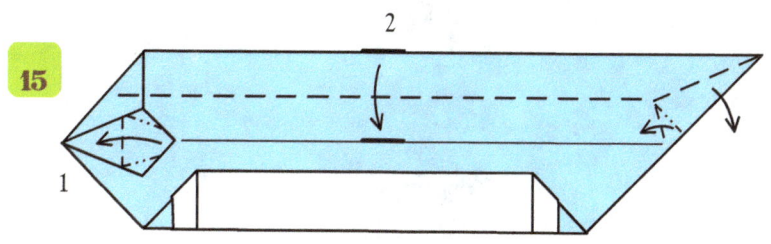

1. Petal-fold.
2. Fold to the center and
   rabbit-ear on the right.

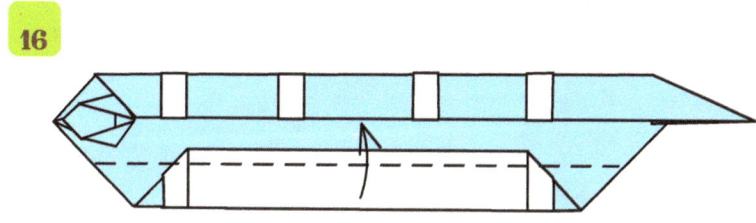

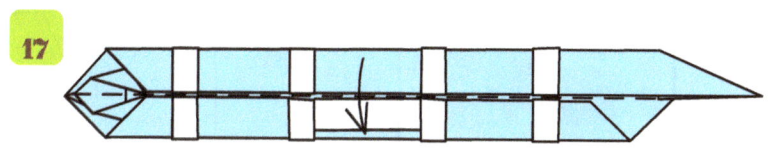

Fold in half.

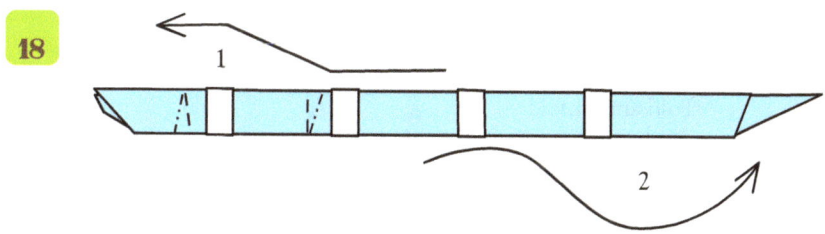

1. Make crimp folds and open the mouth.
2. Curl and shape the snake.
You can shape the snake in many ways.

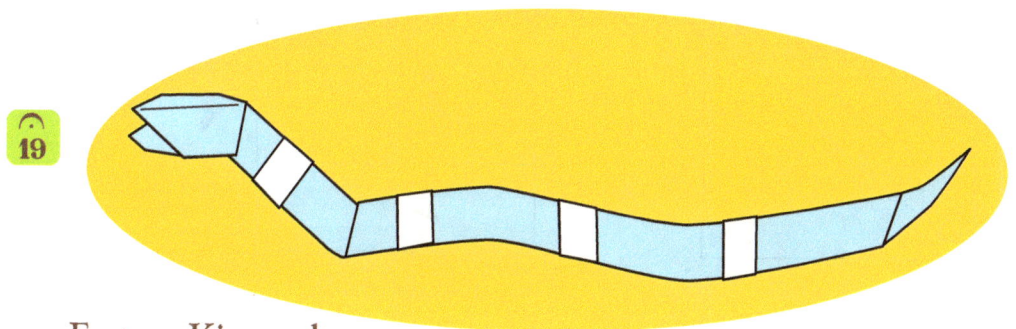

**Eastern Kingsnake**

# 11-Striped Snake

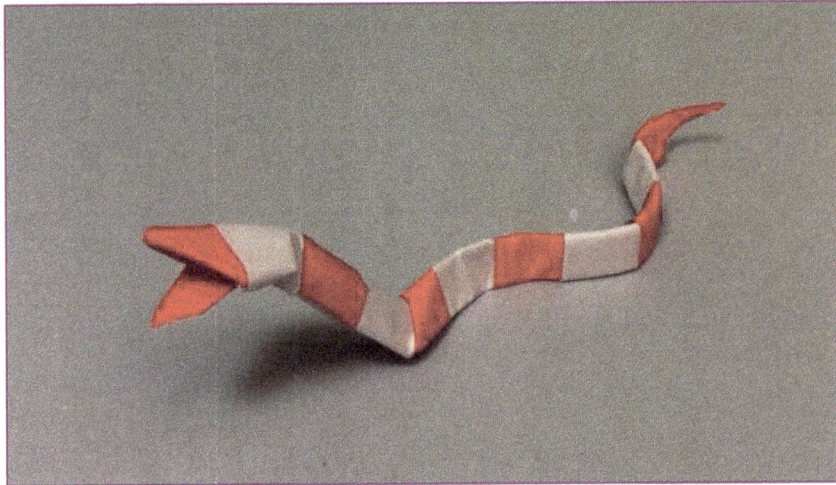

Adding more stripes adds complexity to the design while also creating a more stunning effect. Compared to the 9-Striped Snake with 23 steps, this 11-Striped Snake takes 34 steps. The stripes are equally spaced for this snake.

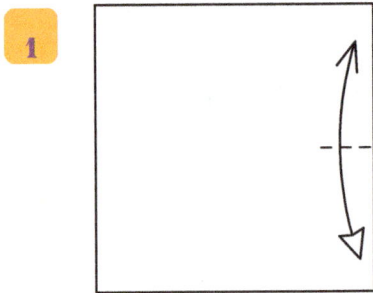

**1**

Fold and unfold on the right.

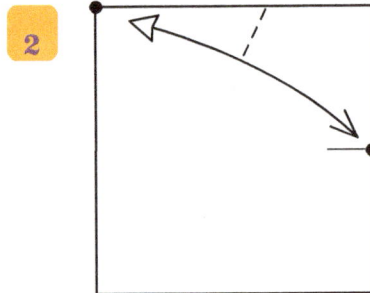

**2**

Fold and unfold on the top.

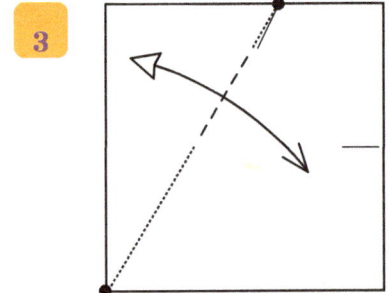

**3**

Fold and unfold in the center.

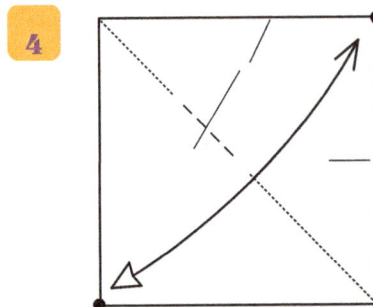

**4**

Fold and unfold through the crease.

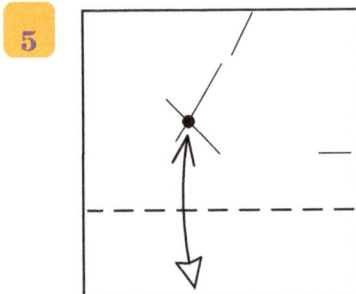

**5**

Fold and unfold.

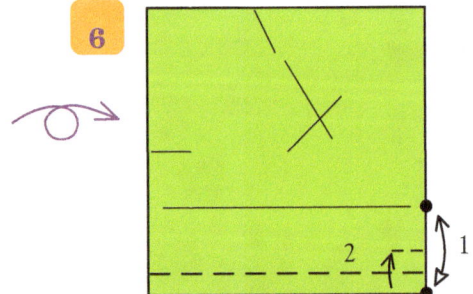

**6**

1. Fold and unfold on the right.
2. Fold up.

**7**

**8**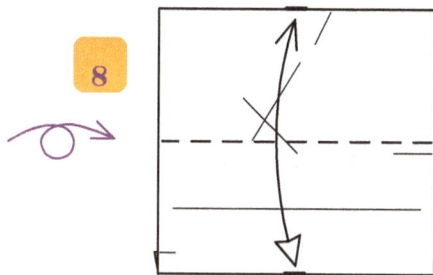

Fold in half and unfold.

**9**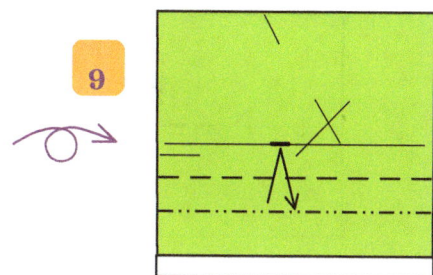

Mountain-fold along the crease for this pleat fold.

**10**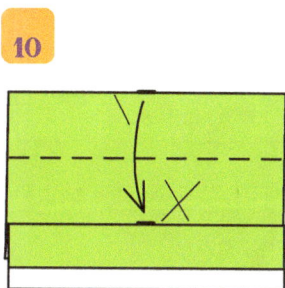

**11**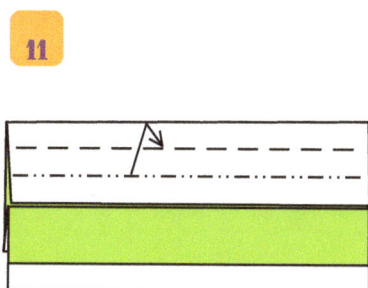

Divide in thirds for this pleat fold.

**12**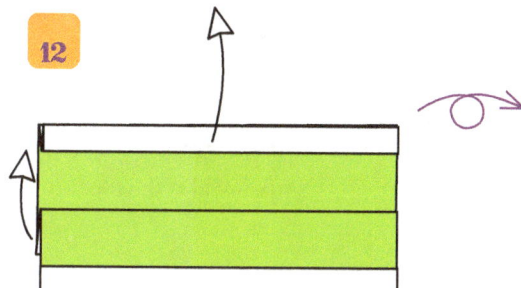

Unfold.

**13**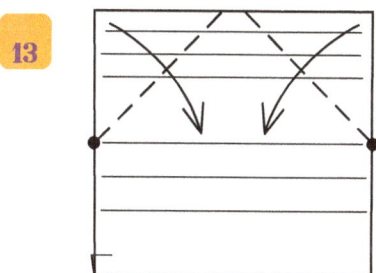

**14**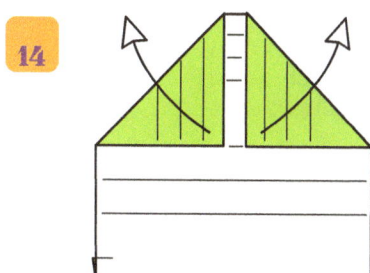

Unfold.

**15**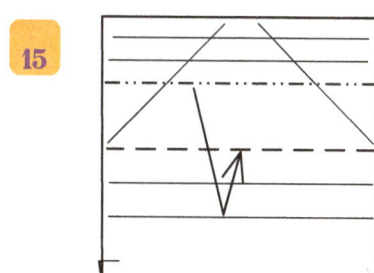

Pleat-fold along the creases.

**16**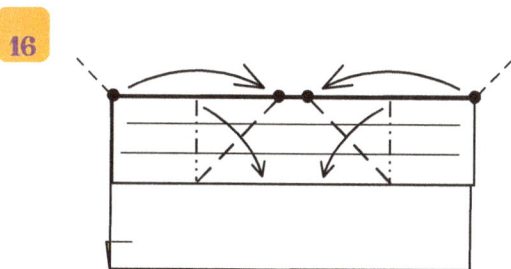

Make squash folds.

**17**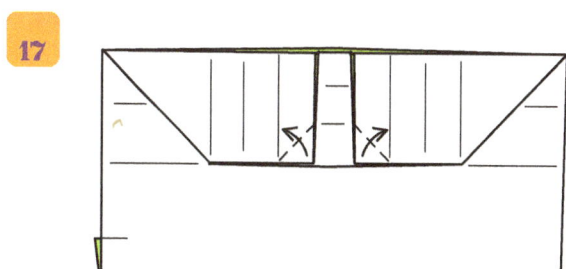

**18**

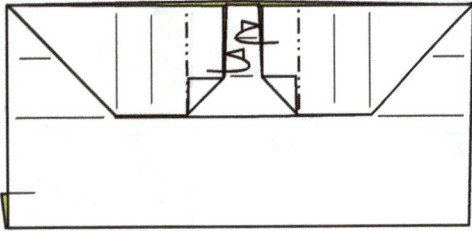

Fold inside.

**19**

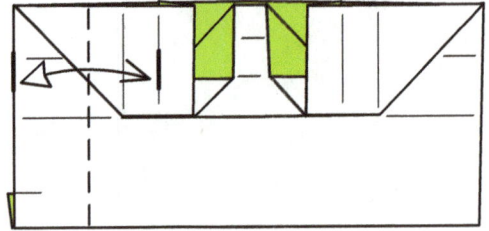

Fold and unfold.

**20**

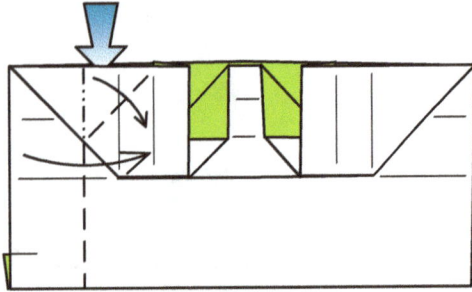

Squash-fold at the top.

**21**

1. Squash-fold.
2. Repeat steps 19–21 on the right.

**22**

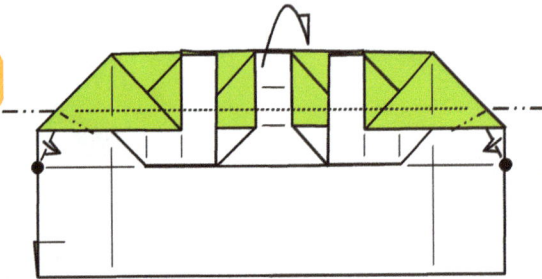

Mountain-fold along a hidden crease. Make small squash folds on the left and right.

**23**

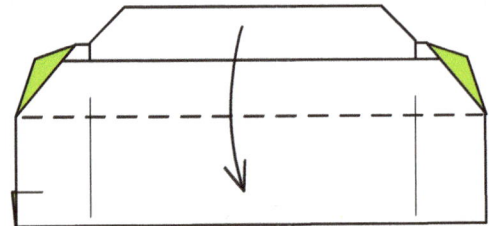

Fold along the crease.

**24**

**25**

**26**

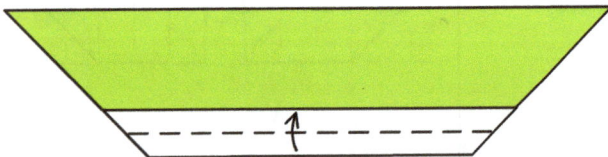

**27**

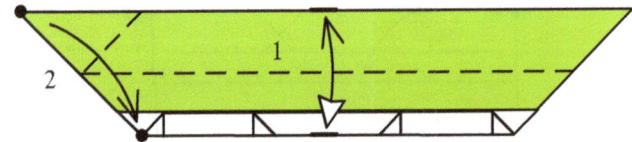

1. Fold and unfold.
2. Valley-fold.

**28**

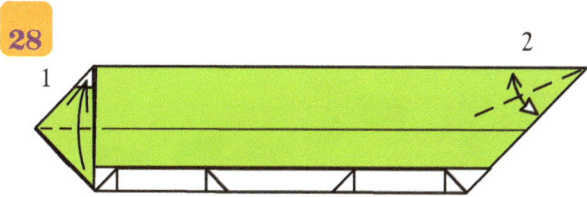

1. Fold up.
2. Fold and unfold.

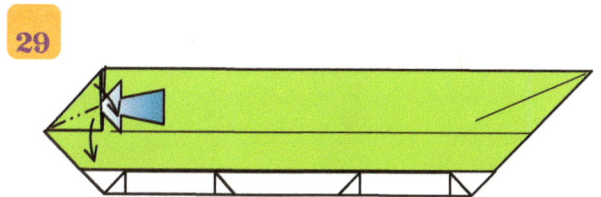

**29**

Squash-fold.

**30**

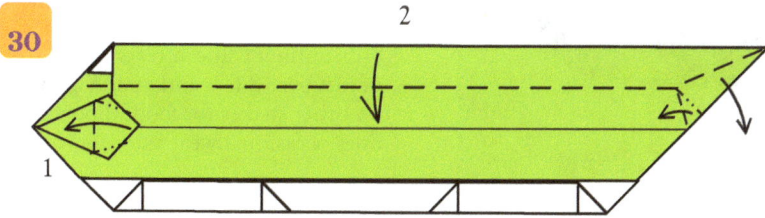

1. Petal-fold.
2. Fold to the center and rabbit-ear on the right.

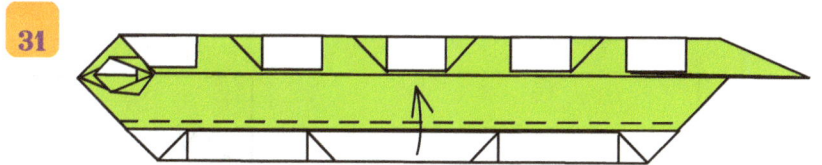

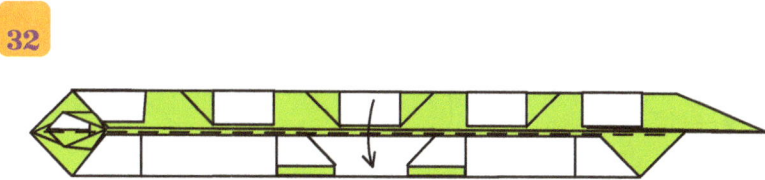

**31**

**32**

Fold in half.

**33**

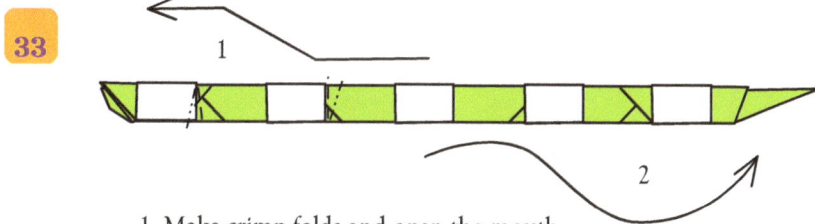

1. Make crimp folds and open the mouth.
2. Curl and shape the snake.
You can shape the snake in many ways.

**34**

11-Striped Snake

# Banded Krait

This poisonous snake is found in India and much of the Asian Subcontinent. It can reach a length of just over 8 feet and mainly preys on other snakes for food, though it does occasionally eat frogs and fish.

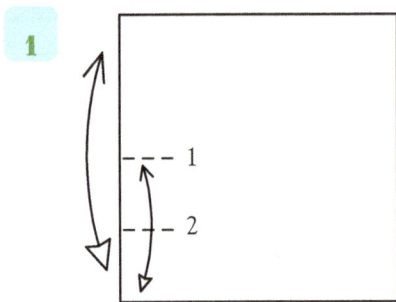

**1**

Fold and unfold twice on the left.

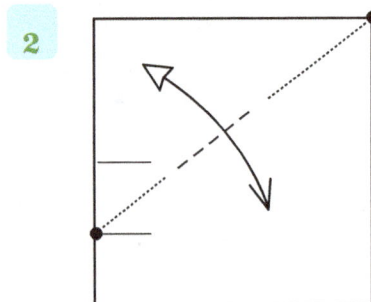

**2**

Fold and unfold in the center.

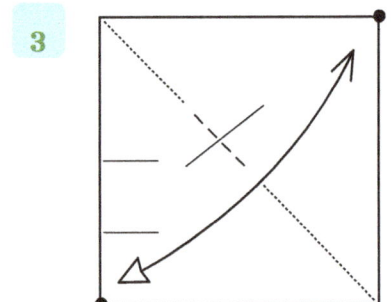

**3**

Fold and unfold through the intersection.

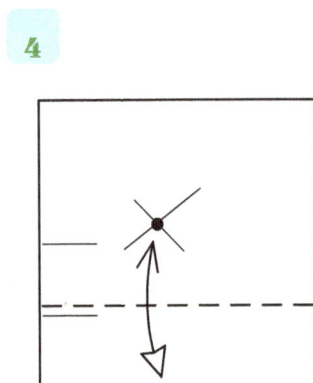

**4**

Fold and unfold.

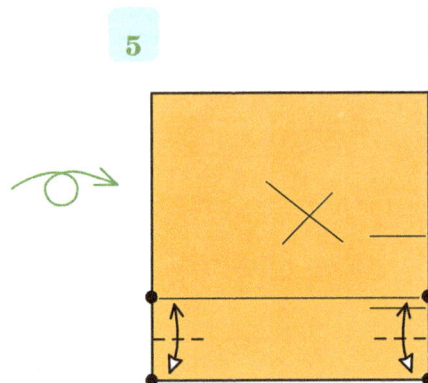

**5**

Fold and unfold on the left and right.

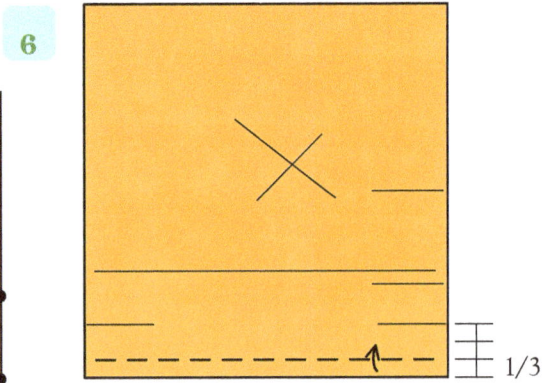

**6**

Fold 1/3 of the way up.

1/3

**7**

**8**

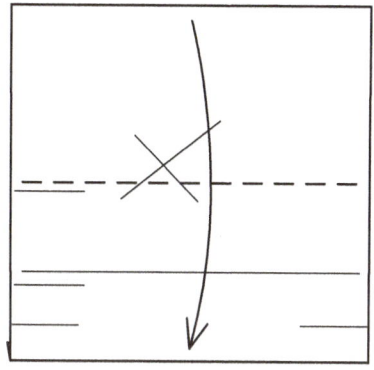

Fold in half.

**9**

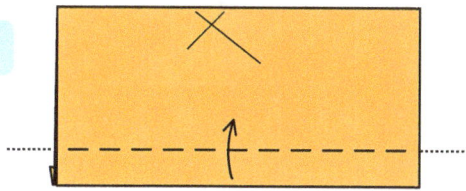

Fold the top layer
along hidden creases.

**10**

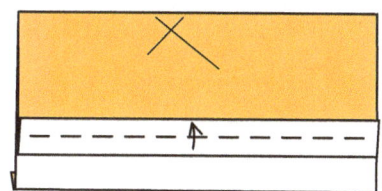

Fold in half.

**11**

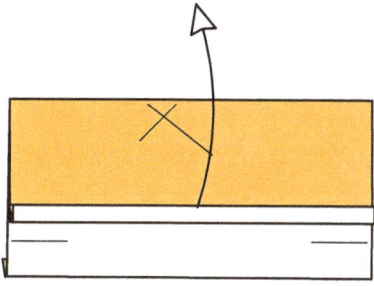

Unfold.

**12**

1. Fold and unfold.
2. Mountain-fold along the
   crease for this pleat fold.

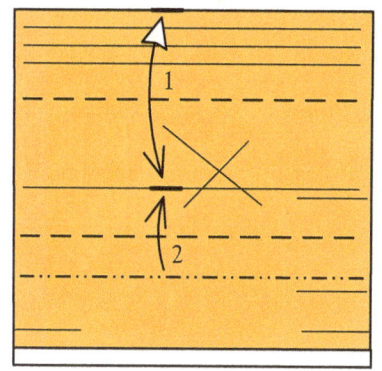

**13**

**14**

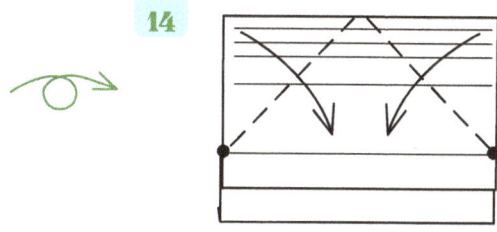

**15**

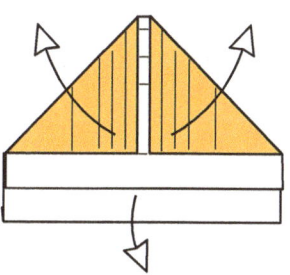

Unfold.

**16**

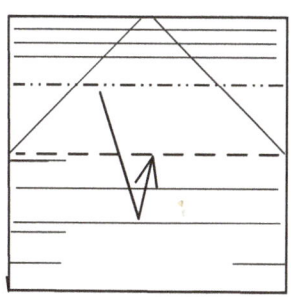

Pleat-fold along
the creases.

**17**

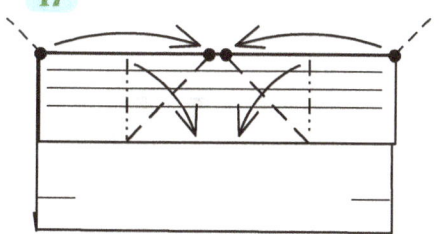

Make squash folds.

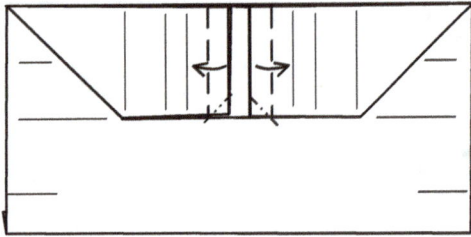

**18**

Valley-fold along the creases
for these squash folds.

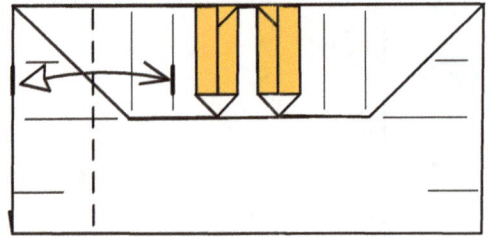

**19**

Fold and unfold.

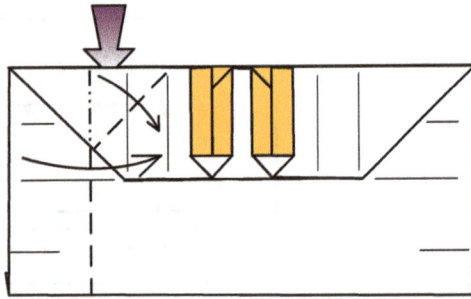

**20**

Squash-fold at the top.

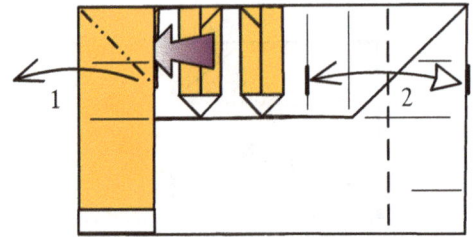

**21**

1. Squash-fold.
2. Repeat steps 19–21
   on the right.

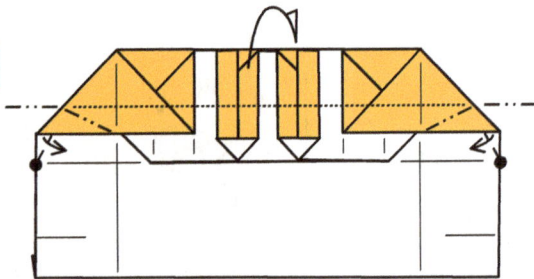

**22**

Mountain-fold along a hidden crease. Make
small squash folds on the left and right.

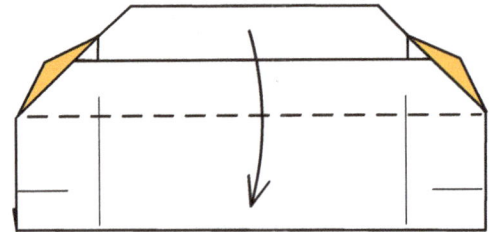

**23**

Fold along the crease.

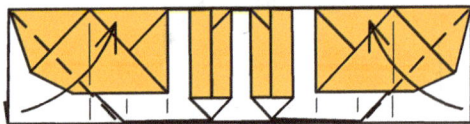

**24**

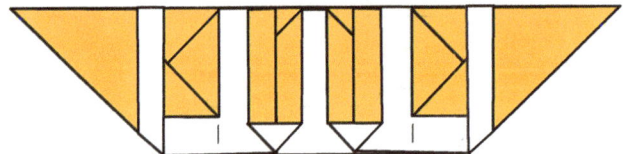

**25**

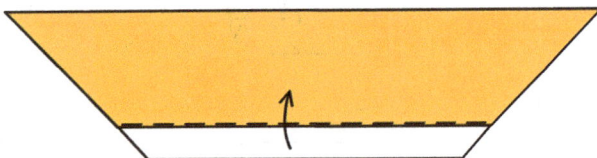

**26**

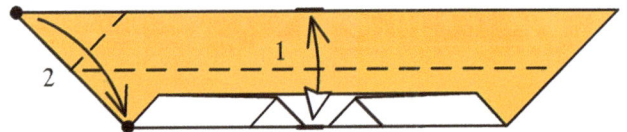

**27**

1. Fold and unfold.
2. Valley-fold.

**28**

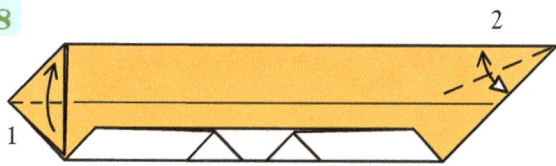

1. Fold up.
2. Fold and unfold.

**29**

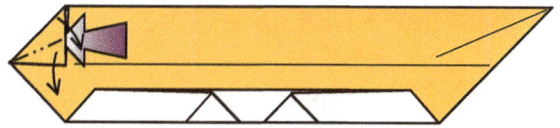

Squash-fold.

**30**

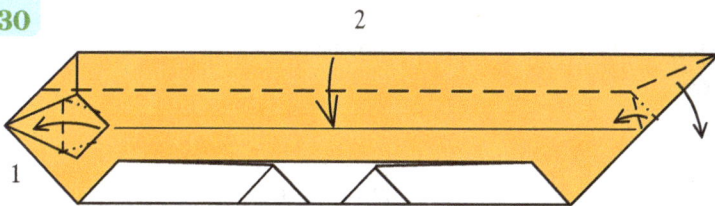

1. Petal-fold.
2. Fold to the center and
   rabbit-ear on the right.

**31**

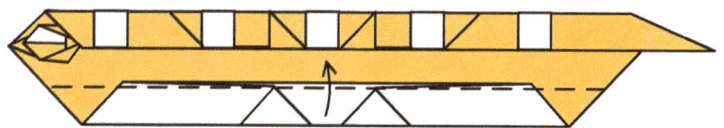

Adjust the layers so
it is not too thick.

**32**

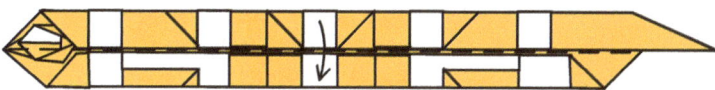

Fold in half.

**33**

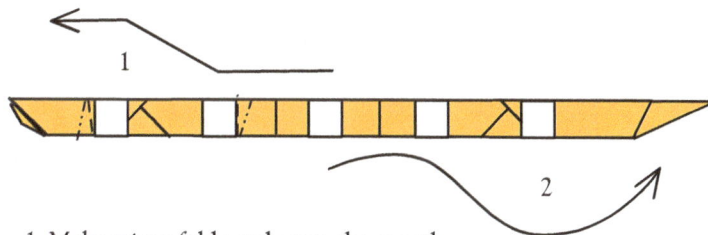

1. Make crimp folds and open the mouth.
2. Curl and shape the snake.
You can shape the snake in many ways.

**34**

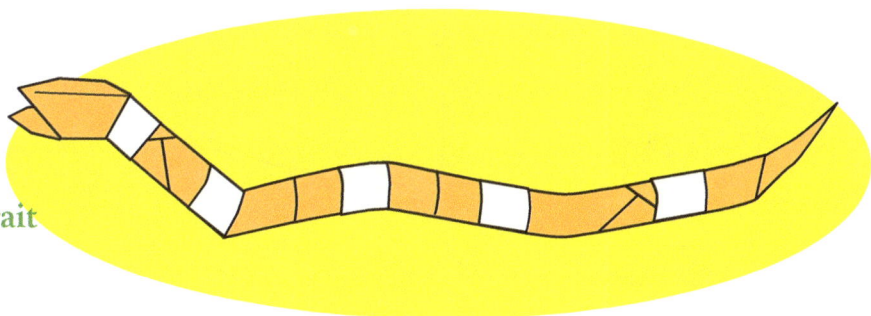

**Banded Krait**

# Bandy-Bandy

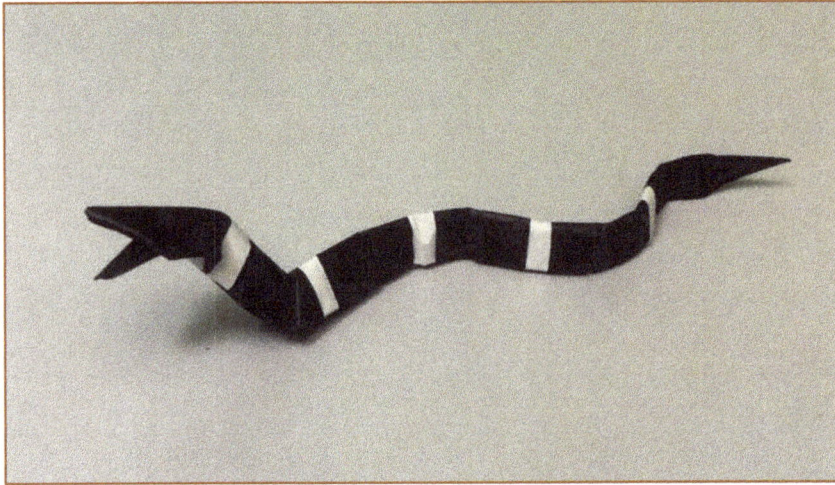

The Bandy Bandy, a mildly venomous snake found in Australia, features many horizontal white bands on a black background as its decoration. It can confuse its predators by raising itself up in loops, thus making it appear taller, as well as making a visual optical illusion of flickering as they move that also makes predators unsure of what they are seeing, giving the Bandy-Bandy a better chance to escape.

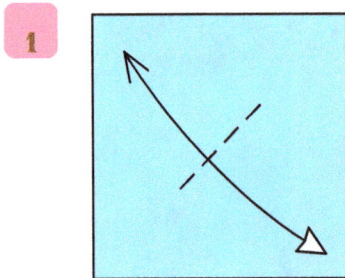

Fold and unfold.

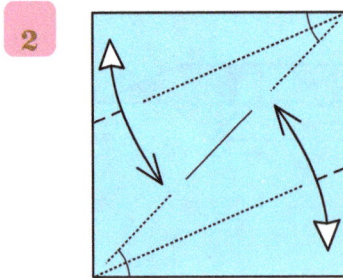

Fold and unfold along the edges.

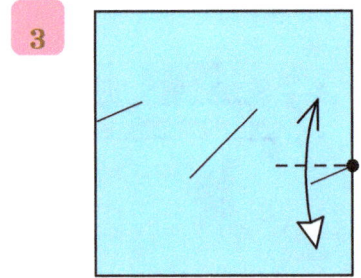

Fold and unfold on the right.

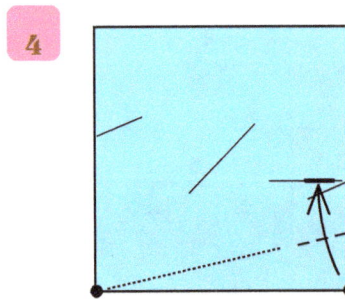

Bring the bottom right corner to the line. Crease on the right.

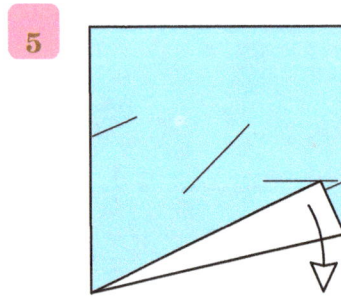

Unfold.

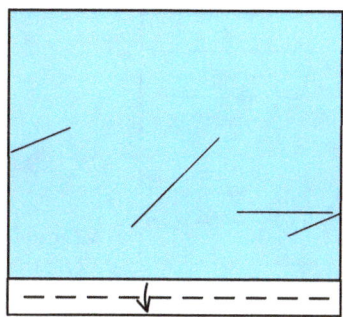

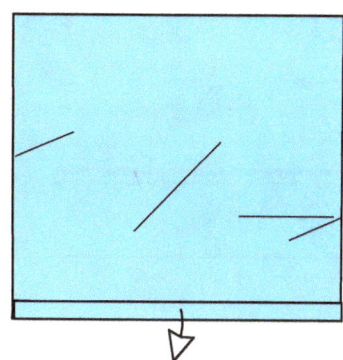

Unfold and rotate 180°.

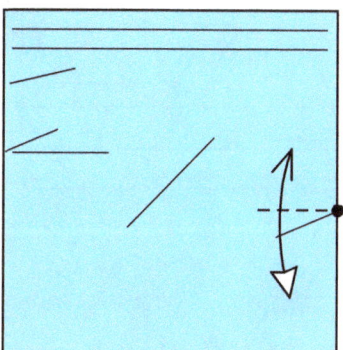

Repeat steps 3–5.

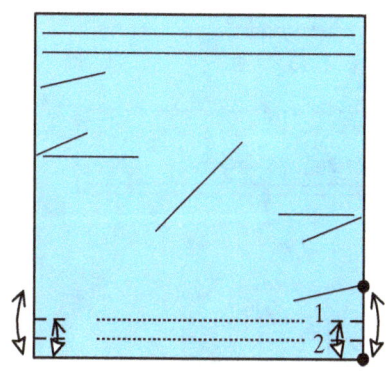

Fold and unfold on
the left and right.

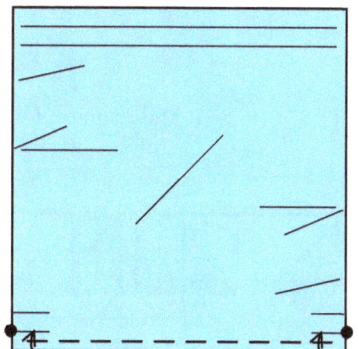

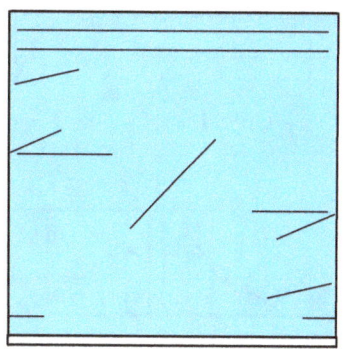

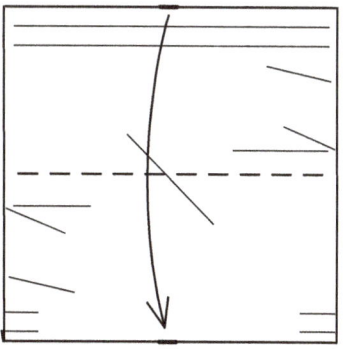

Fold in half.

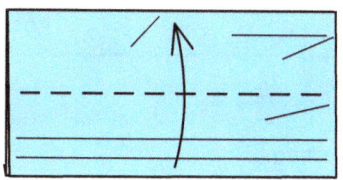

Fold all the layers in half.

**15**

Unfold.

**16**

Mountain-fold
along the crease
for this pleat fold.

**17**

**18**

**19**

Unfold.

**20**

Pleat-fold along
the creases.

**21**

1. Make squash folds.
2. Unfold.

**22**

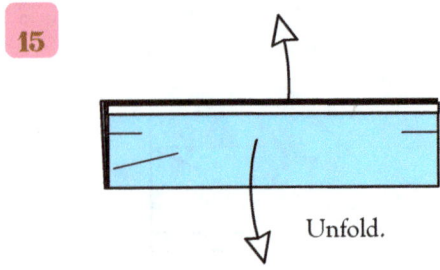

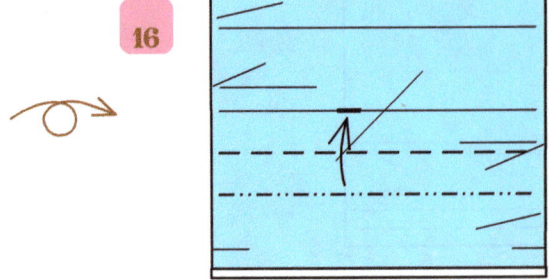

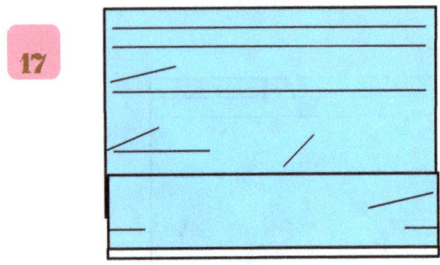

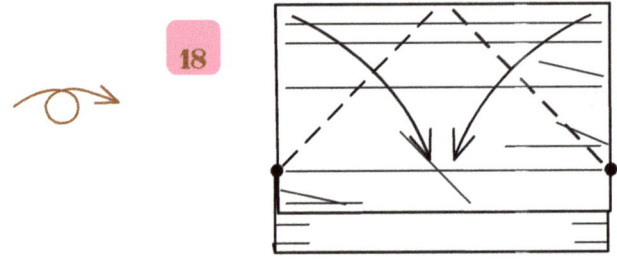

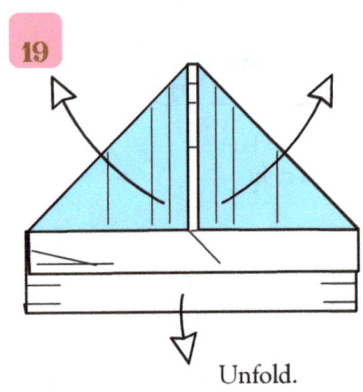

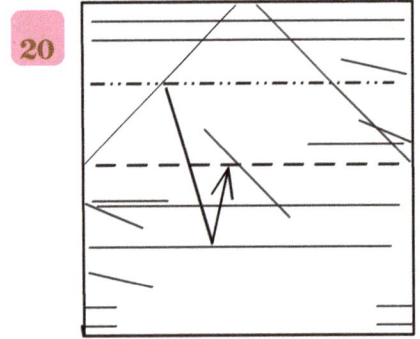

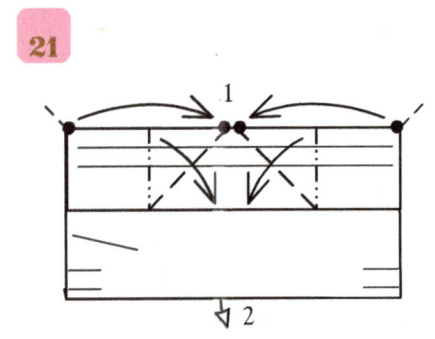

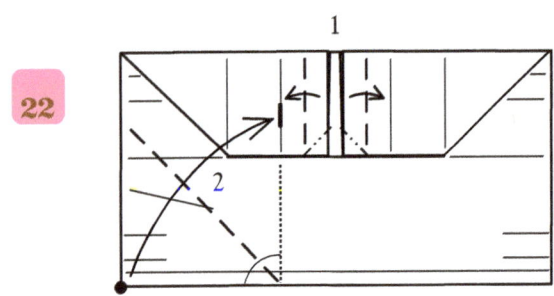

1. Valley-fold along the crease
   for these squash fold.
2. The dot will meet the bold line.

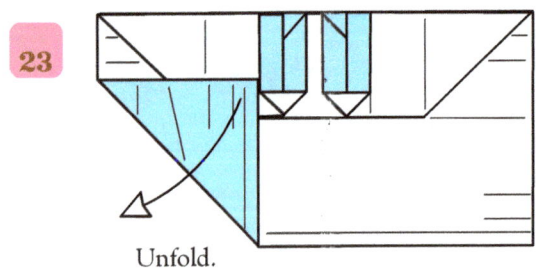

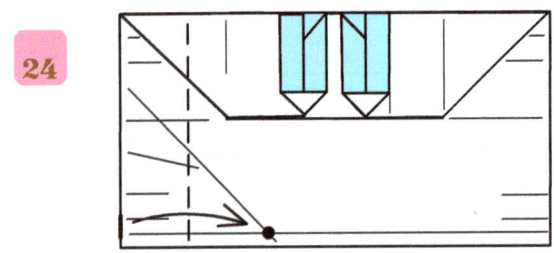

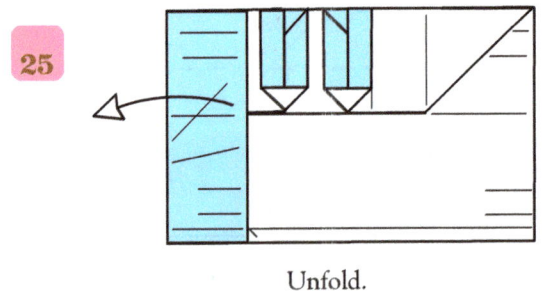

**23**

Unfold.

**24**

The edge will meet the dot.

**25**

Unfold.

**26**

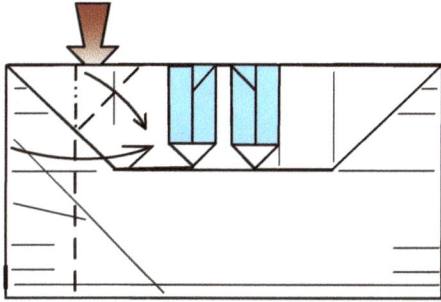

Squash-fold at the top.

**27**

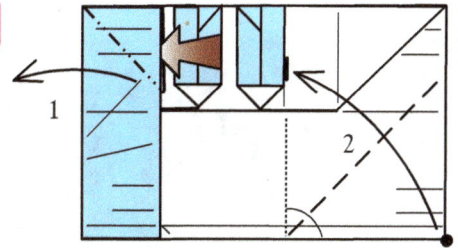

1. Squash-fold.
2. Repeat steps 22–27
   on the right.

**28**

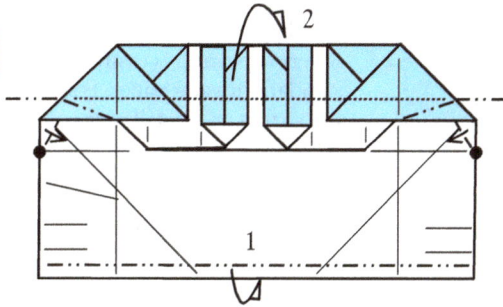

1. Fold along the crease.
2. Mountain-fold along a hidden crease.
   Make small squash folds on the left
   and right.

**29**

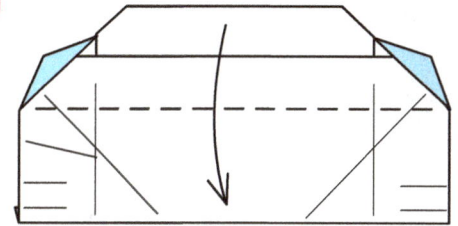

Fold along the crease.

**30**

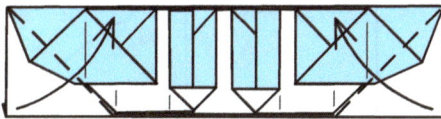

**31**

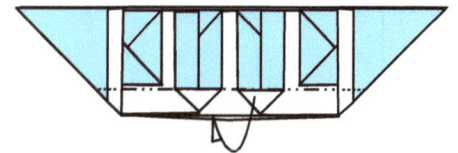

Tuck inside.

**32**

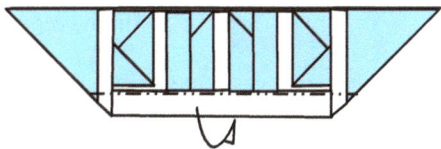

**33**

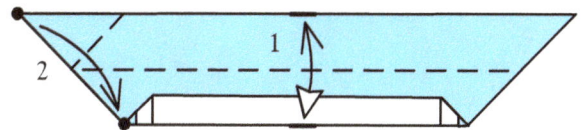

1. Fold and unfold.
2. Valley-fold.
3. Continue...

**34**

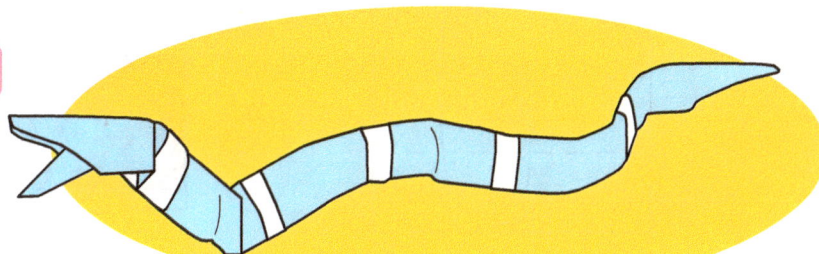

Bandy-Bandy

# 13-Striped Snake

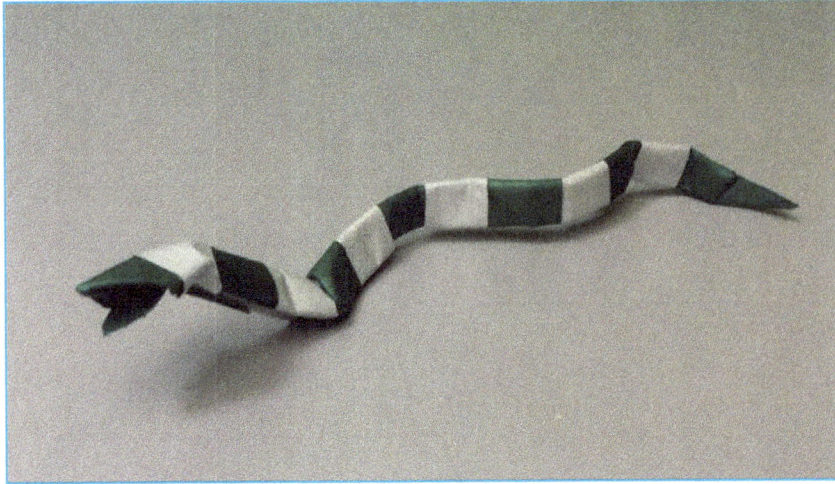

As more stripes are added, the effects become more astonishing. Still, this has the same length as snakes with fewer stripes and is easily foldable from standard origami paper. For this snake, the stripes are equally spaced.

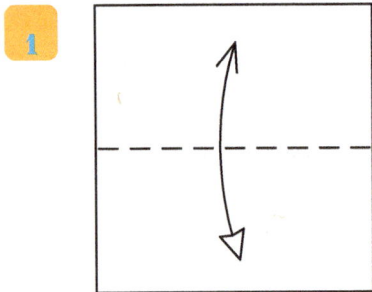

1 Fold and unfold.

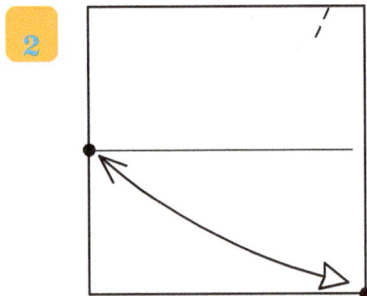

2 Fold and unfold on the top.

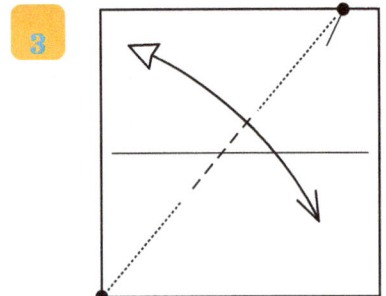

3 Fold and unfold in the center.

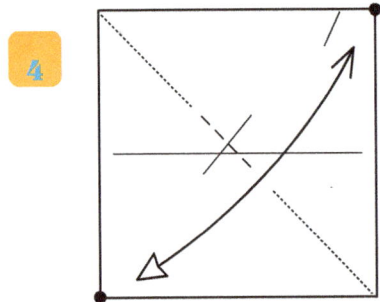

4 Fold and unfold in the center, along the diagonal.

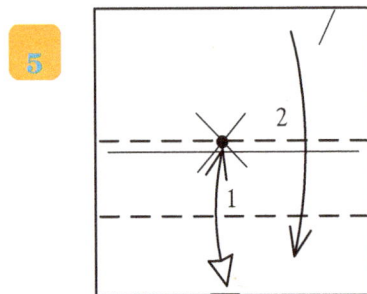

5 1. Fold and unfold.
2. Fold down.

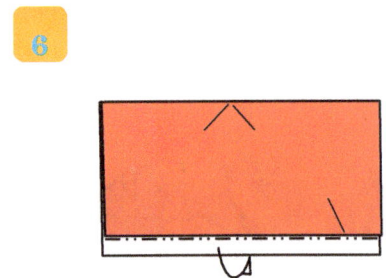

6 Fold behind along the edge.

**7**

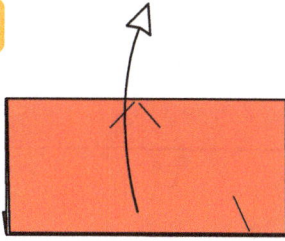

Unfold.

**8**

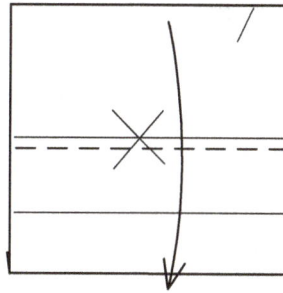

Fold along the crease.

**9**

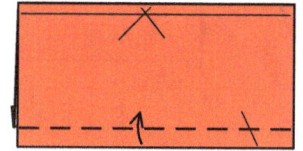

Fold along the
hidden edge.

**10**

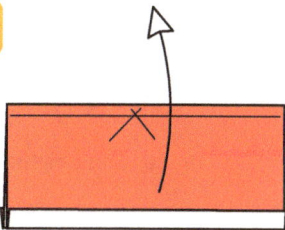

Unfold and rotate 180°.

**11**

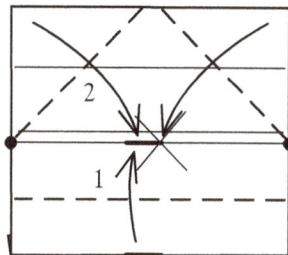

1. Fold up to the line.
2. Bring the top corners
   to the line.

**12**

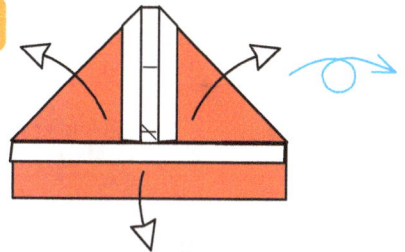

Unfold.

**13**

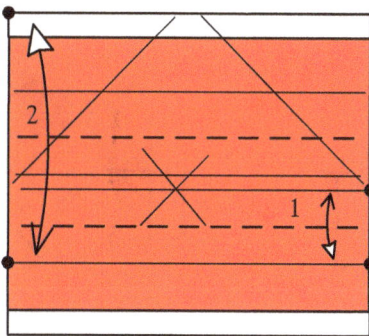

Fold and unfold.

**14**

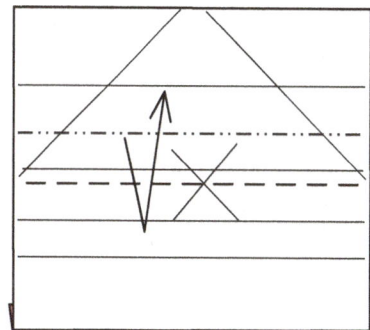

Pleat-fold along
the creases.

**15**

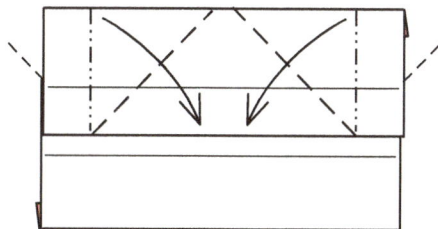

Valley-fold along the creases
for these squash folds.

**16**

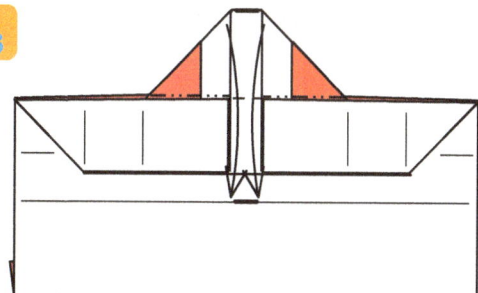

Make reverse folds.

**17**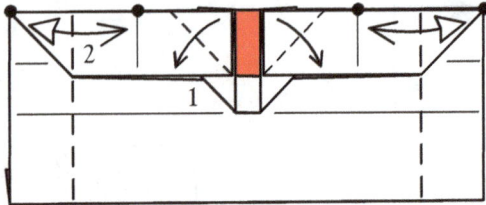

1. Fold down in the center.
2. Fold and unfold on the left and right.

**18**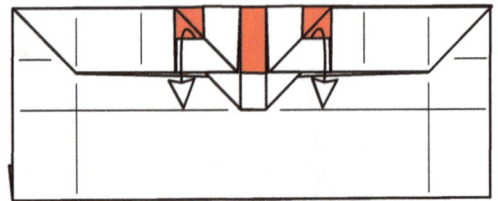

Unlock the top layers.

**19**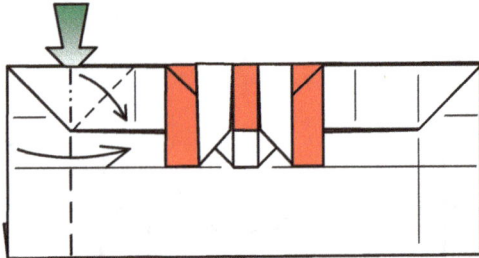

Squash-fold at the top.

**20**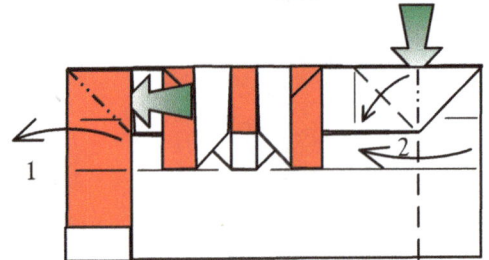

1. Squash-fold.
2. Repeat steps 19–20 on the right.

**21**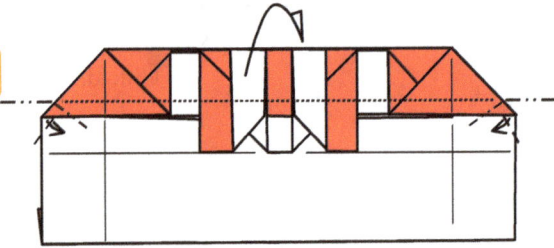

Mountain-fold along a hidden crease. Make small squash folds on the left and right.

**22**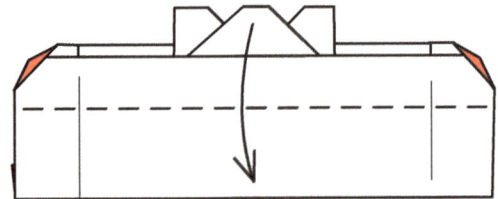

Fold along the crease.

**23**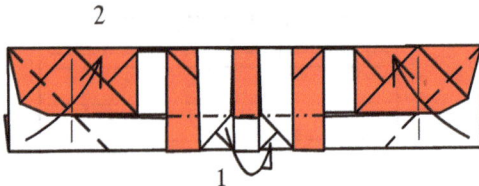

1. Tuck the flaps inside.
2. Fold up on the left and right.

**24**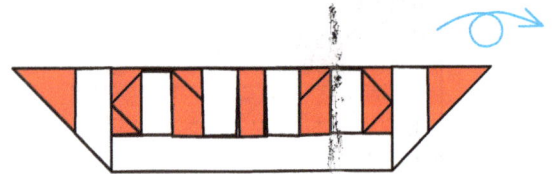

**25**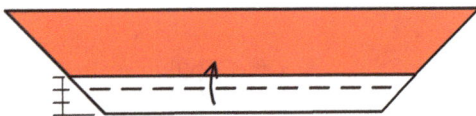

Fold up about 2/3 of the way.

**26**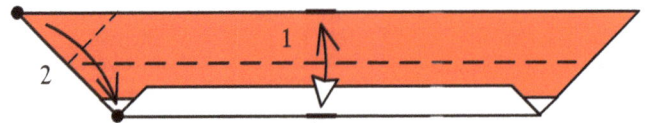

1. Fold and unfold.
2. Valley-fold.
3. Continue...

**27**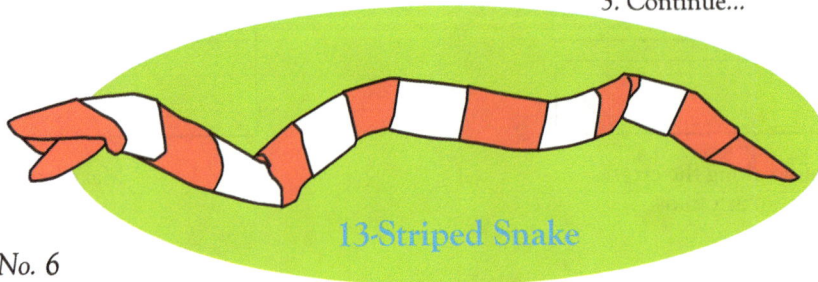

13-Striped Snake

# Kingsnake

This variety of snake uses mimicry and a foul odor to ward off predators, shaking its tail like a rattlesnake and emitting an unpleasant smell when provoked. Though it can bite, this snake is not poisonous.

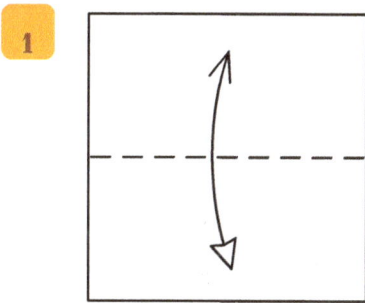

**1**

Fold and unfold.

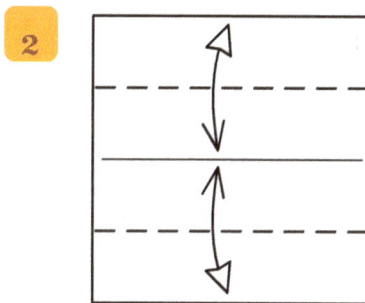

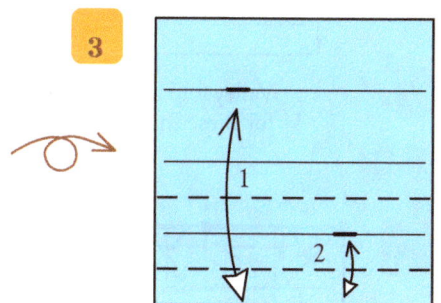

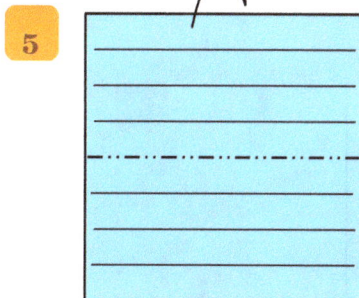

**2**

Fold and unfold.

**3**

Fold and unfold.
Rotate 180°.

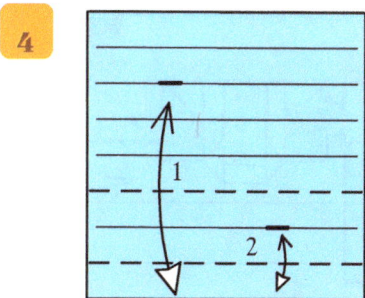

**4**

Fold and unfold.

**5**

Fold in half along the crease.

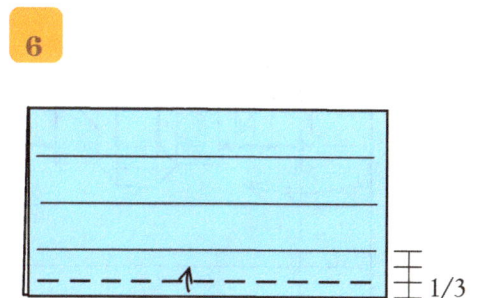

**6**

Fold up 1/3 of the way. Repeat behind.

1/3

**7**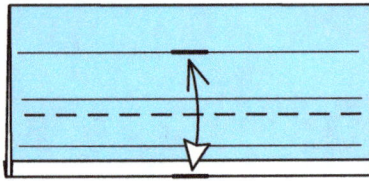

Fold and unfold
the top layer.

**8**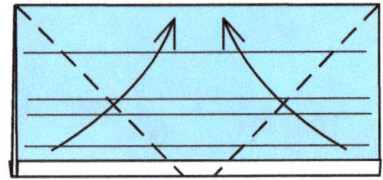

**9**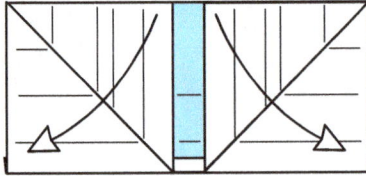

Unfold.

**10**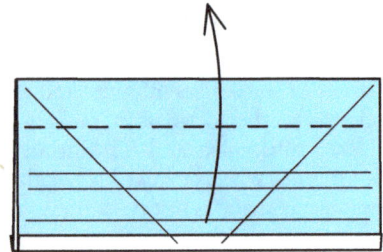

Fold the top layer
along the crease.

**11**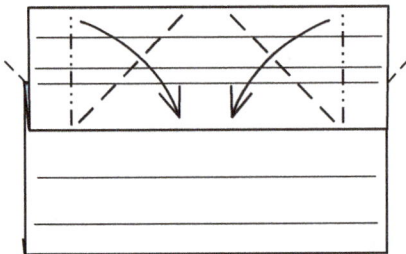

Valley-fold along the creases
for these squash folds.

**12**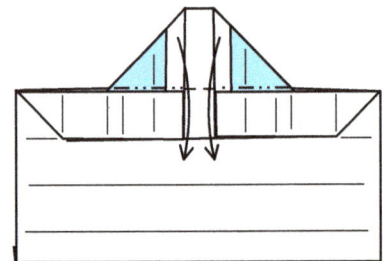

Make reverse folds
along the creases.

**13**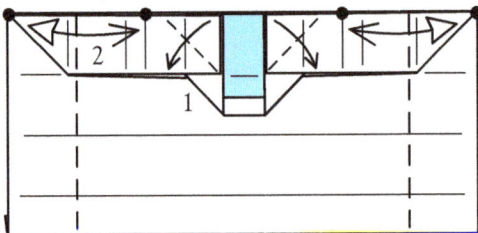

1. Fold down in the center.
2. Fold and unfold on the
   left and right.

**14**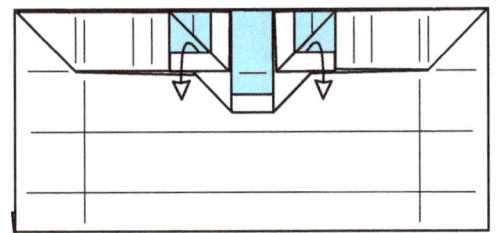

Unlock the top layers.

**15**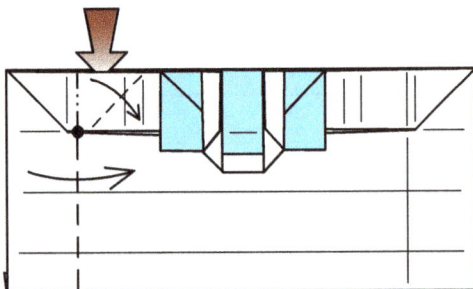

Squash-fold. Small folds
will happen at the dot.

**16**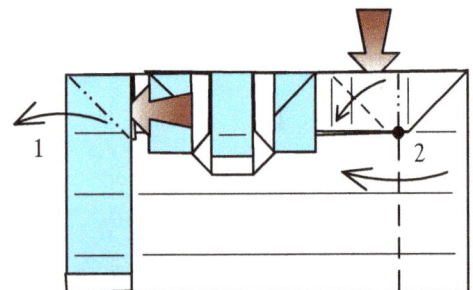

1. Squash-fold.
2. Repeat steps 15–16 on the right.

**17**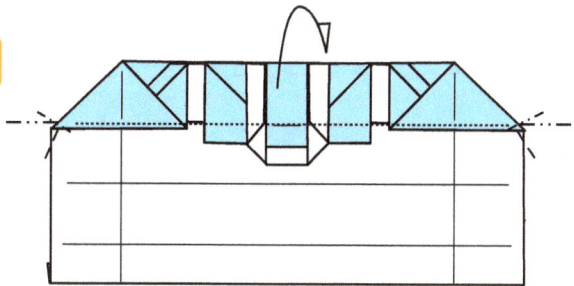

Mountain-fold along a hidden crease. Make small squash folds on the left and right.

**18**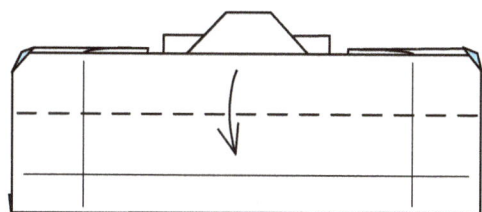

Fold along the crease.

**19**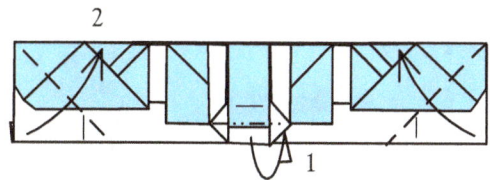

1. Fold inside.
2. Fold up on the left and right.

**20**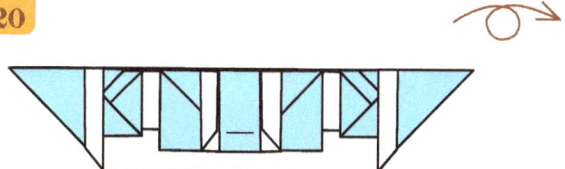

**21**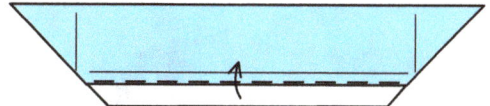

**22**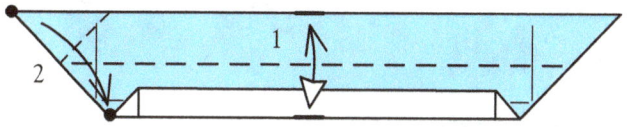

1. Fold and unfold.
2. Valley-fold.
3. Continue...

**23**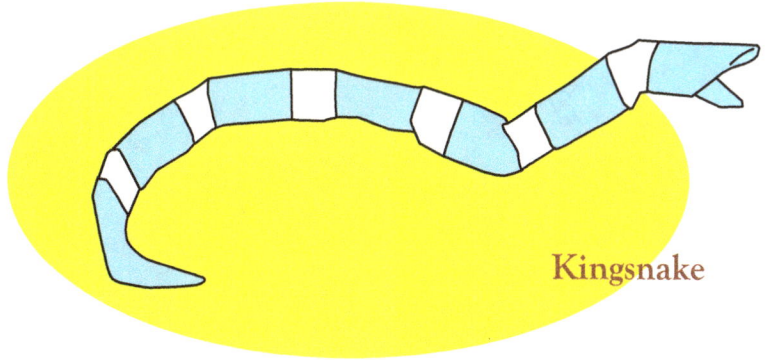

Kingsnake

# Second Movement

## Andante: Frolicking in the Jungle

The intersection of jungle animals and origami has always been a favorite topic. Great care was taken to keep these designs in the intermediate level with most folded in around two dozen steps. Two Hippos frolic with a two-horned Rhino, a duo-colored Tapir meets an Anteater and Lion, while a Giraffe and Okapi keep watch in the safari. Elephants and Oxpeckers lead the way as you join these jungle animals.

## Lion

Regal, fierce and commanding, the Lion is known in popular culture as "King of the Jungle", though in reality, lions mainly live in desert areas and forests. In Sanskrit, the word for "Jungle" means an uninhabited area, so the term "King of the Jungle" was likely meant to suggest that the Lion held a high status amongst other animals in areas not inhabited by humans.

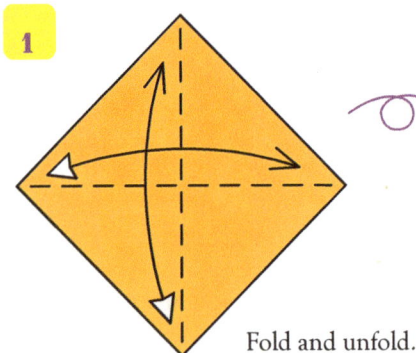

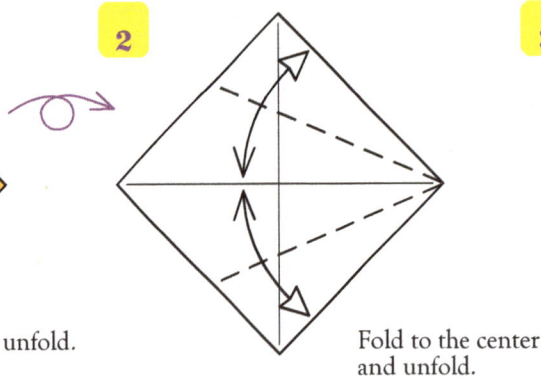

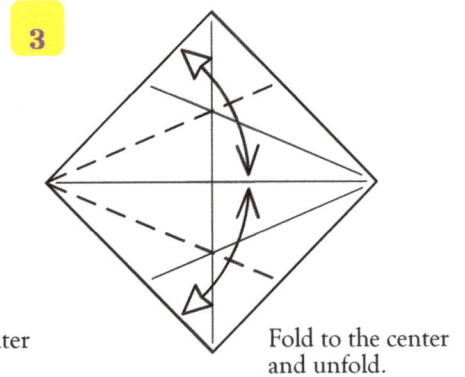

**1**

Fold and unfold.

**2**

Fold to the center and unfold.

**3**

Fold to the center and unfold.

**4**

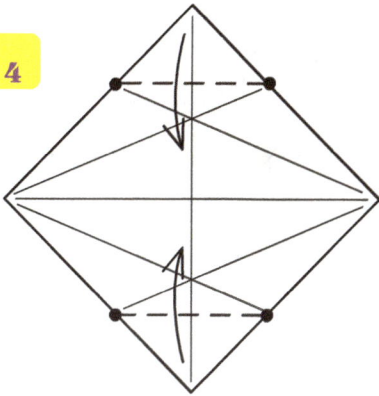

**5**

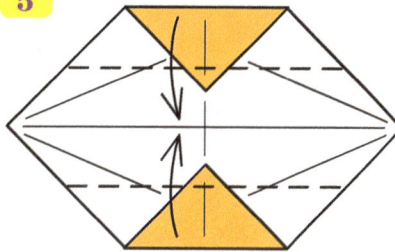

Fold to the center.

**6**

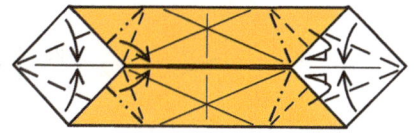

Make squash folds on the left
and reverse folds on the right.

**7**

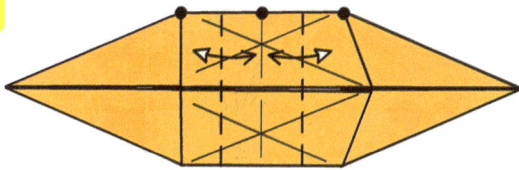

Fold and unfold.

**8**

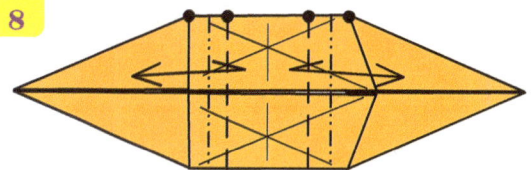

Valley-fold along the creases
for these pleat folds.

**9**

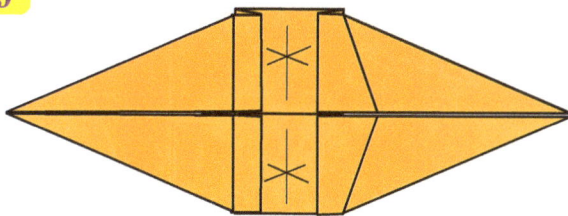

**10**

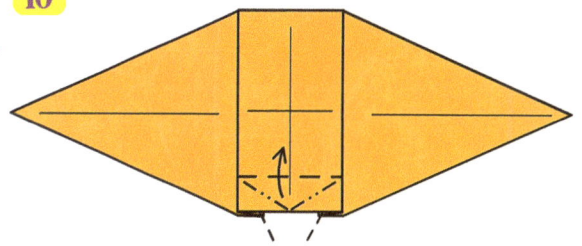

Petal-fold.

**11**

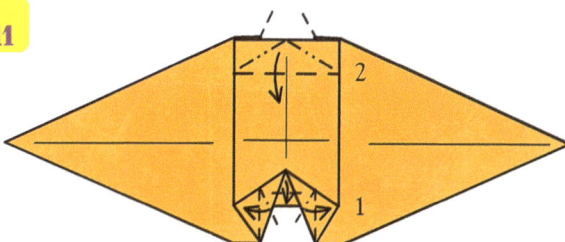

1. Petal-fold.
2. Repeat steps 10–11 on the top.

**12**

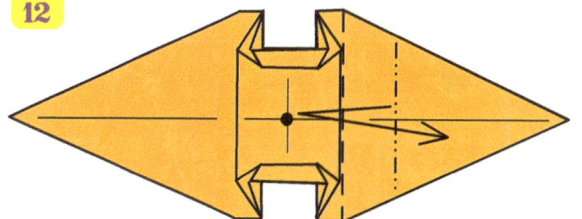

Pleat-fold to the center.

*Lion* **41**

**13**

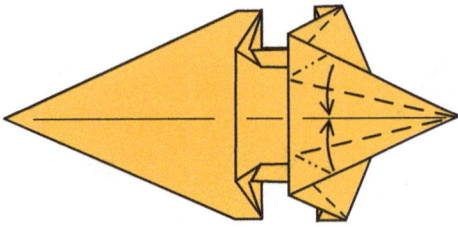

Make squash folds.

**14**

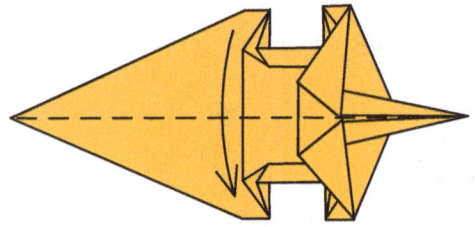

**15**

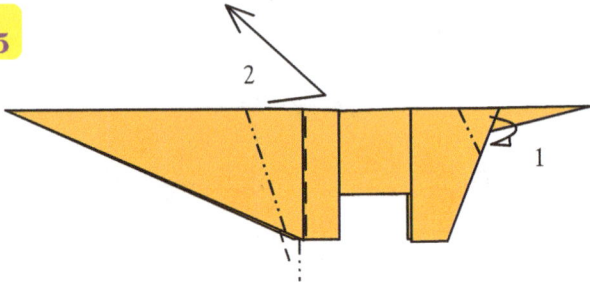

1. Repeat behind.
2. Crimp-fold.

**16**

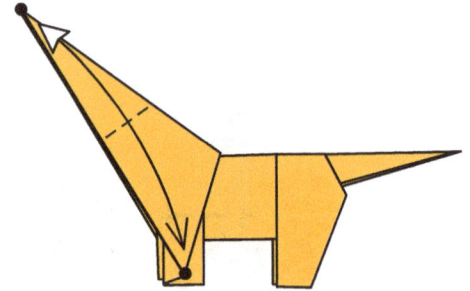

Fold and unfold.

**17**

1. Make reverse folds.
2. Mountain-fold along the crease for this crimp fold.

**18**

1. Crimp-fold.
2. Repeat behind.

**19**

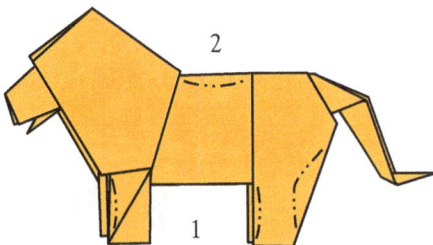

1. Shape the legs, repeat behind.
2. Shape the back.

**20**

Lion

# Anteater

With their distinctive long snouts and tongues, Anteaters search for food such as ants and termites by sense of smell due to their having poor eyesight. They eat their food whole since they have no teeth with which to chew.

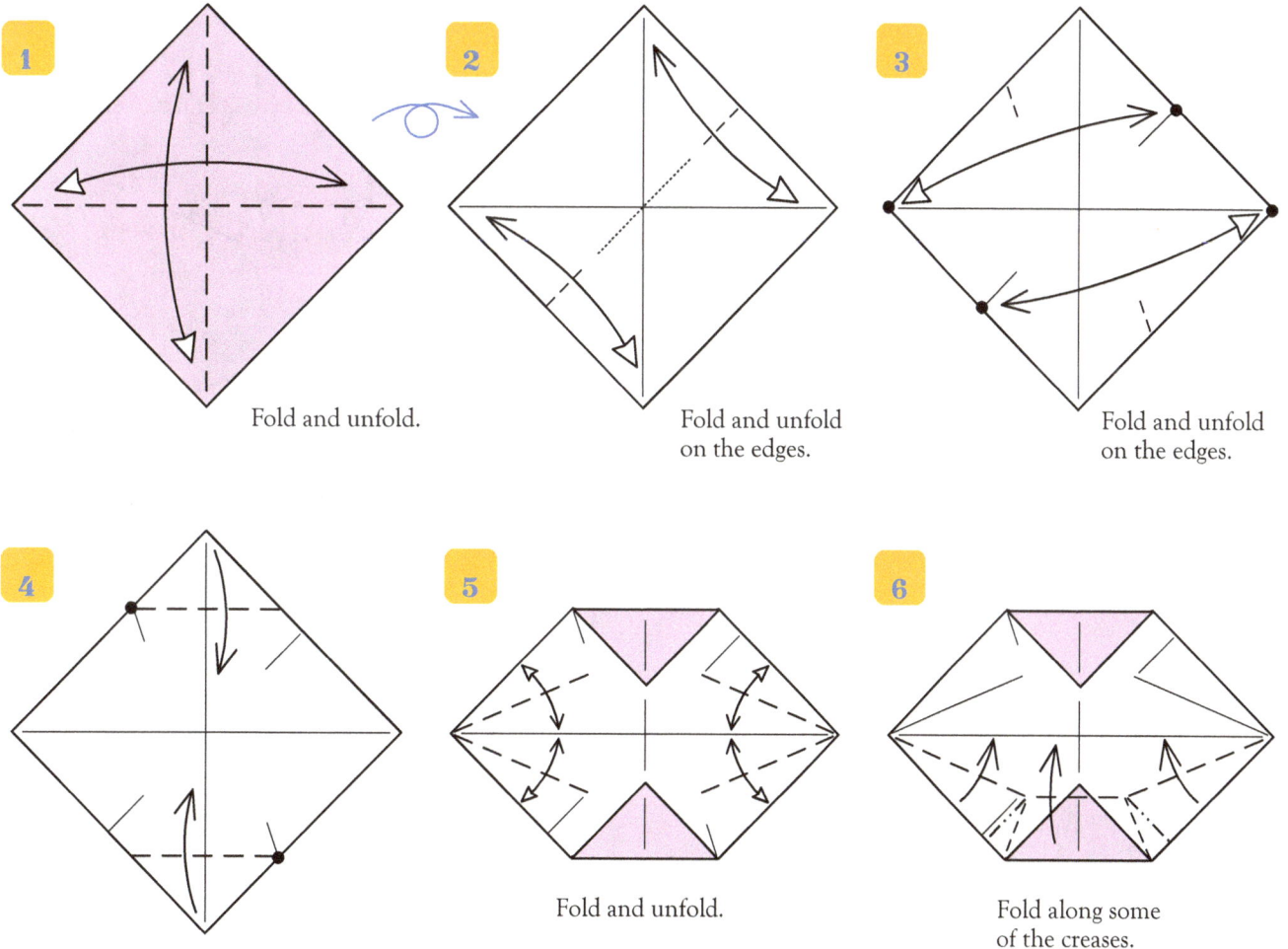

**1** Fold and unfold.

**2** Fold and unfold on the edges.

**3** Fold and unfold on the edges.

**4**

**5** Fold and unfold.

**6** Fold along some of the creases.

**7**

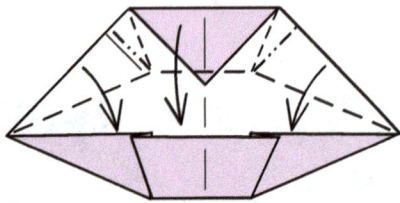

**8**

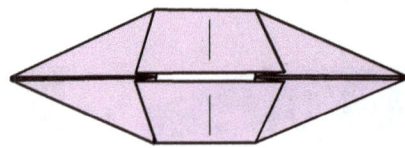

**9**

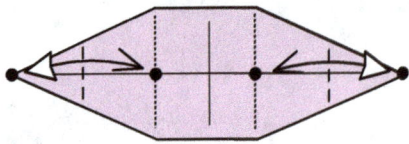

Fold and unfold.

**10**

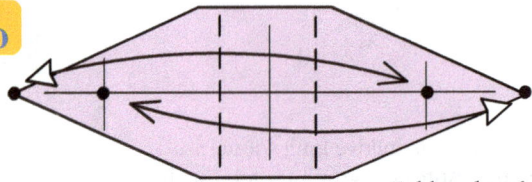

Fold and unfold.

**11**

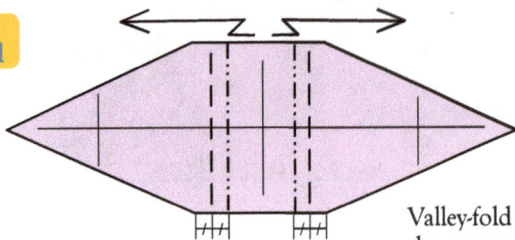

Valley-fold along
the creases for
these pleat folds.

**12**

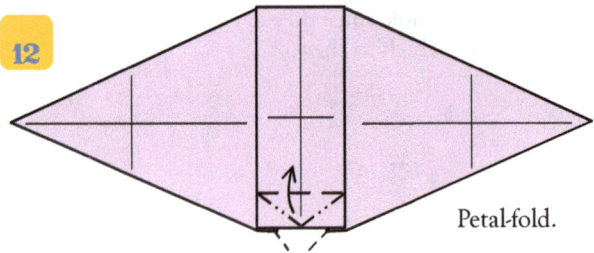

Petal-fold.

**13**

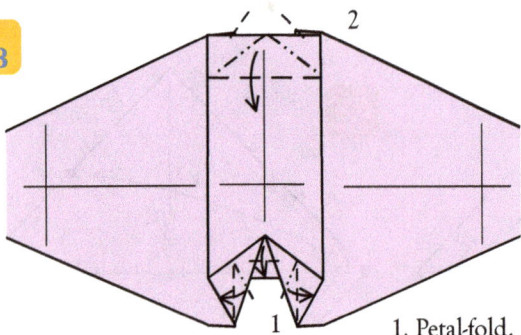

1. Petal-fold.
2. Repeat steps 12–13 on the top.

**14**

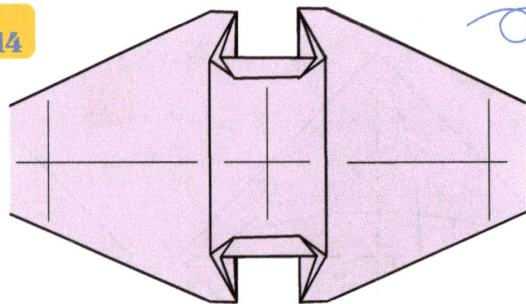

**15**

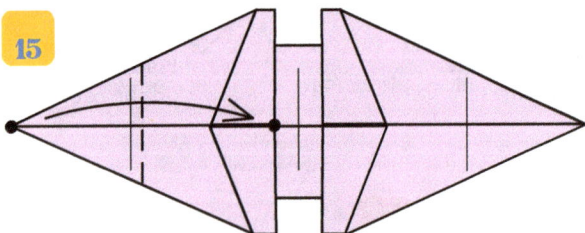

**16**

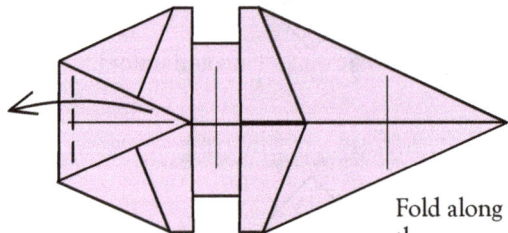

Fold along
the crease.

**17**

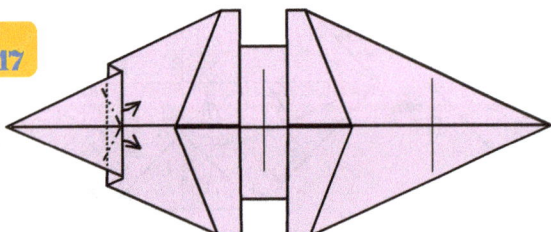

Make small reverse folds between
the layers to form the ears.

**18**

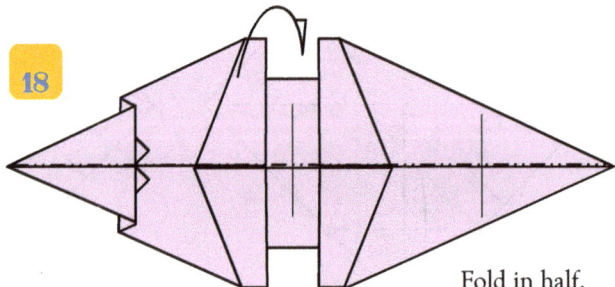

Fold in half.

**19**

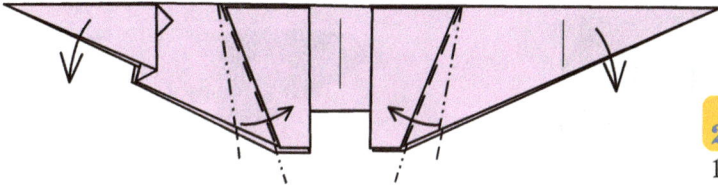

Make crimp folds.

**20**

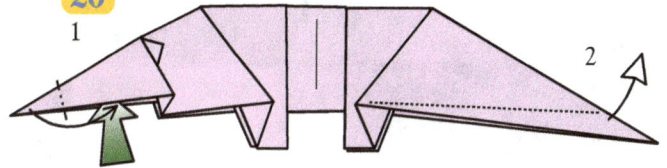

1. Reverse-fold.
2. Spread the tail. Fold along hidden layers at the dotted line.

**21**

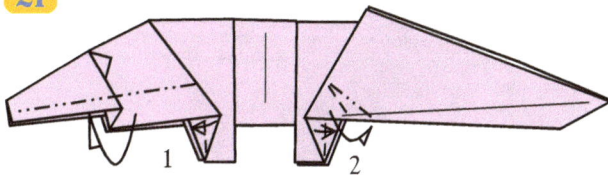

1. Thin the head.
2. Shape the tail.
Repeat behind.

**22**

Tuck under the flaps.
Repeat behind.

**23**

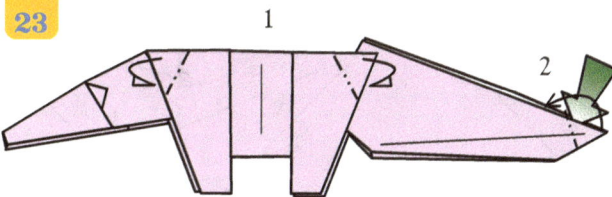

1. Fold behind on the left and right. Repeat behind.
2. Reverse-fold.

**24**

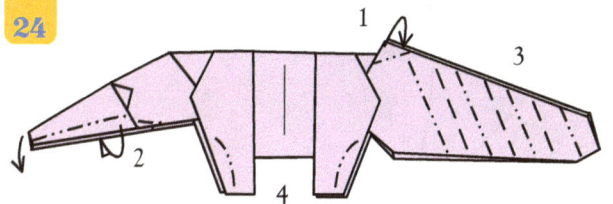

1. Reverse-fold.
2. Shape and round the head.
3. Pleat-fold the tail.
4. Shape the legs.
Repeat behind.

**25**

Anteater

# Malayan Tapir

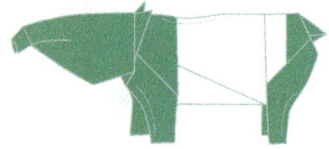

These animals look like across between a pig and an anteater, with a porcine body and a long snout. Interestingly, Tapirs are relatives of both rhinoceroses and horses, as all of them are odd-toed ungulates.

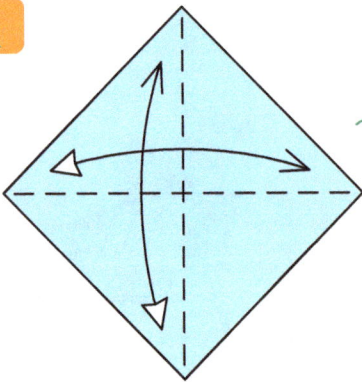

Fold and unfold.

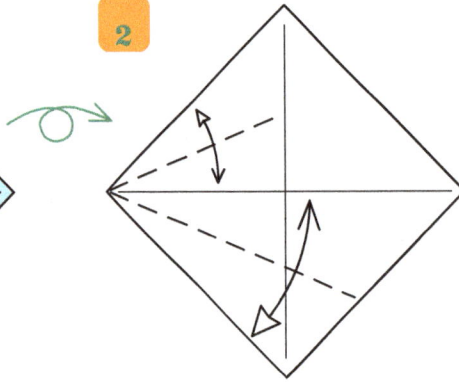

Fold to the center and unfold.

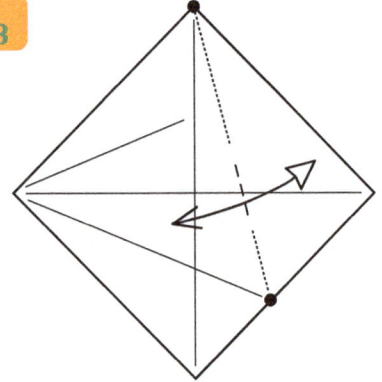

Fold and unfold on the diagonal.

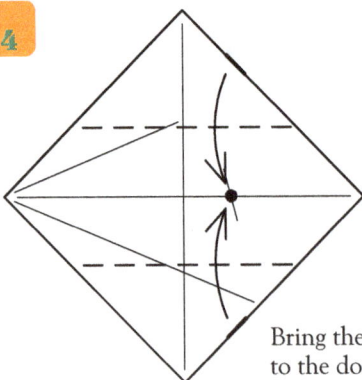

Bring the edges to the dot.

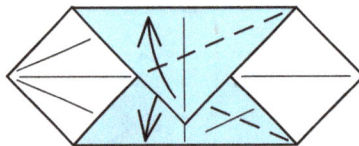

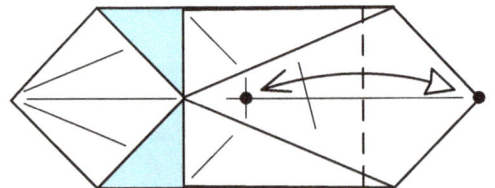

Fold and unfold.

**7**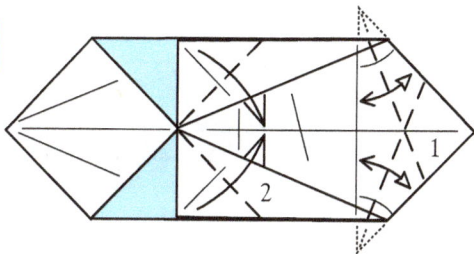

1. Fold to the crease and unfold.
2. Fold to the center.

**8**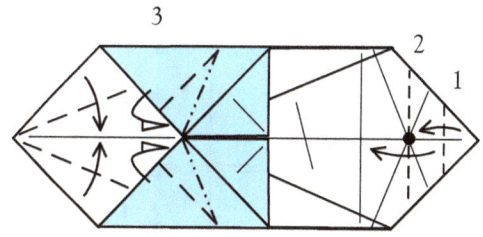

1. Fold to the dot.
2. Continue.
3. Fold along some of the creases.

**9**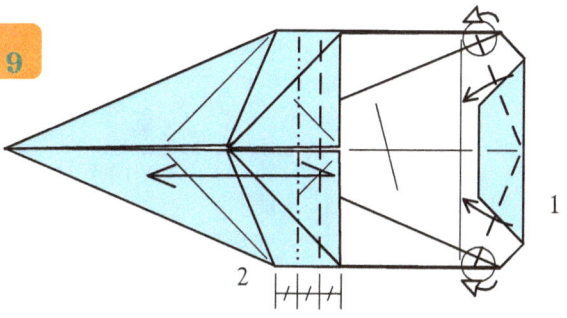

1. Fold along the creases and spread the layers at the top and bottom.
2. Pleat-fold in thirds.

**10**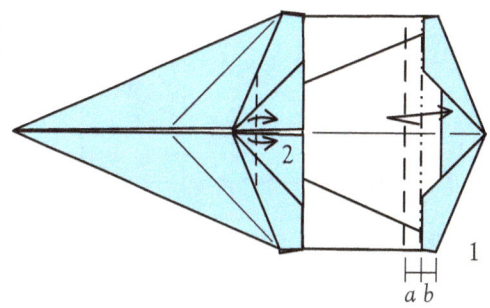

1. Pleat-fold so *a* is slightly larger than *b*.
2. Fold the ears.

**11**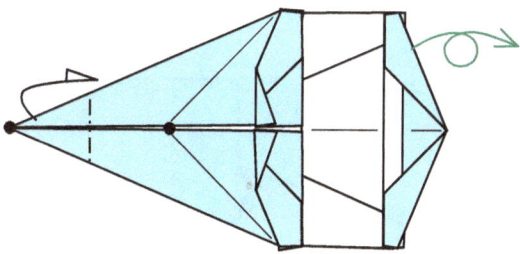

The dots will meet.

**12**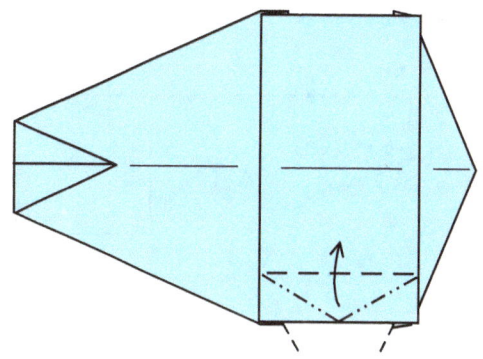

Petal-fold.

**13**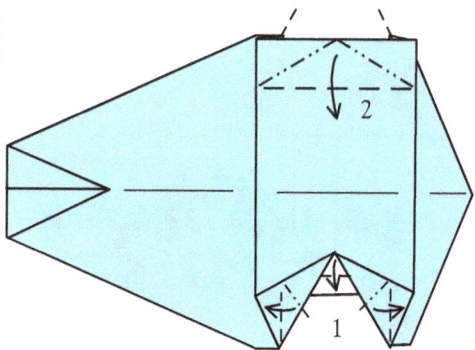

1. Petal-fold.
2. Repeat steps 12–13 on the top.

**14**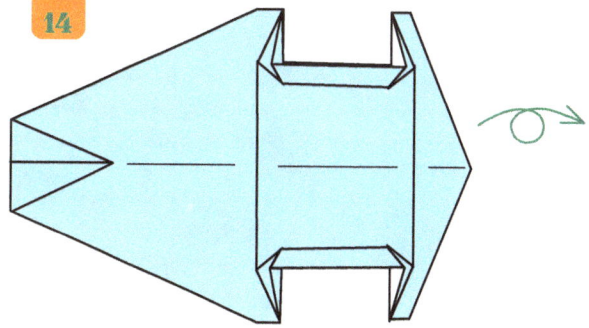

*Malayan Tapir* **47**

**15**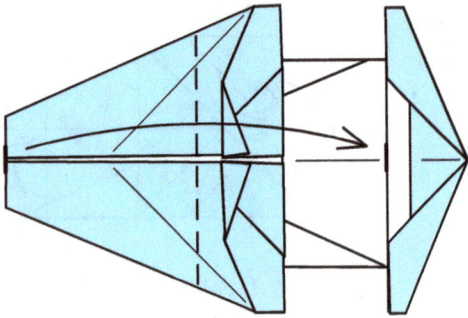

**16**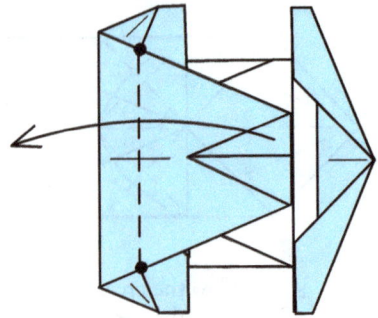

**17**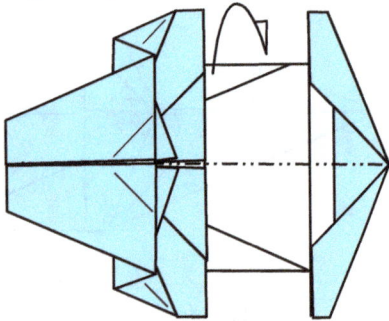

Fold in half.

**18**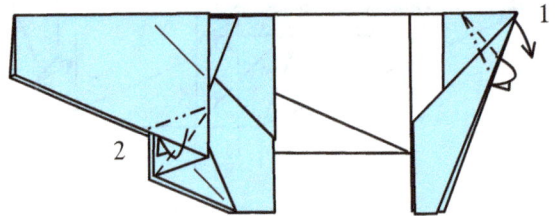

1. Crimp-fold.
2. Fold inside, repeat behind.

**19**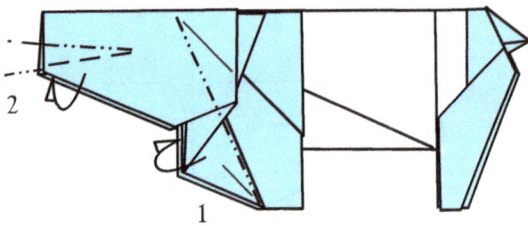

1. Fold inside, repeat behind.
2. Crimp-fold.

**20**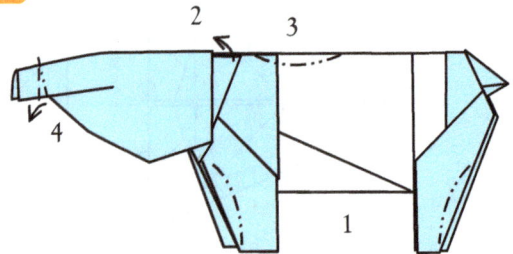

1. Shape the legs, repeat behind.
2. Spread the ears, repeat behind.
3. Shape the back.
4. Shape the head.

**21**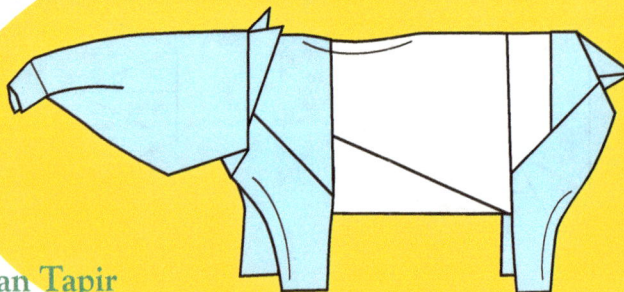

Malayan Tapir

# Hippo with Mouth

Hippos are amongst the deadliest animals on Earth due to their aggressive nature, size and sharp teeth. They are not territorial on land but when provoked or threatened, can wreak havoc on their enemies.

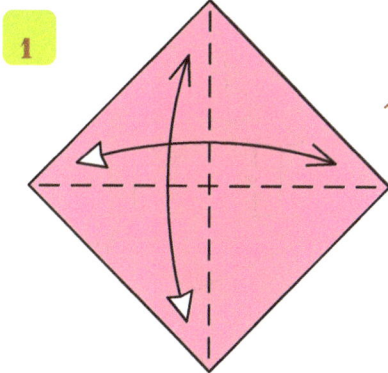

**1**

Fold and unfold.

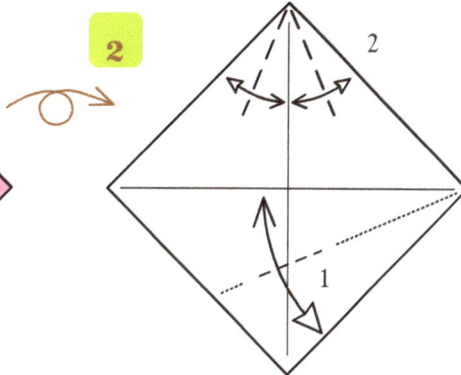

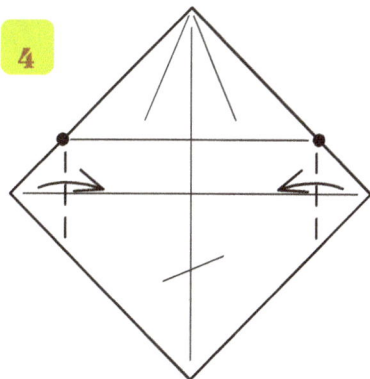

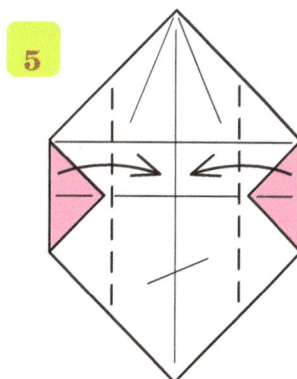

**2**

Fold to the center and unfold.
1. Along the diagonal.
2. At the top.

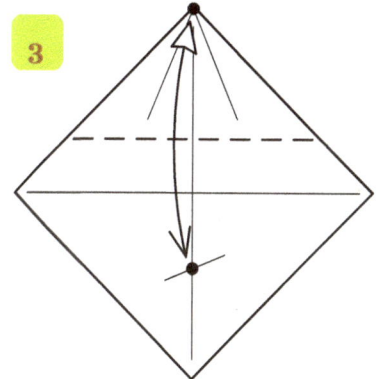

**3**

Fold and unfold.

**4**

**5**

Fold to the center.

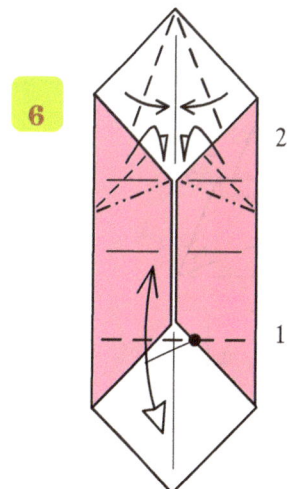

**6**

1. Fold and unfold.
2. Fold along some of the creases.

**7**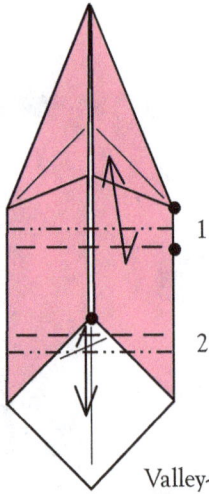

Valley-fold along the creases for these pleat folds.

**8**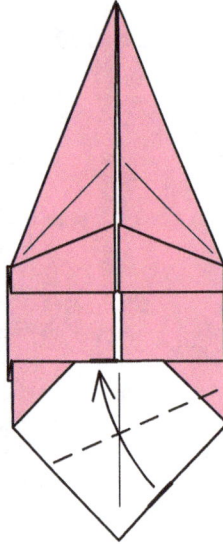

**9**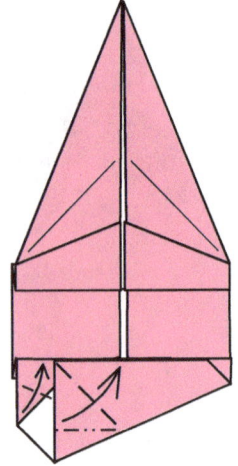

Squash-fold.

**10**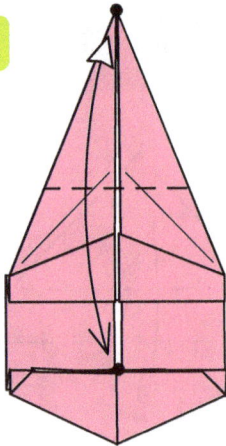

Fold and unfold.

**11**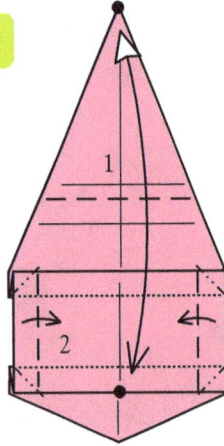

1. Fold and unfold.
2. Make petal folds.

**12**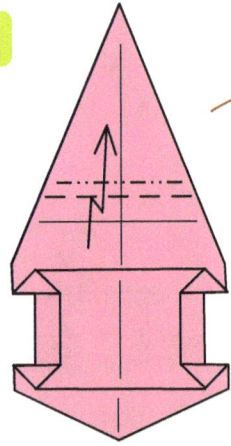

Pleat-fold along the creases.

**13**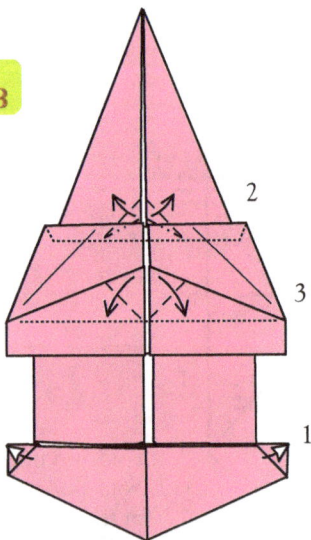

1. Pull out the inner layers.
2. Make small squash folds to form the eyes.
3. Fold the ears.

**14**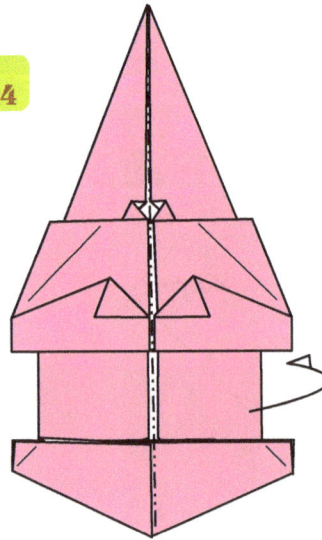

Fold in half and rotate 90°.

**15**

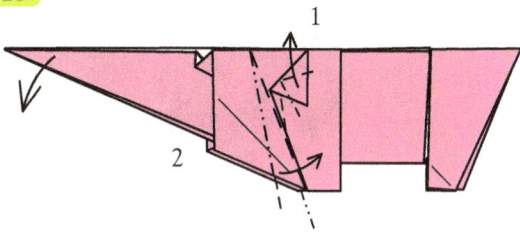

1. Squash-fold, repeat behind.
2. Crimp-fold.

**16**

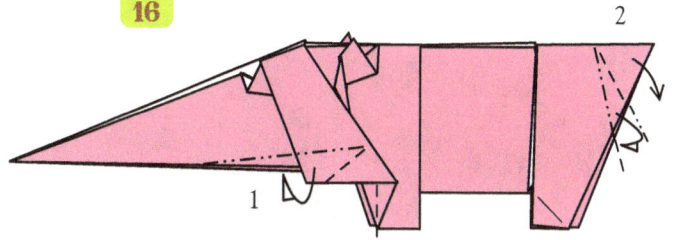

1. Fold inside, repeat behind.
2. Crimp-fold.

**17**

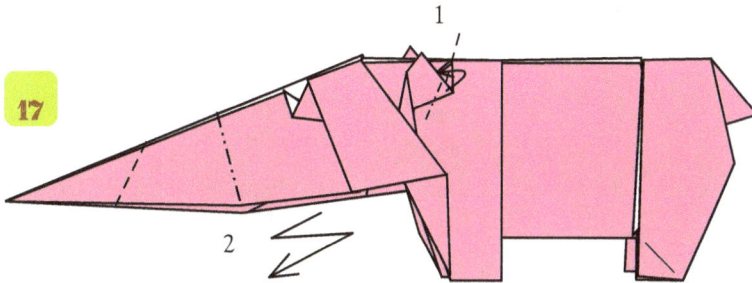

1. Reverse-fold, repeat behind.
2. Crimp-fold.

**18**

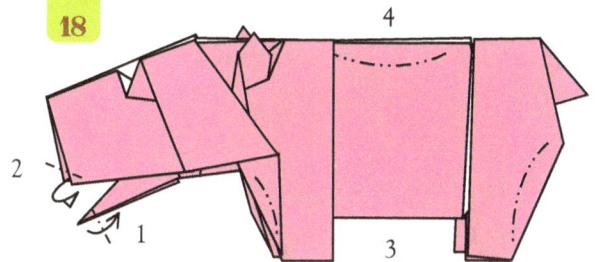

1. Reverse-fold.
2. Fold inside, repeat behind.
3. Shape the legs, repeat behind.
4. Shape the back.

**19**

Hippo with Mouth

# Hippopotamus

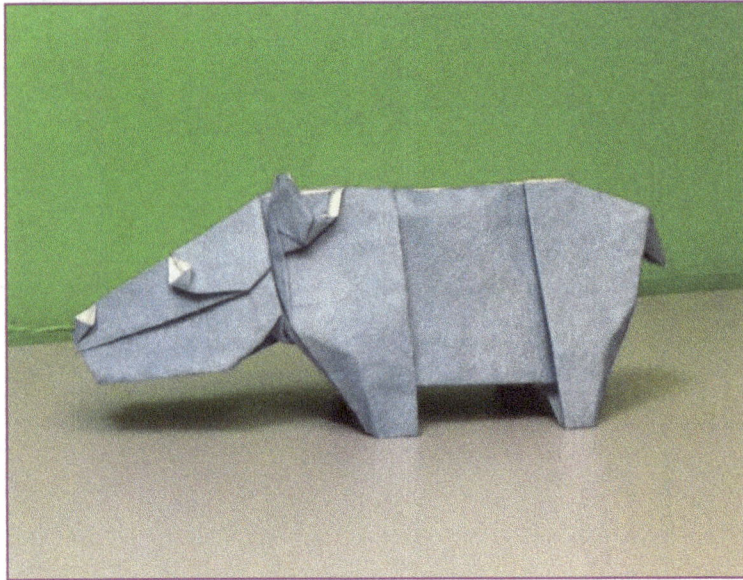

Though they have an ungainly appearance on land, Hippos are quite graceful under water and are good swimmers. They mainly eat vegetation and spend around two thirds of the day in the water to keep cool.

**1**

Fold and unfold.

**2**

Fold and unfold.

**3**

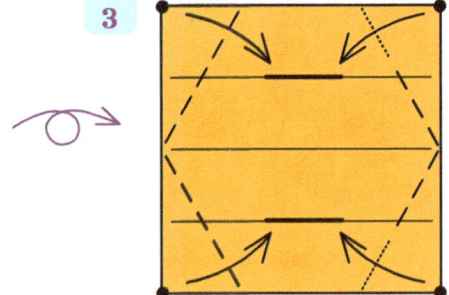

Bring the corners to the creases.

**4**

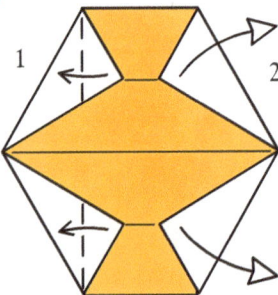

1. Fold to the left.
2. Unfold.

**5**

**6**

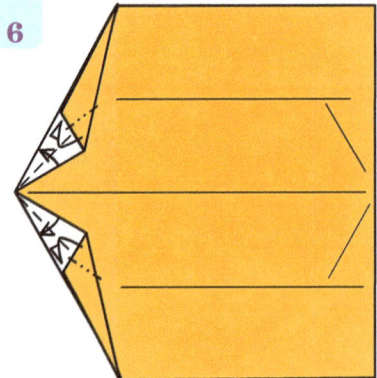

Make reverse folds.

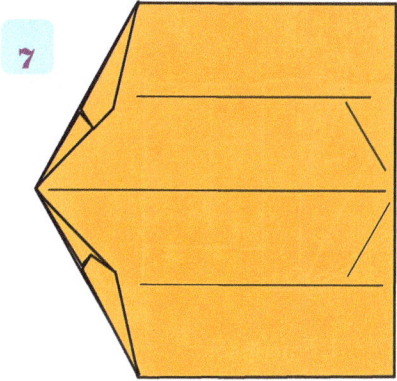

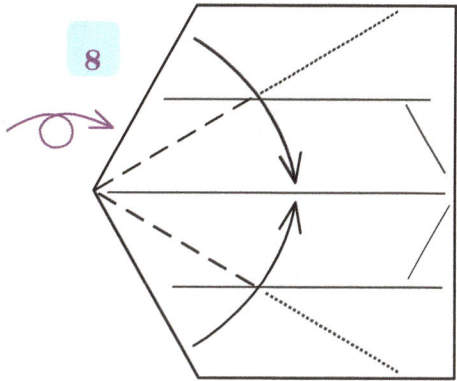

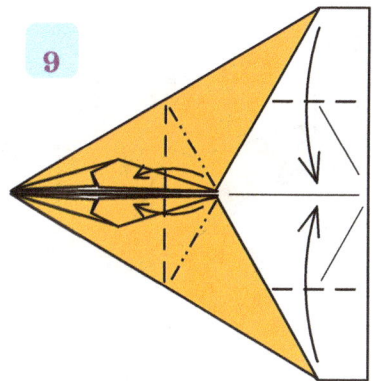

Make squash folds.

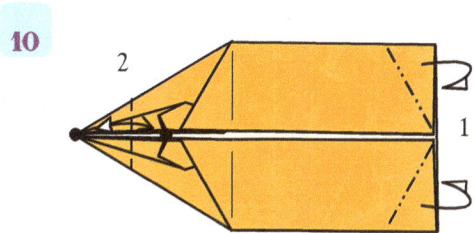

1. Fold along the hidden creases.
2. Fold and unfold.

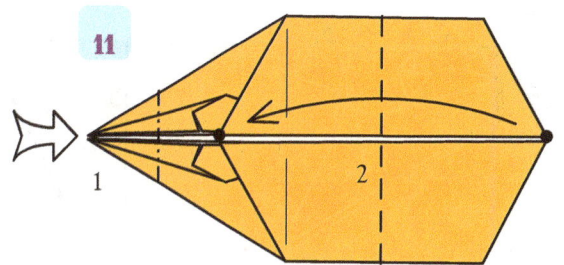

1. Sink.
2. The dots will meet.

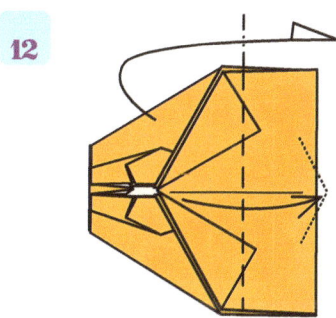

Fold slightly to the right
of the right side. Repeat
behind on the same line.

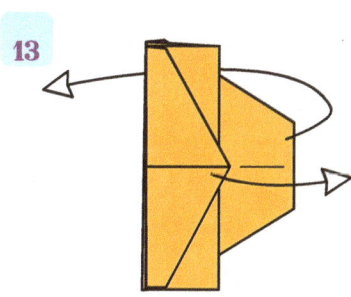

Unfold.

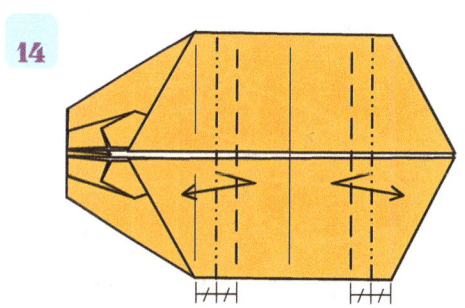

Make pleat folds.
Mountain-fold
along the creases.

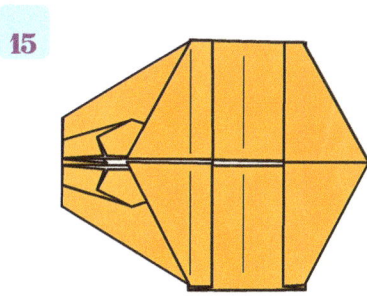

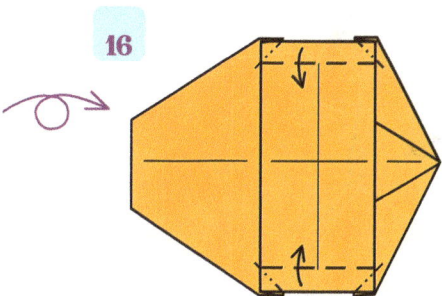

Make petal folds.

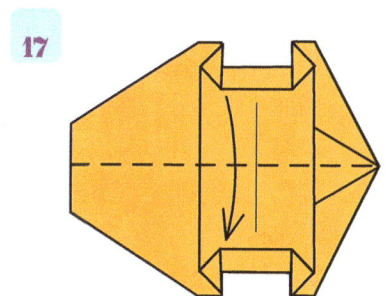

**18**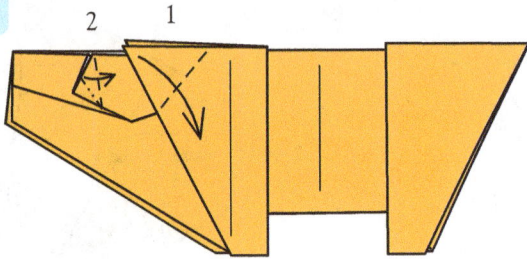

1. Fold down.
2. Squash-fold.
Repeat behind.

**19**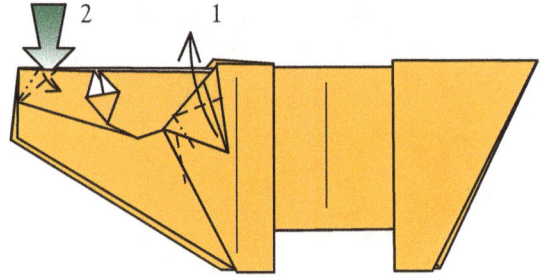

1. Squash-fold.
2. Squash-fold.
Repeat behind.

**20**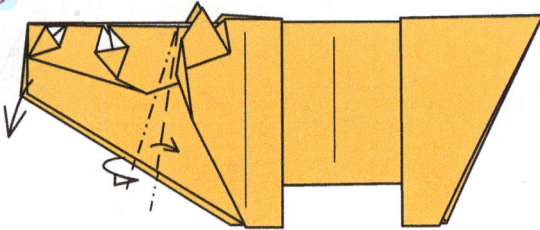

Crimp-fold.

**21**

1. Reverse-fold, repeat behind.
2. Double-rabbit-ear.

**22**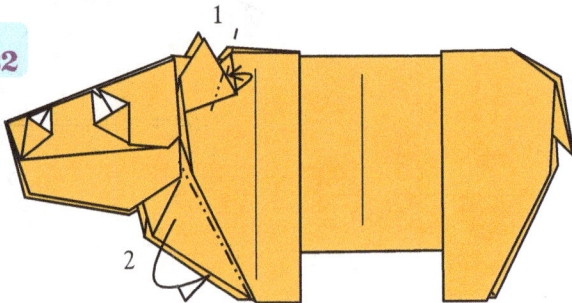

1. Reverse-fold.
2. Fold inside.
Repeat behind.

**23**

Shape the Hippo with soft folds.

**24**

**Hippopotamus**

# Rhinoceros

The Rhinoceros is a fierce, large animal, easily identified by the two horns on its nose. The horns, which can be wielded as weapons in a fight, are actually made of keratin, the same substance that human hair and nails are made of. There are five species of Rhino, the Black Rhino, the Indian Rhino, the Sumatran Rhino, the Javan Rhino and the Indian Rhino. All are endangered due to poaching, the Javan Rhino having the least remaining numbers.

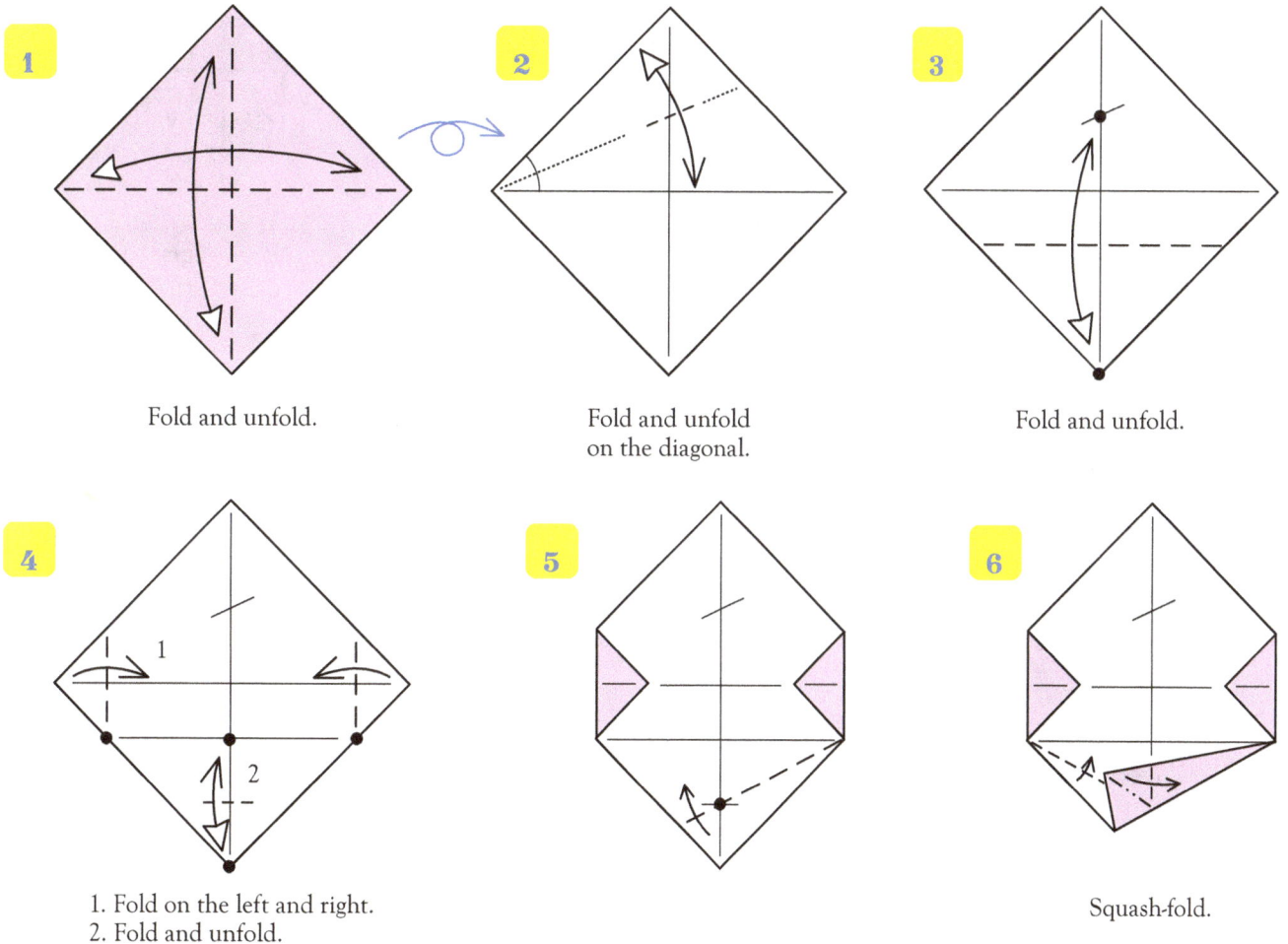

**1**

Fold and unfold.

**2**

Fold and unfold
on the diagonal.

**3**

Fold and unfold.

**4**

1. Fold on the left and right.
2. Fold and unfold.

**5**

**6**

Squash-fold.

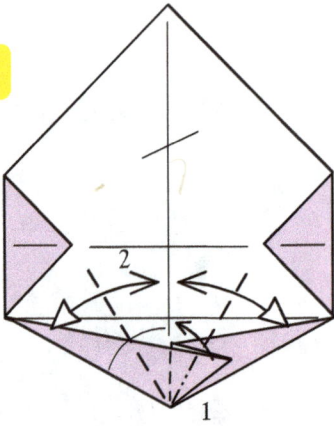

**7**

1. Squash-fold.
2. Fold to the center
   and unfold.

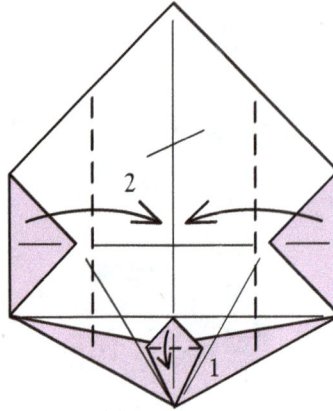

**8**

1. Fold down.
2. Fold to the center.
   Rotate 180°.

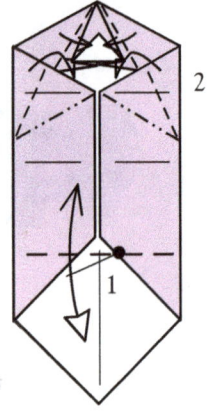

**9**

1. Fold and unfold.
2. Fold along some
   of the creases.

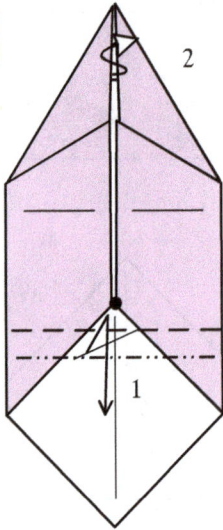

**10**

1. Valley-fold along the
   crease for this pleat fold.
2. Pull out.

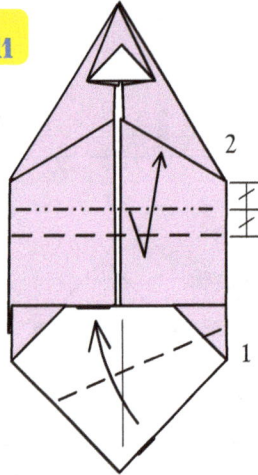

**11**

1. The edges will meet.
2. Mountain-fold along the
   crease for this pleat fold.

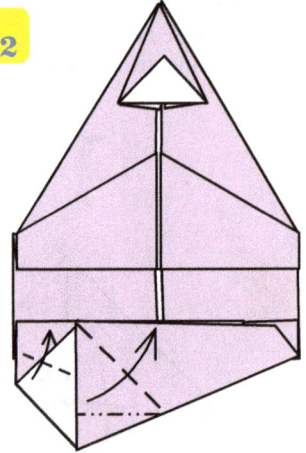

**12**

Squash-fold.

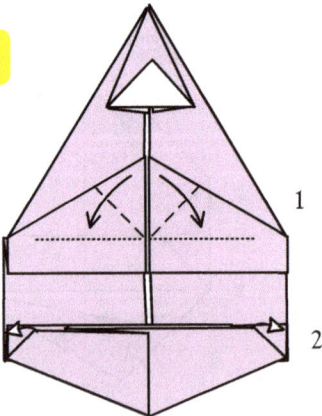

**13**

1. Fold the ears.
2. Pull out the inner layers.

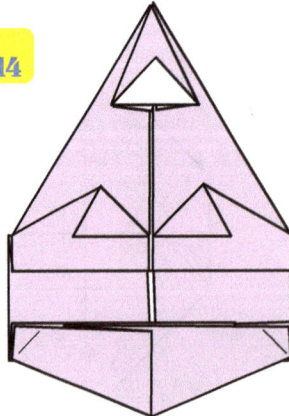

**14**

Rotate 90°.

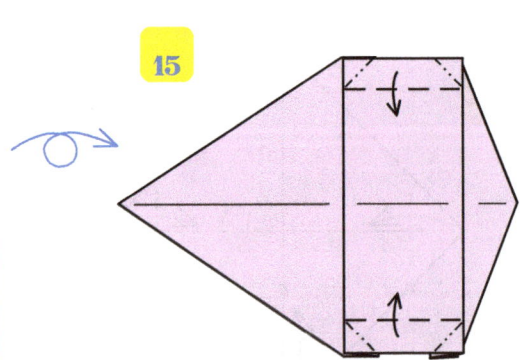

**15**

Make petal folds.

**16**

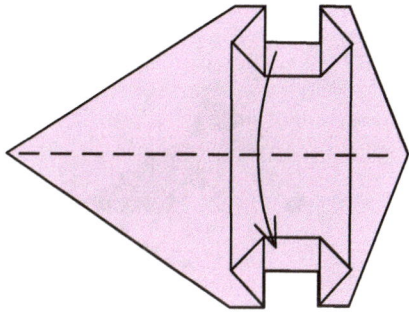

Fold in half.

**17**

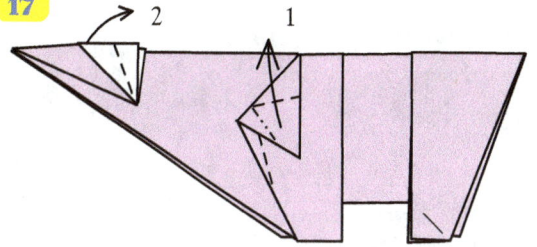

1. Squash-fold, repeat behind.
2. Outside-reverse-fold.

**18**

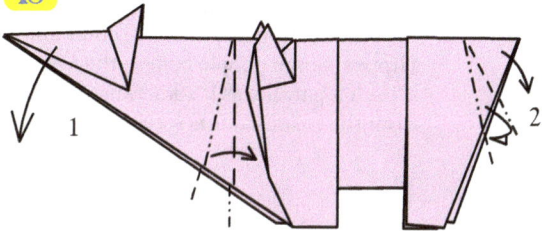

Make crimp folds.

**19**

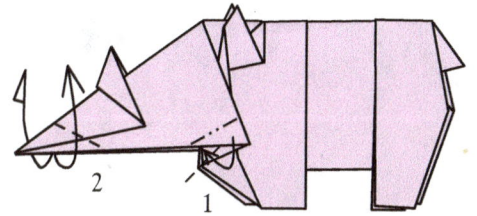

1. Reverse-fold, repeat behind.
2. Outside-reverse-fold.

**20**

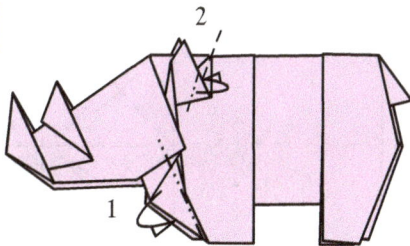

1. Fold inside.
2. Reverse-fold.
Repeat behind.

**21**

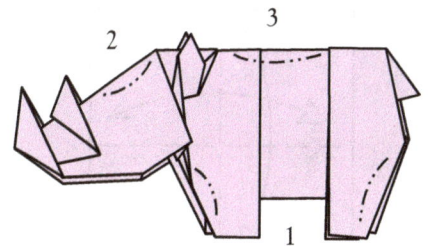

1. Shape the legs, repeat behind.
2. Shape the head.
3. Shape the body.

**22**

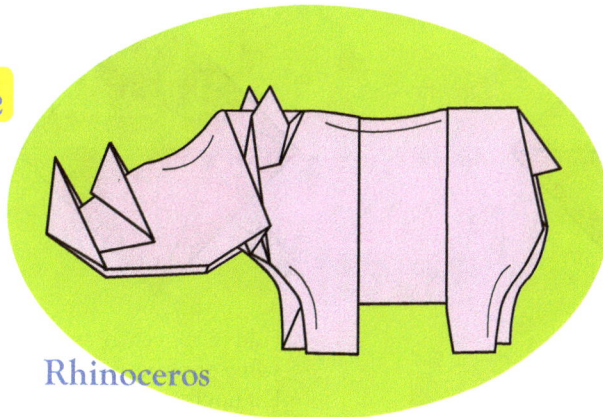

Rhinoceros

# Oxpecker

This small bird often serves as the Rhino's personal housecleaner, perching on its back and eating small insects and other parasites. The Oxpecker also provides the same service for other mammals, such as Zebras and Hippos. Some people believe the Oxpecker is itself a parasite as it sometimes draws blood from the mammal it is serving.

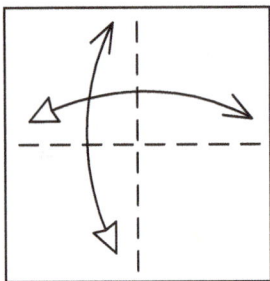

1    Fold and unfold.

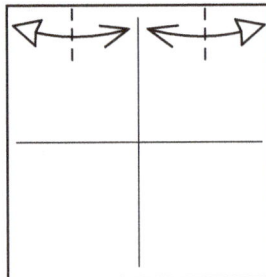

2    Fold and unfold.

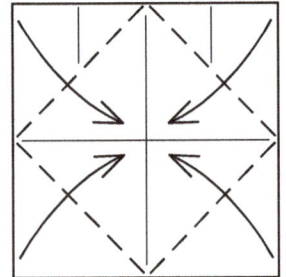

3    Fold to the center.

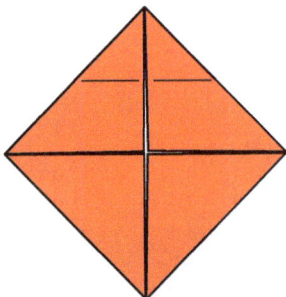

4

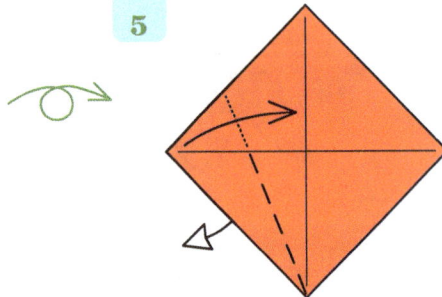

5    Fold to the center and swing out from behind. Do not crease at the top.

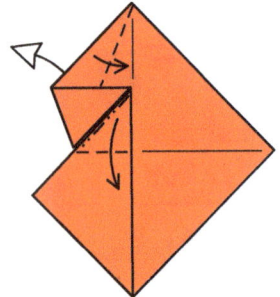

6    Squash-fold and swing out from behind.

**7**

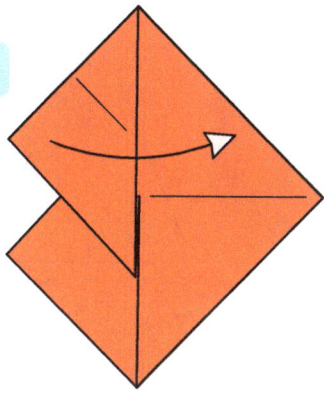

Unfold.

**8**

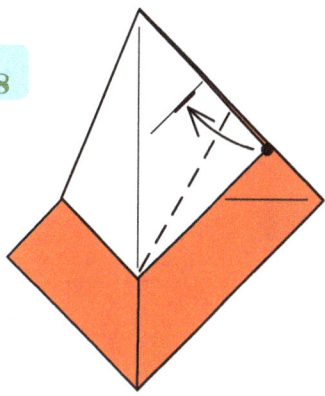

Bring the dot
to the line.

**9**

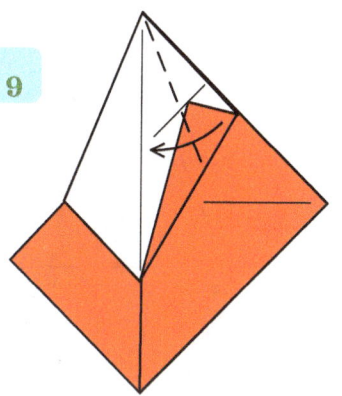

**10**

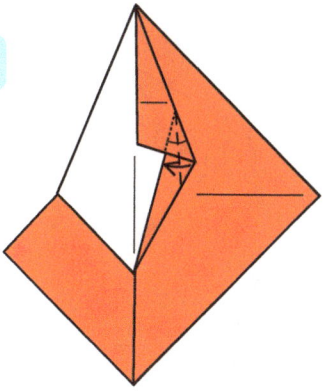

**11**

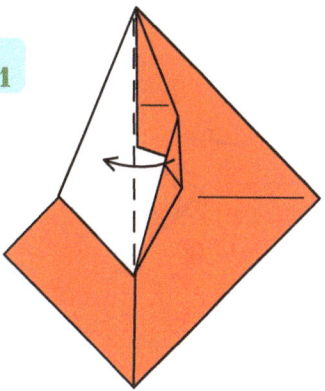

**12**

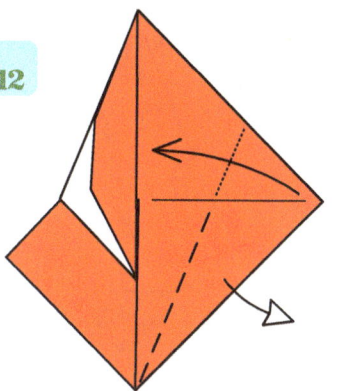

Repeat steps 5–11
on the right.

**13**

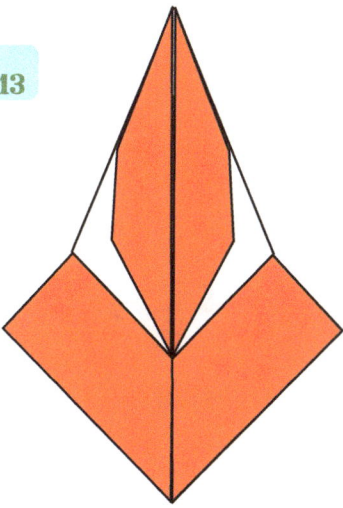

**14**

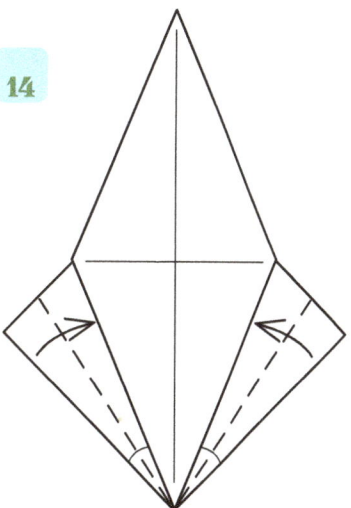

**15**

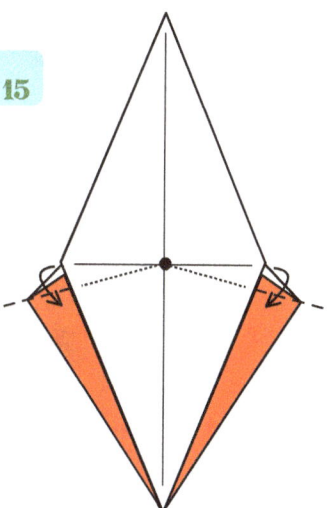

**16**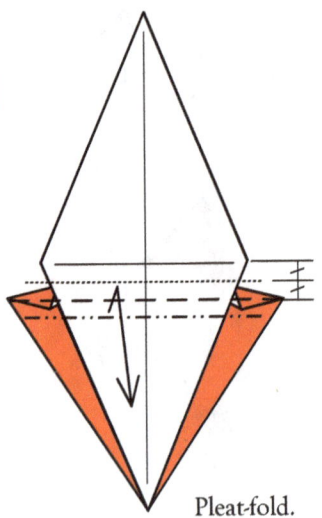

Pleat-fold.

**17**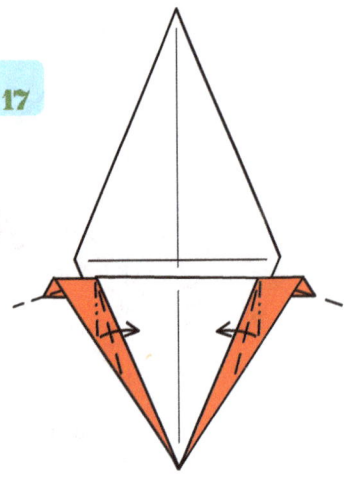

Make squash folds.

**18**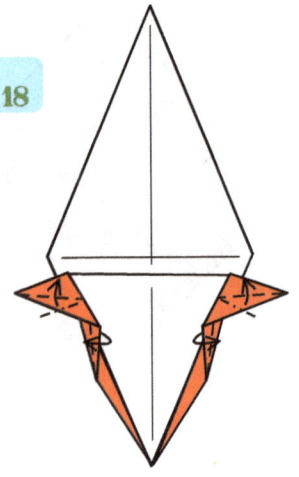

Make squash folds.

**19**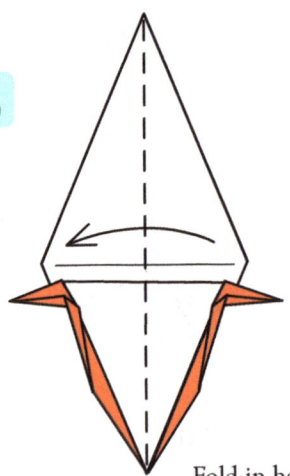

Fold in half and rotate.

**20**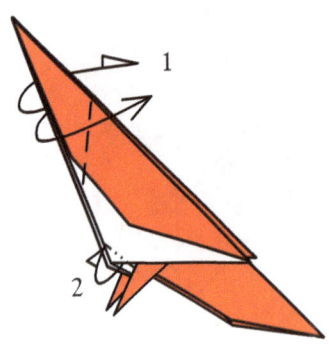

1. Outside-reverse-fold.
2. Fold inside, repeat behind.

**21**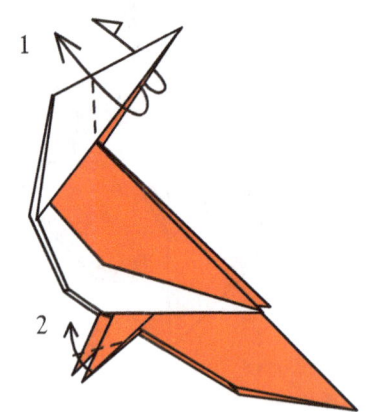

1. Outside-reverse-fold.
2. Outside-reverse-fold, repeat behind.

**22**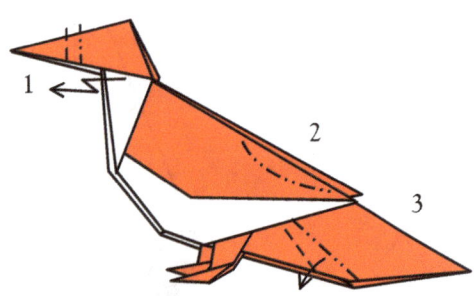

1. Crimp-fold.
2. Shape the wings, repeat behind.
3. Crimp-fold.

**23**

Oxpecker

# Elephant

The Elephant is know for its long trunk and ivory tusks, and of all the Elephant species, the African Bush Elephant is the largest living land mammal on Earth. Elephants have excellent memories and are also known for displaying very complex feelings and emotions, including happiness, grief and love.

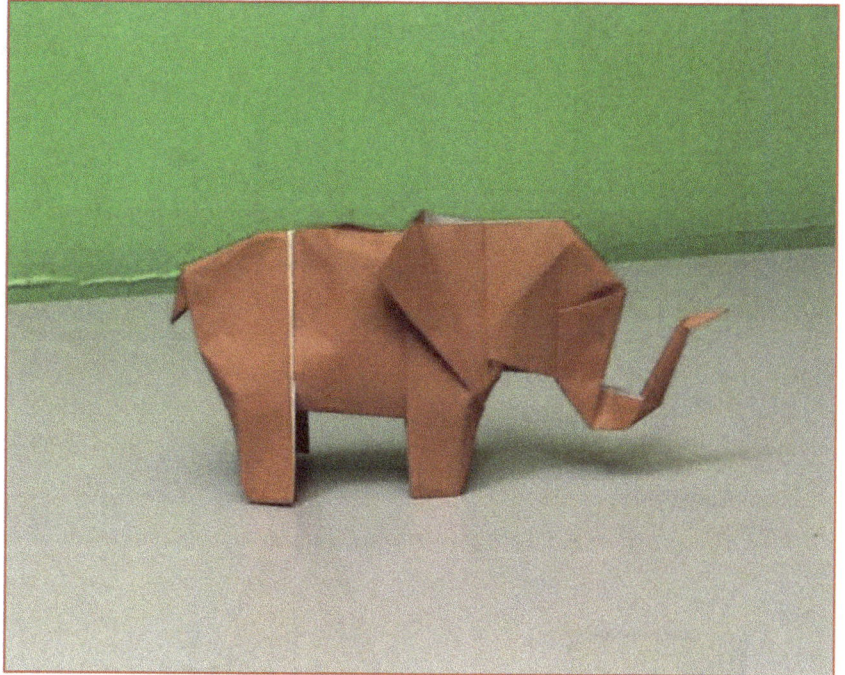

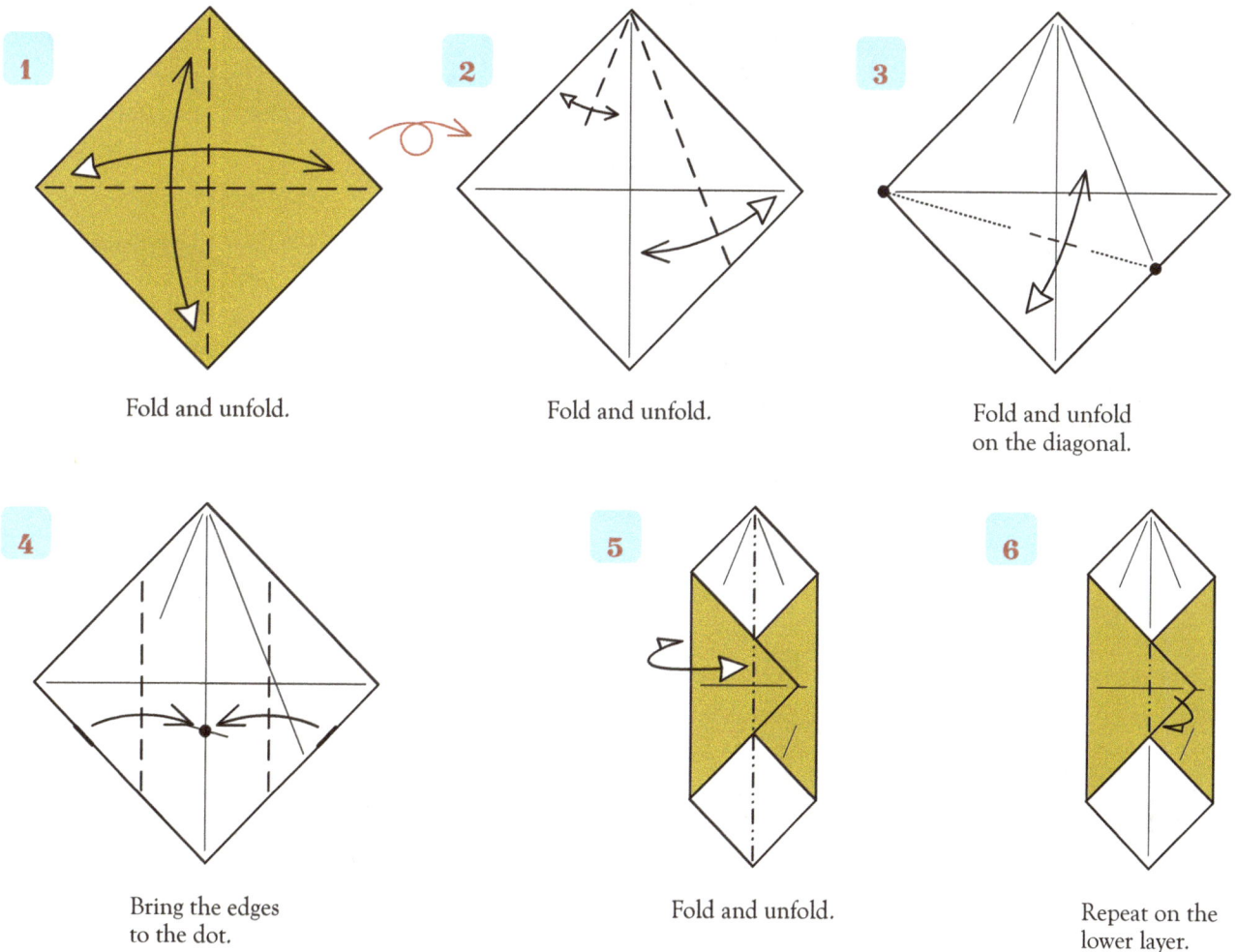

**1**

Fold and unfold.

**2**

Fold and unfold.

**3**

Fold and unfold on the diagonal.

**4**

Bring the edges to the dot.

**5**

Fold and unfold.

**6**

Repeat on the lower layer.

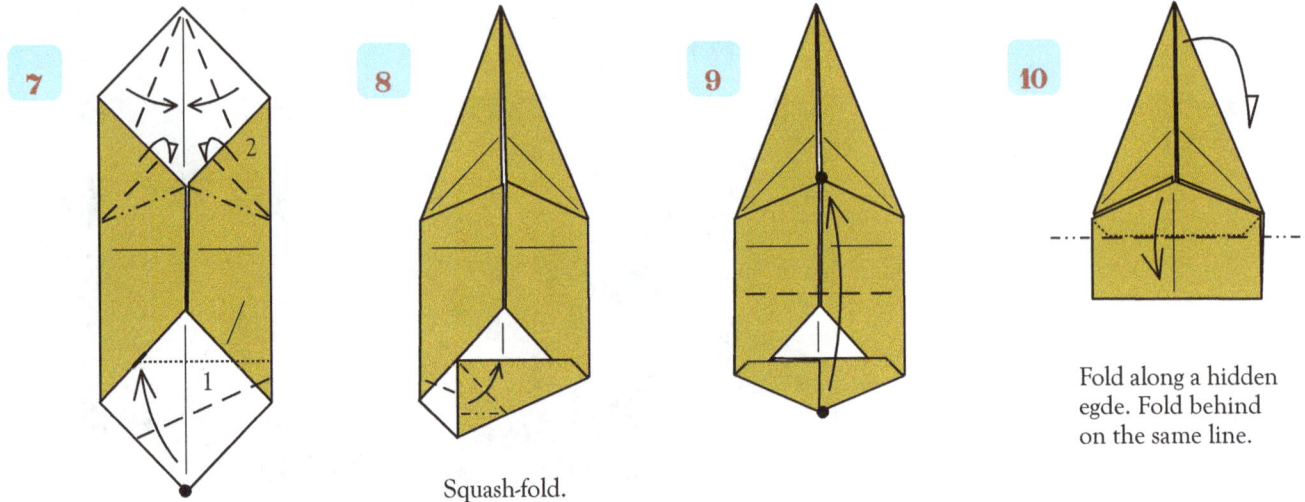

**7**

1. Bring the dot to the line so one side is horizontal.
2. Fold along some of the creases.

**8**

Squash-fold.

**9**

**10**

Fold along a hidden egde. Fold behind on the same line.

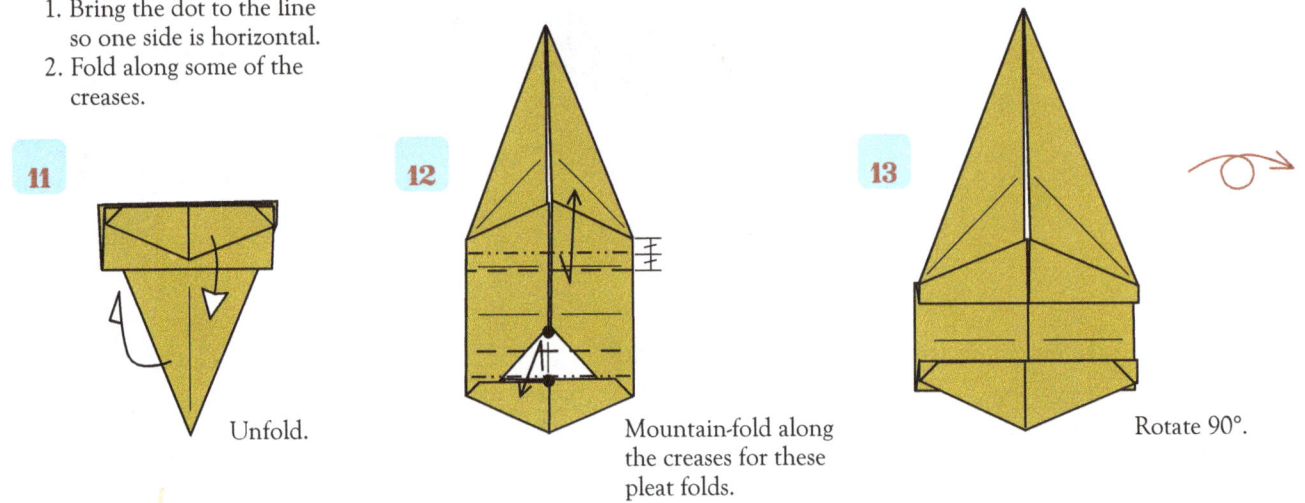

**11**

Unfold.

**12**

Mountain-fold along the creases for these pleat folds.

**13**

Rotate 90°.

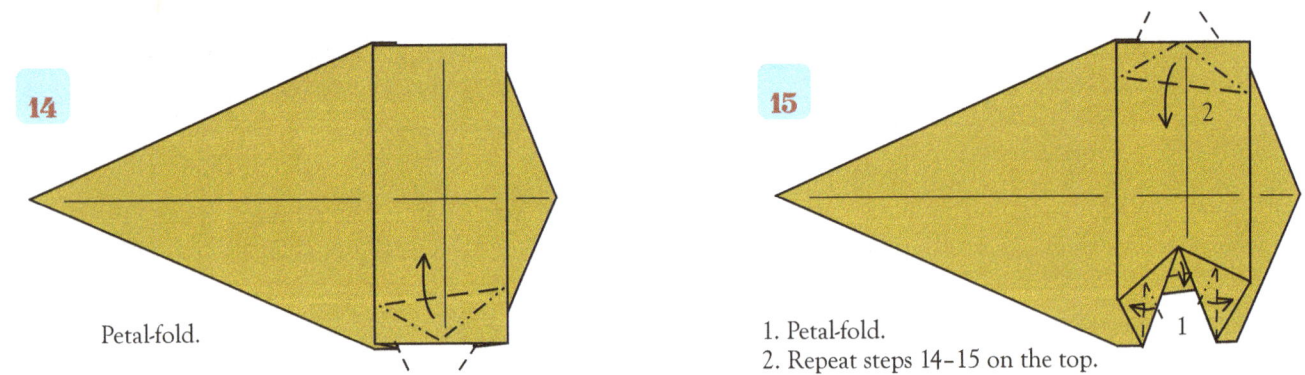

**14**

Petal-fold.

**15**

1. Petal-fold.
2. Repeat steps 14–15 on the top.

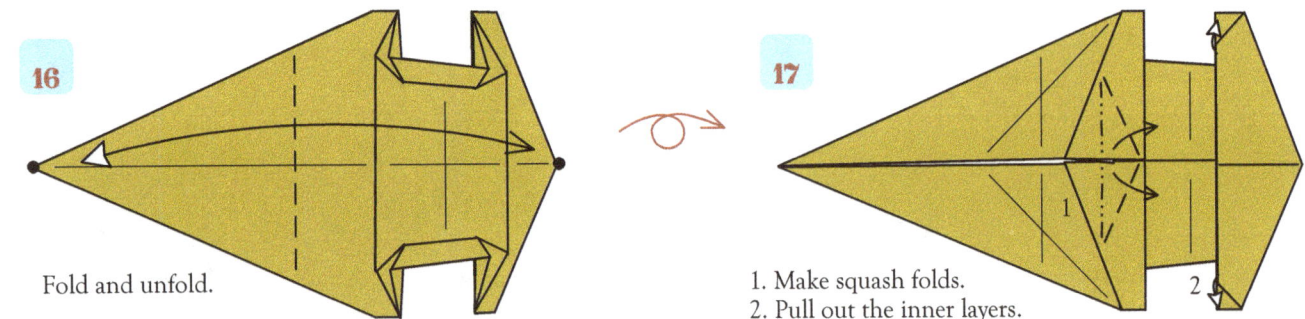

**16**

Fold and unfold.

**17**

1. Make squash folds.
2. Pull out the inner layers.

**18**

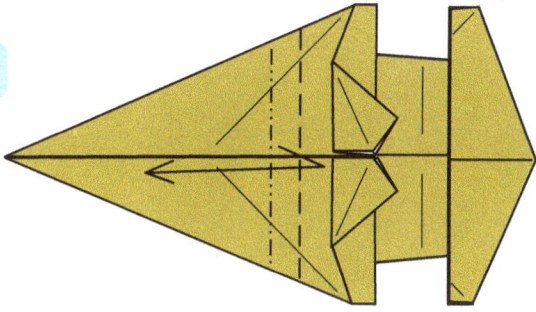

Mountain-fold along the
crease for this pleat fold.

**19**

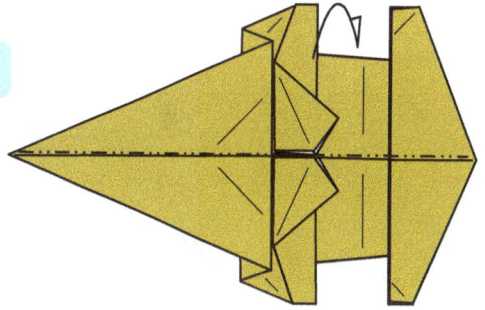

Fold in half.

**20**

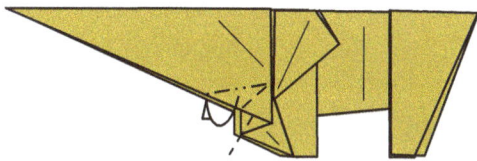

Fold inside, repeat behind.

**21**

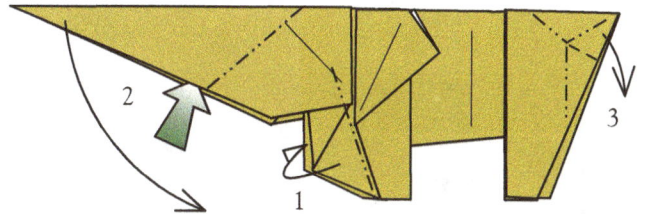

1. Fold inside, repeat behind.
2. Reverse-fold.
3. Double-rabbit-ear.

**22**

Repeat behind.

**23**

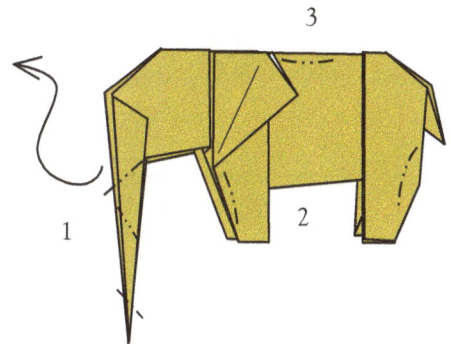

1. Shape the trunk with reverse folds.
2. Shape the legs, repeat behind.
3. Shape the back.

**24**

Elephant

# Giraffe

The Giraffe, with its **very** long neck, is the tallest living land mammal on Earth. Giraffes have very long tongues that are purple or black in color, which allows them to feed for many hours a day without their tongues getting sunburnt. While it seems like Giraffes are very quiet animals, they actually communicate using sounds too low to be heard by human ears, as well as through non-verbal communication.

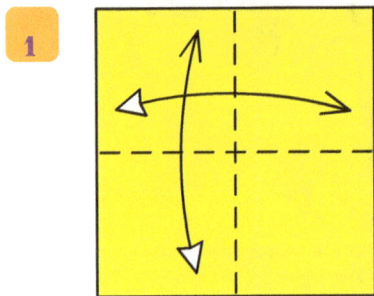

**1**

Fold and unfold.

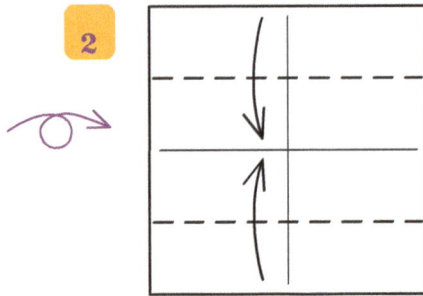

**2**

Fold to the center.

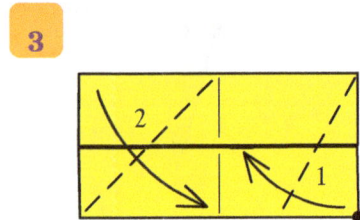

**3**

1. Bring the corner to the line.
2. Fold to the crease.

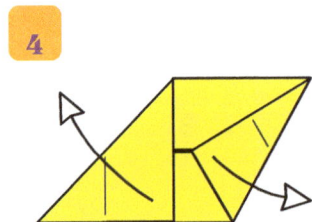

**4**

Unfold.

**5**

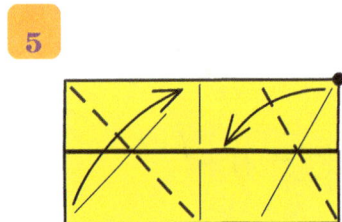

Repeat steps 3-4 in the opposite direction.

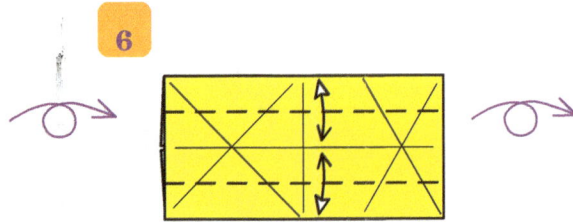

**6**

Fold and unfold.

**7**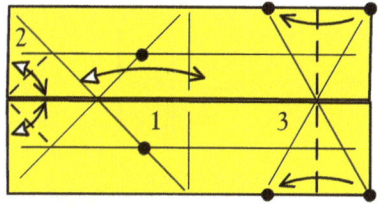

1. Fold and unfold.
2. Fold and unfold.
3. The dots will meet.

**8**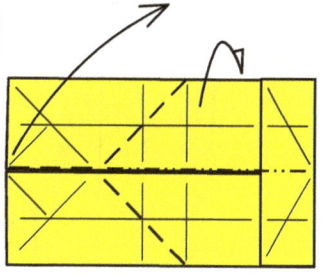

Fold along the creases.

**9**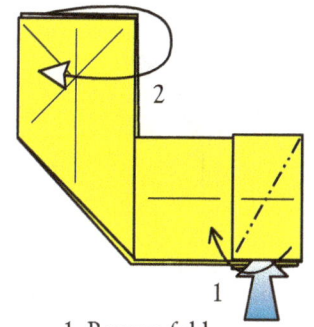

1. Reverse-fold.
2. Wrap around
Repeat behind.

**10**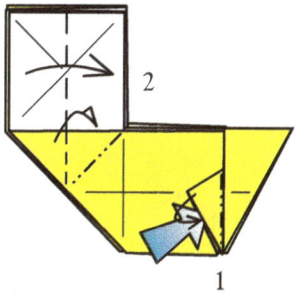

1. Reverse-fold.
2. Reverse-fold.
Repeat behind.

**11**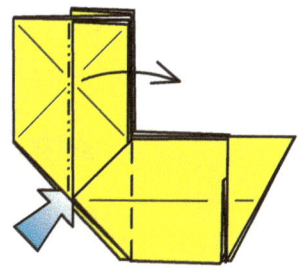

Spread-squash-fold.

**12**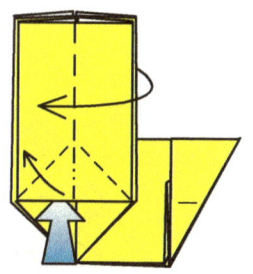

**13**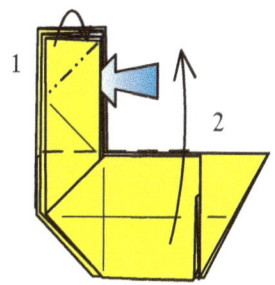

1. Make four reverse folds.
2. Fold up.

**14**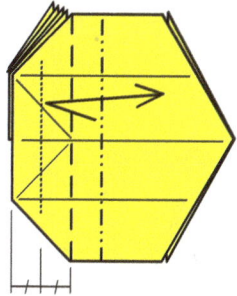

Pleat-fold to the
half-way mark.

**15**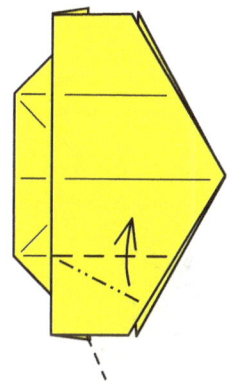

Valley-fold along the crease
for this squash fold.

**16**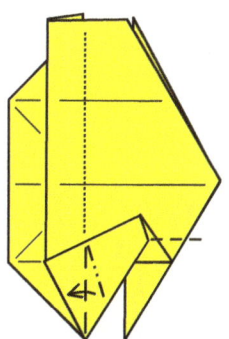

Squash-fold.

**17**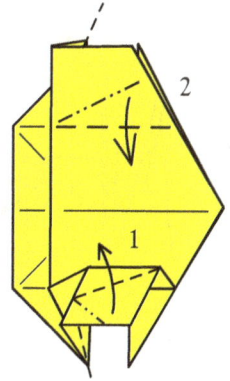

1. Squash-fold.
2. Repeat steps 15–17
on the top.

**18**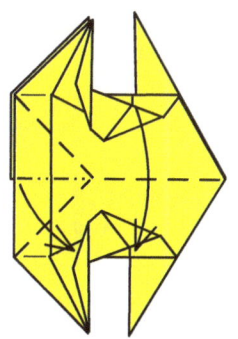

Push in on the left
while folding in half.

**19**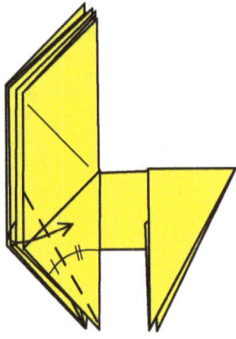

Fold two flaps at an angle of 1/3. Repeat behind.

**20**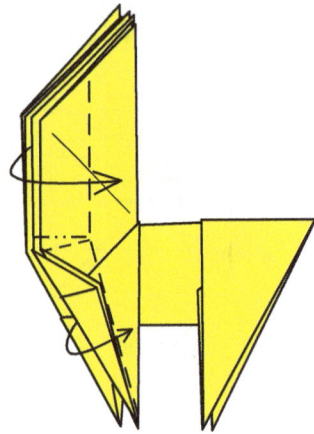

Fold in half at the top and bottom. Repeat behind.

**21**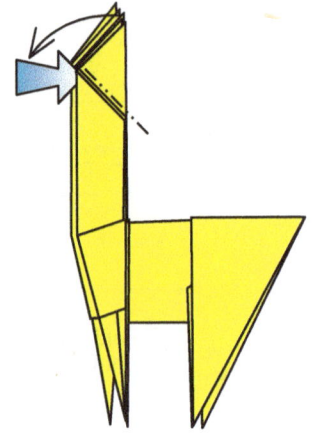

Reverse-fold the middle flap.

**22**

Head detail.

Fold one flap, repeat behind.

**23**

Rabbit-ear, repeat behind.

**24**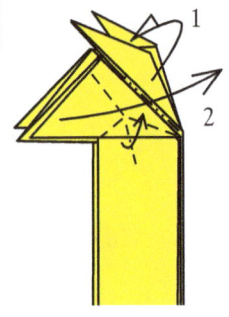

1. Fold inside.
2. Fold the ear.
Repeat behind.

**25**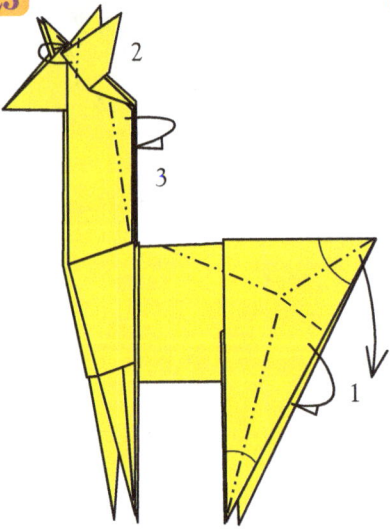

1. Double-rabbit-ear.
2. Reverse-fold, repeat behind.
3. Fold two flaps inside, repeat behind.

**26**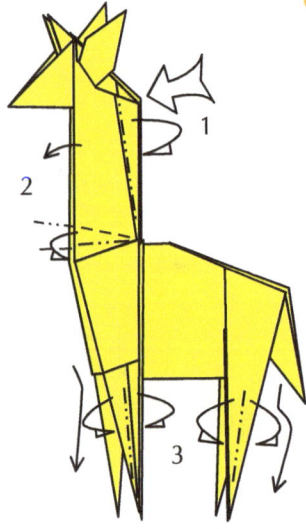

1. Sink.
2. Crimp-fold.
3. Shape the legs, repeat behind.

**27**

Giraffe

# Okapi

Looking like a cross between a Zebra, Horse and Giraffe, these animals share the Giraffe's long tongue and have stripes on their legs and hindquarters. Okapis are related to Giraffes and have excellent hearing and live in Central Africa in the Ituri Rainforest.

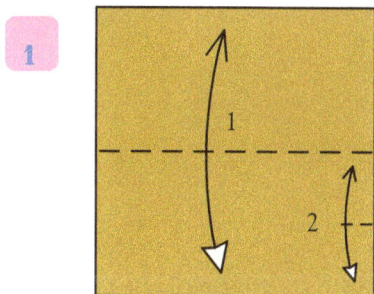

**1**
Fold and unfold.

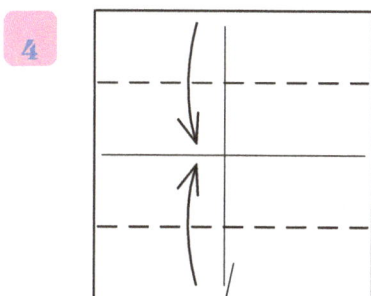

**2**
Fold and unfold on the bottom.

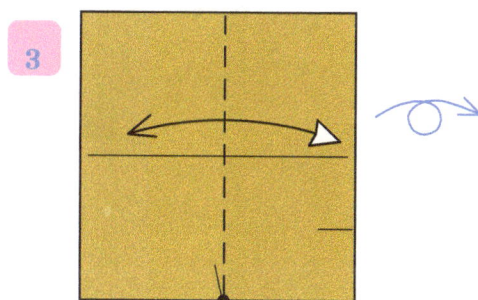

**3**
Fold and unfold.

**4**
Fold to the center.

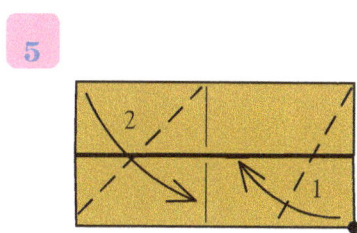

**5**
1. Bring the corner to the line.
2. Fold to the crease.

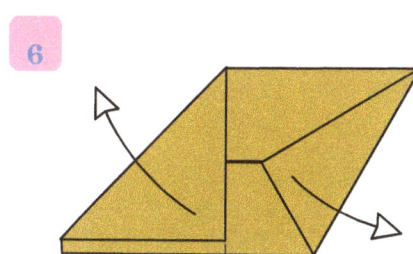

**6**
Unfold.

**7**

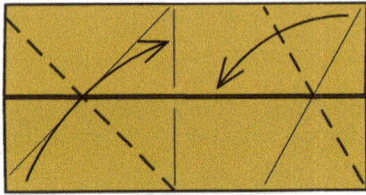

Repeat steps 5–6 in
the opposite direction.

**8**

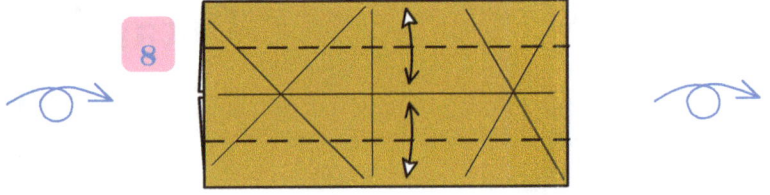

Fold and unfold.

**9**

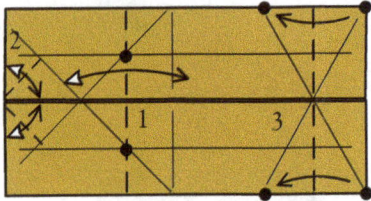

1. Fold and unfold.
2. Fold and unfold.
3. The dots will meet.

**10**

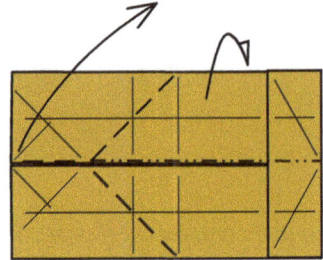

Fold along the creases.

**11**

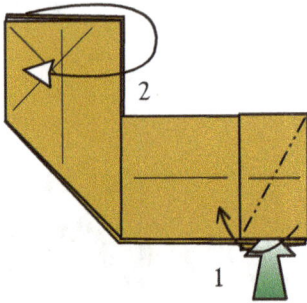

1. Reverse-fold.
2. Wrap around
Repeat behind.

**12**

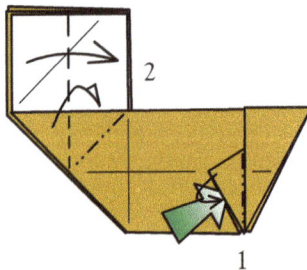

Continue with steps 10 through
the end of the Giraffe (page 64).

**13**

Okapi

# Third Movement

## Minuet: An Octet of Colorful Tetrahedra with a Trio of Grand Pyramids

The tetrahedron is one of the simplest of pyramids. Here are eight tetrahedra with color-change patterns, including a Tetrahedron of Triangles and a Capped Tetrahedron. The models were designed with simplicity in folding, more than half of these are accomplished in under 20 steps. These duo-colored shapes complement the striped snakes in colorful scenes.

## Double-Banded Tetrahedron

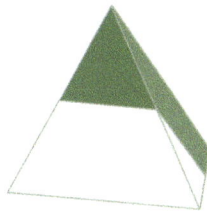

The Double-Banded Tetrahedron has a band of four triangles. The paper is divided into thirds.

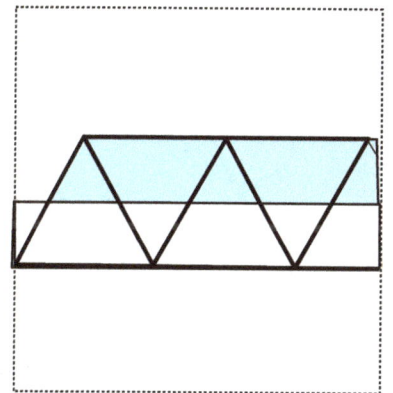

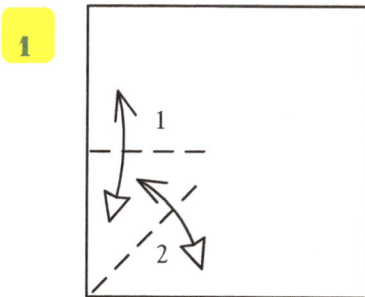

**1**

Fold and unfold.

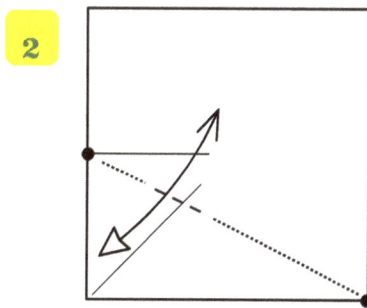

**2**

Fold and unfold at the intersection.

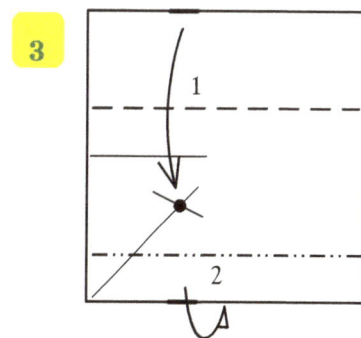

**3**

Fold to the dot.

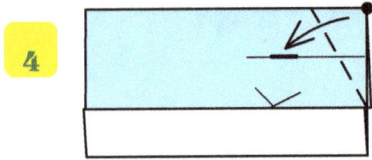

Bring the corner
to the line.

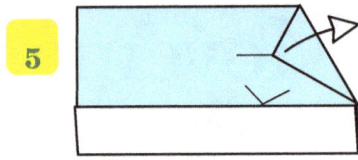

Unfold.

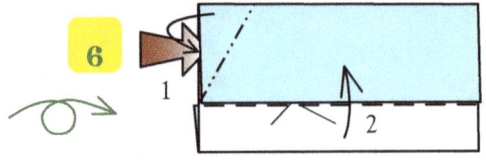

1. Reverse-fold.
2. Fold up.

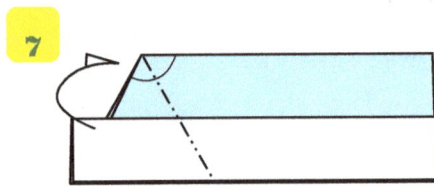

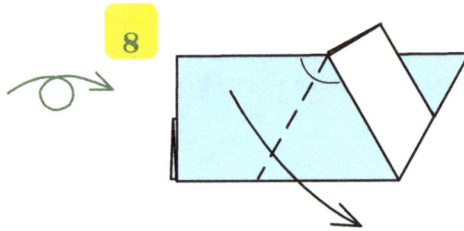

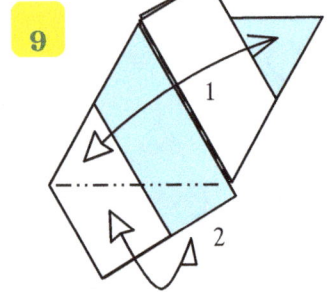

Fold and unfold.

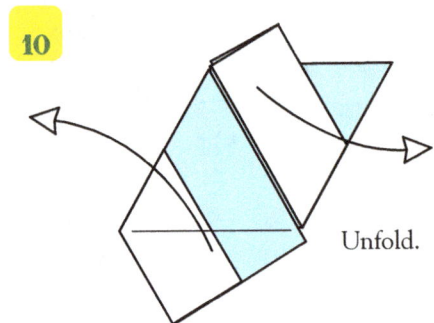

Unfold.

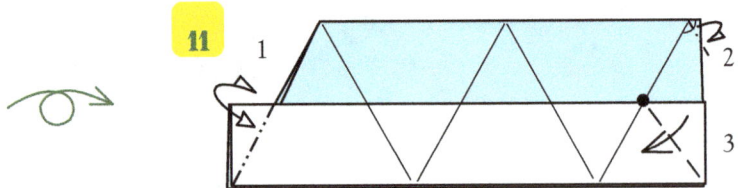

1. Fold and unfold.
2. Fold behind.
3. Valley-fold.

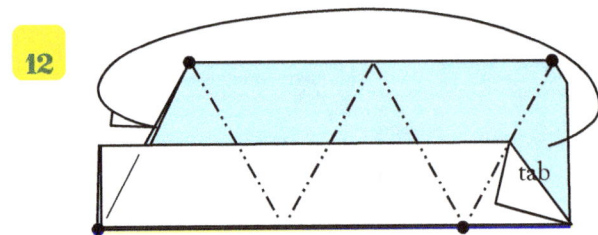

Tuck the tab into pocket.
The pairs of dots will meet.

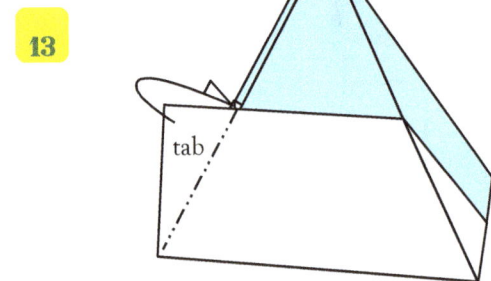

tab

Tuck the tab into pocket.

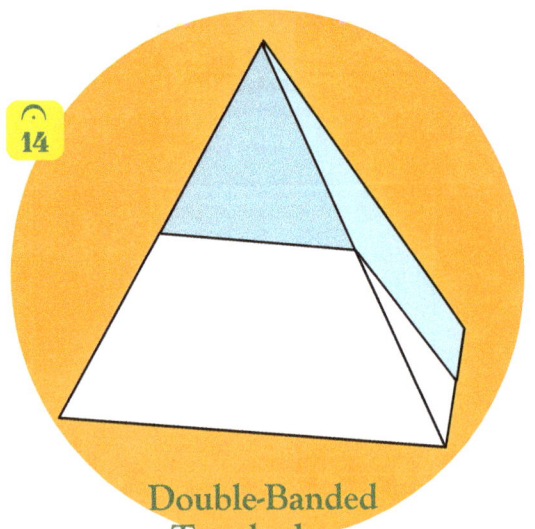

**Double-Banded
Tetrahedron**

# Triple-Banded Tetrahedron

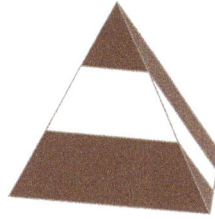

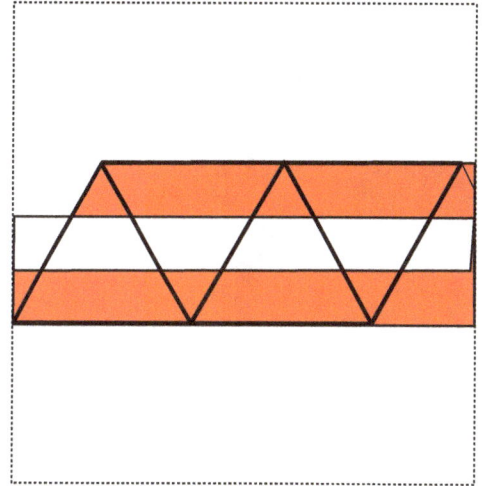

The Triple-Banded Tetrahedron has a band of four triangles. The paper is divided into 9ths.

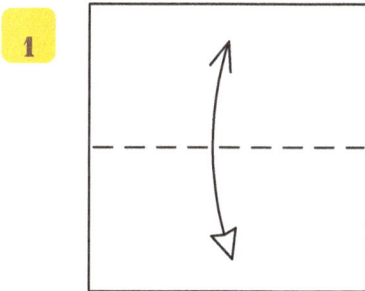

**1** Fold and unfold.

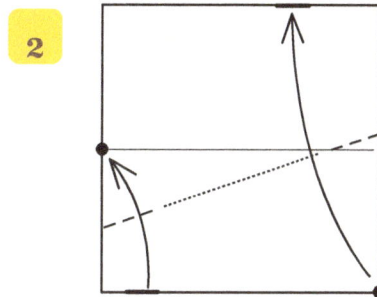

**2** Bring the lower right corner to the top edge and the bottom edge to the left center. Crease on the edges.

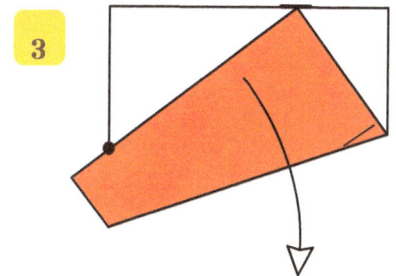

**3** Unfold.

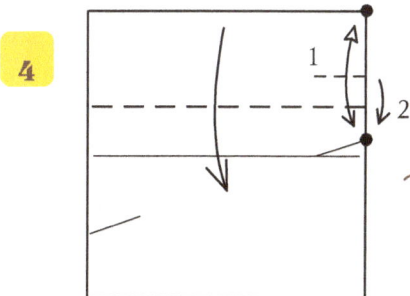

**4**
1. Fold and unfold on the right.
2. Use the new crease for the valley fold.

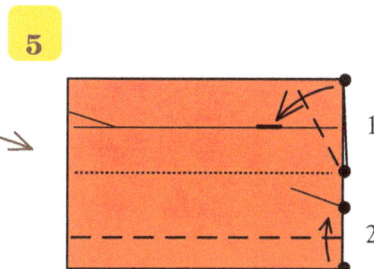

**5**
1. Bring the corner to the line.
2. Fold up to the dot.

**6** Unfold.

**7**

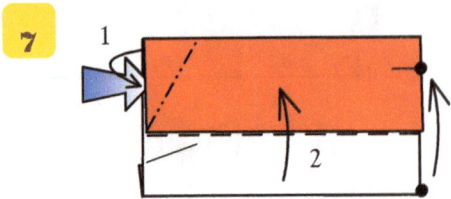

1. Reverse-fold.
2. Fold up.

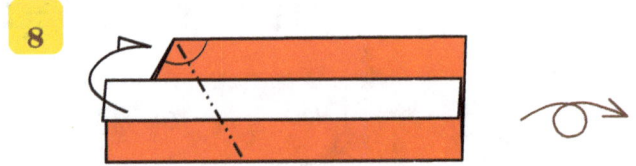

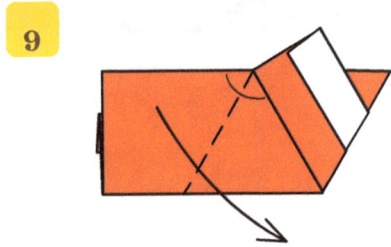

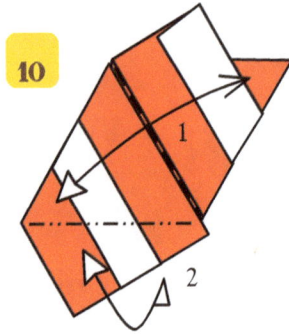

**8**

**9**

**10**

Fold and unfold.

**11**

Unfold.

**12**

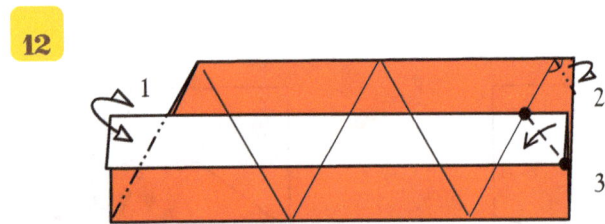

1. Fold and unfold.
2. Fold behind.
3. Valley-fold.

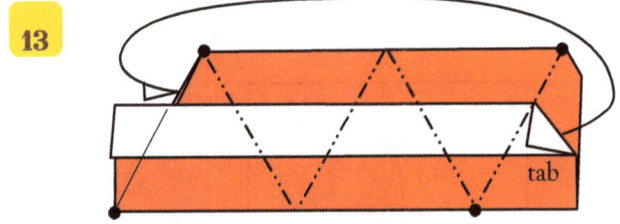

**13**

Tuck the tab into pocket.
The pairs of dots will meet.

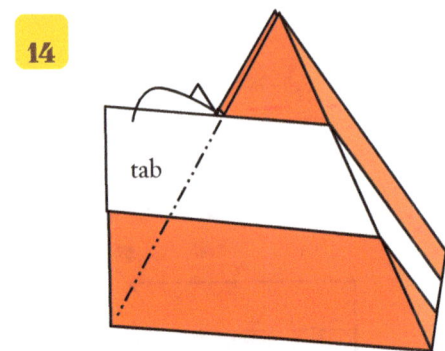

tab

**14**

tab

Tuck the tab into pocket.

**15**

Triple-Banded
Tetrahedron

# Snow-Capped Mountain

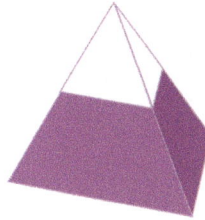

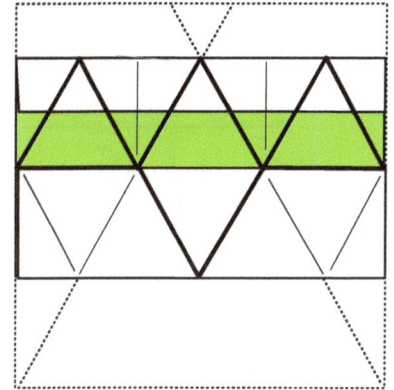

The Snow-Capped Mountain has white triangles on top. The layout uses even symmetry.

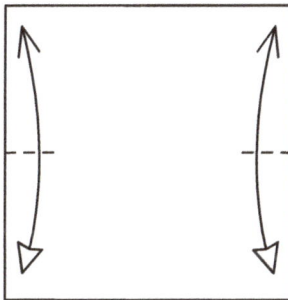

**1**

Fold and unfold on the edges.

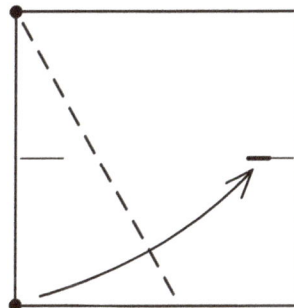

**2**

Bring the corner to the line.

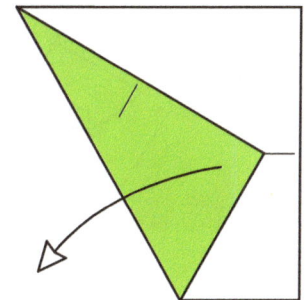

**3**

Unfold.

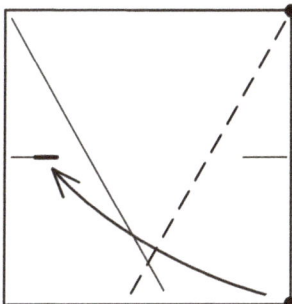

**4**

Repeat steps 2–3 on the right.

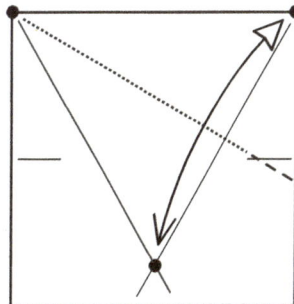

**5**

Fold and unfold on the right. Rotate 180°.

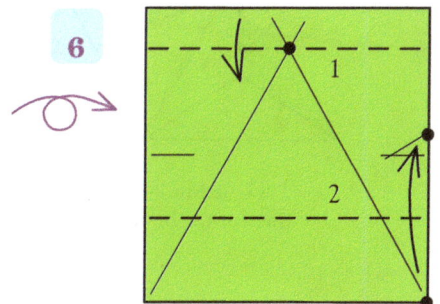

**6**

**7**

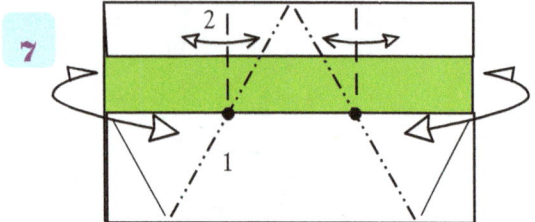

1. Fold and unfold along the partially hidden creases.
2. Fold and unfold on the top half.

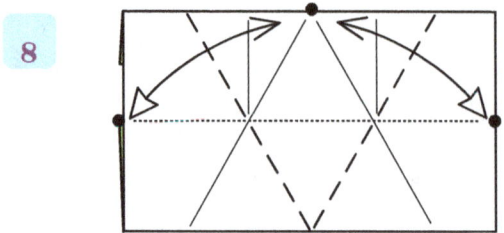

**8**

Fold and unfold.

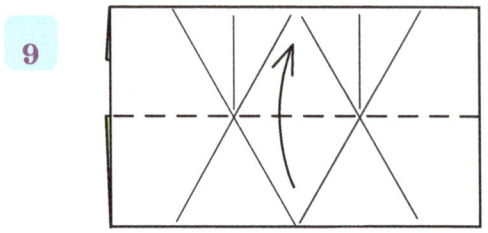

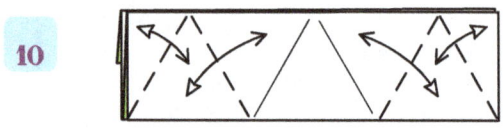

**9**

**10**

Fold and unfold along the creases.

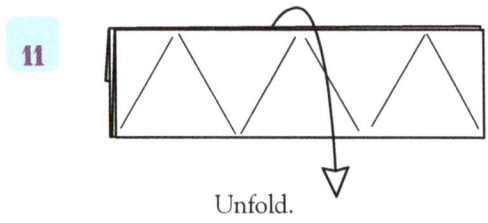

**11**

Unfold.

**12**

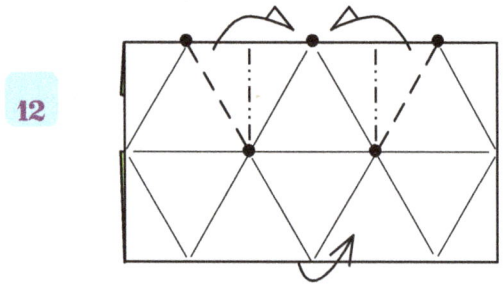

Push in at the lower dots. The upper dots will meet.

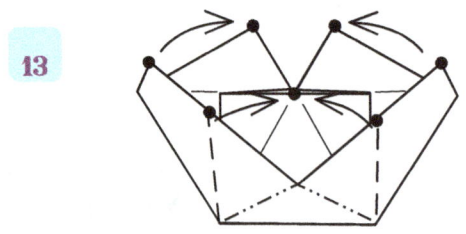

**13**

This is 3D. The groups of dots will meet.

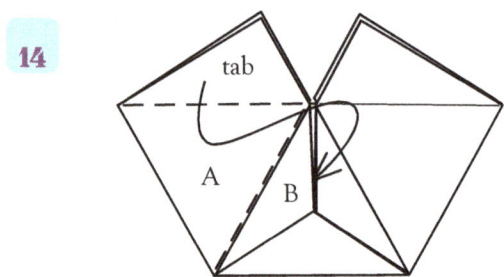

**14**

tab

A   B

Fold all the layers together to tuck the tab inside. Region A will cover B.

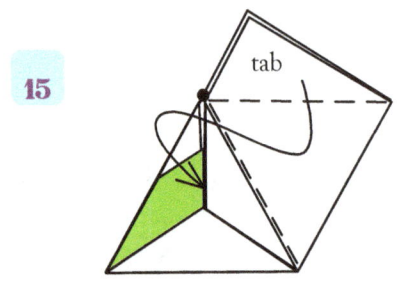

**15**

tab

Tuck inside. Rotate the dot to the top.

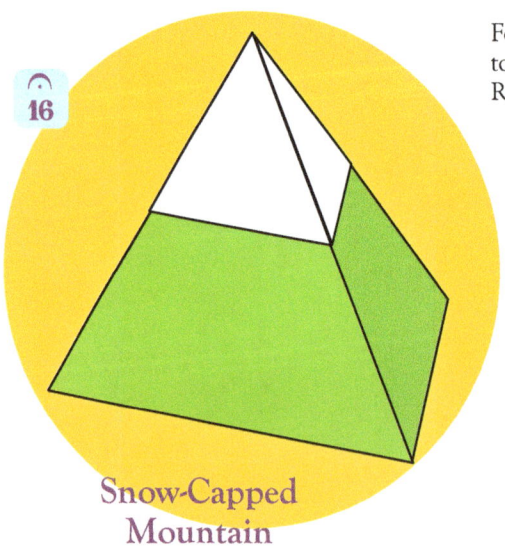

**16**

Snow-Capped Mountain

# Striped Tetrahedron

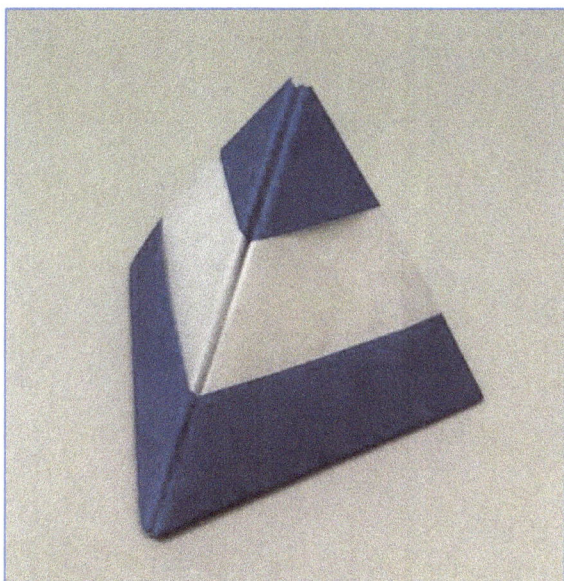

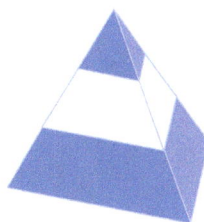

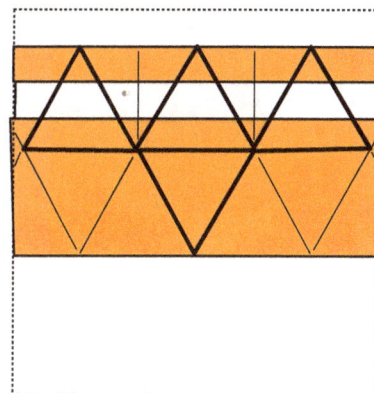

A few folds set up the three stripes. The paper is divided into 11ths and even symmetry is used.

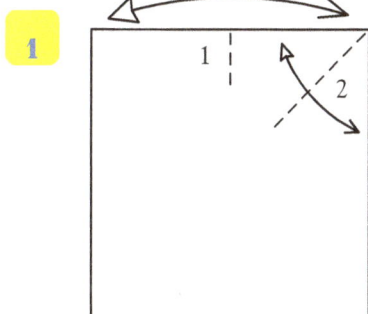

**1**

Fold and unfold
at 1 and 2.

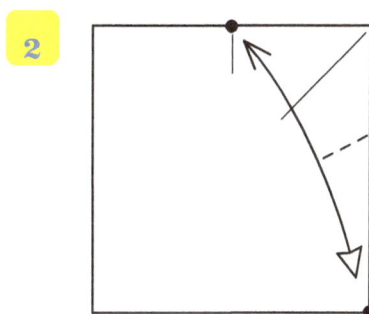

**2**

Fold and unfold
on the right.

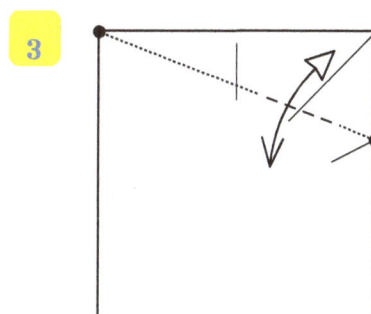

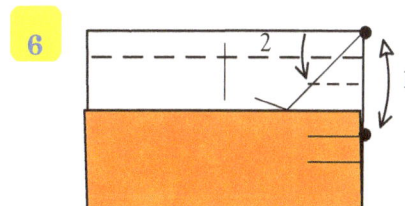

**3**

Fold and unfold along
the intersection.

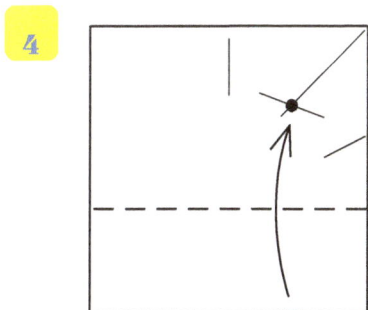

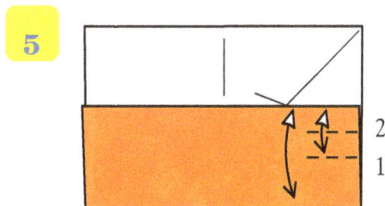

**4**

**5**

Fold and unfold
on the right.

**6**

1. Fold and unfold.
2. Fold to the crease.

**7**

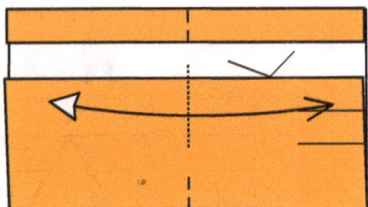

Fold and unfold at
the top and bottom.

**8**

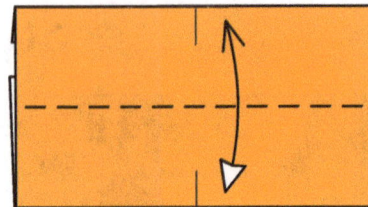

Fold in half and unfold.

**9**

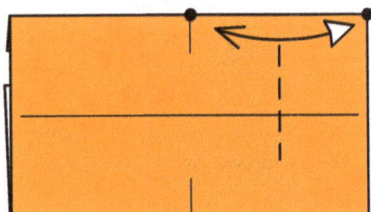

Fold and unfold.

**10**

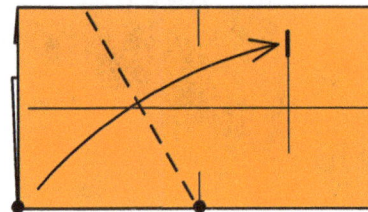

Bring the lower left
corner to the line.

**11**

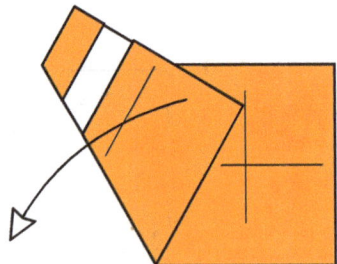

Unfold.

**12**

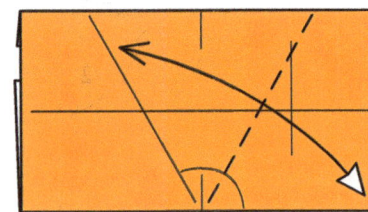

Fold and unfold.

**13**

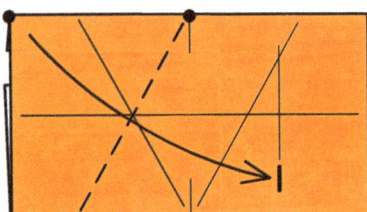

Repeat steps 10–12 in
the opposite direction.

**14**

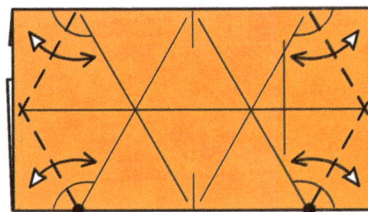

Fold and unfold.

**15**

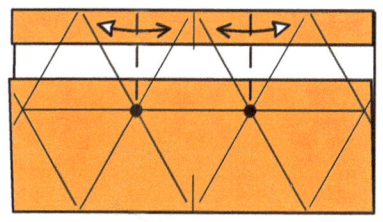

Fold and unfold.

**16**

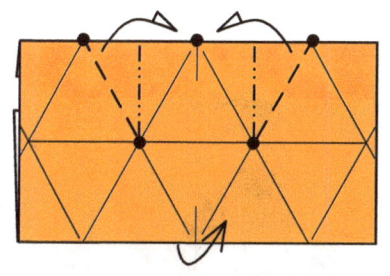

Push in at the lower dots.
The upper dots will meet.

**17**

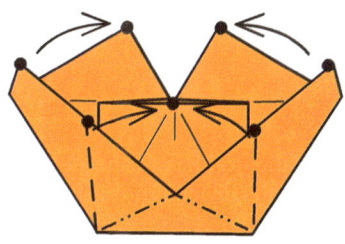

This is 3D. The groups
of dots will meet.

**18**

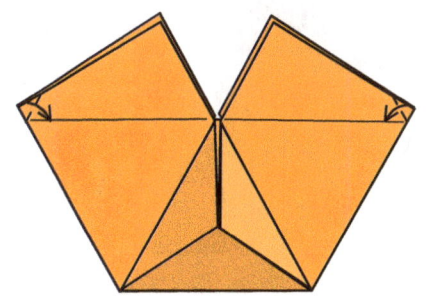

Fold along the creases.

**19**

tab

A

B

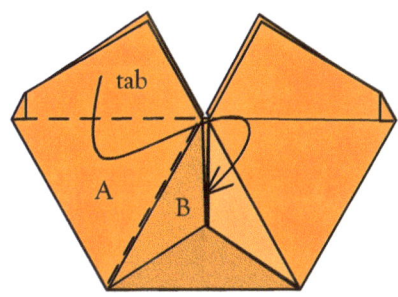

Fold all the layers together
to tuck the tab inside.
Region A will cover B.

**20**

tab

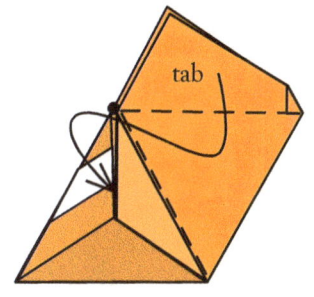

Tuck inside. Rotate
the dot to the top.

**21**

Striped Tetrahedron

# Radiant Tetrahedron

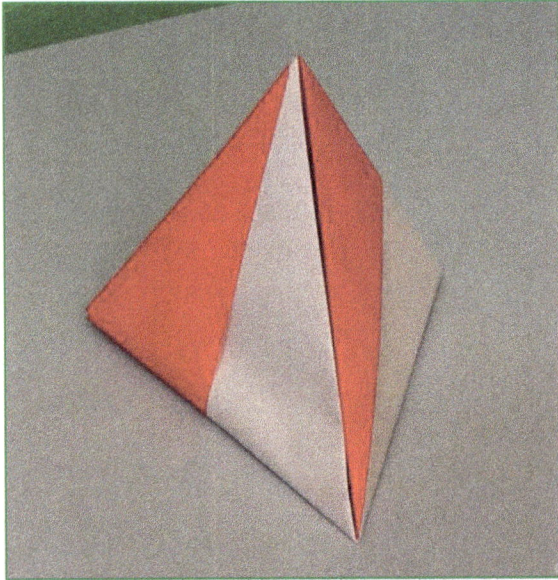

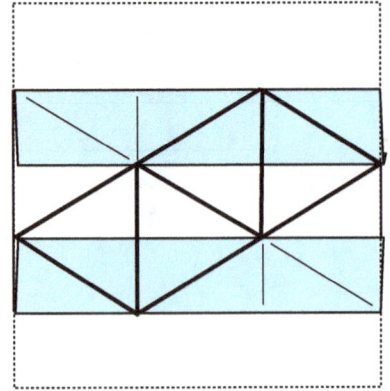

The Radiant Tetrahedron has a band of four triangles. The paper is divided in thirds.

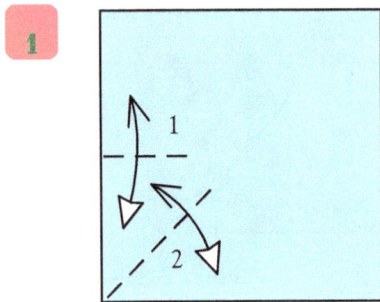

**1** Fold and unfold.

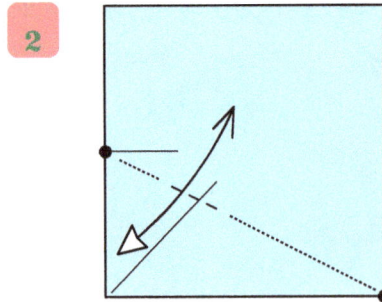

**2** Fold and unfold at the intersection.

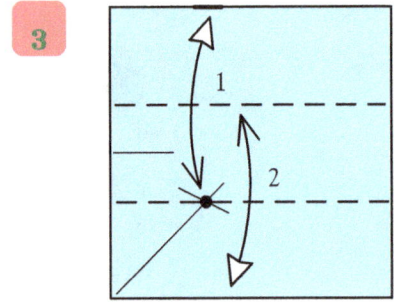

**3** Fold and unfold. Rotate 90°.

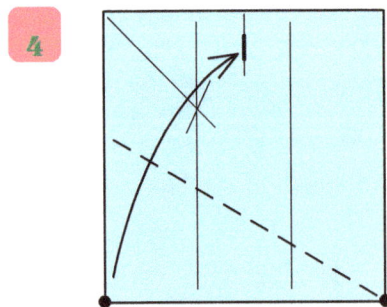

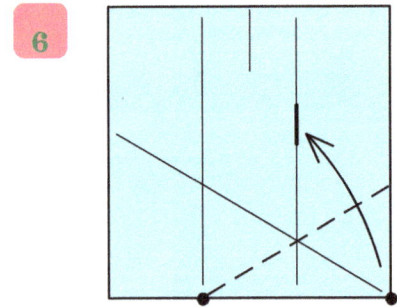

**4** Bring the corner to the line.

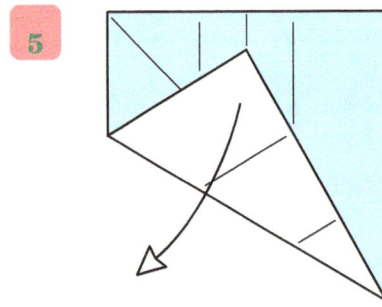

**5** Unfold.

**6** Bring the corner to the line.

**7**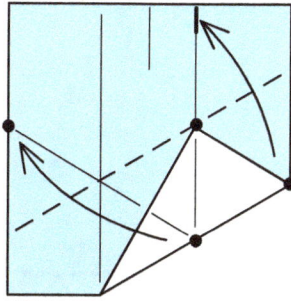

**8**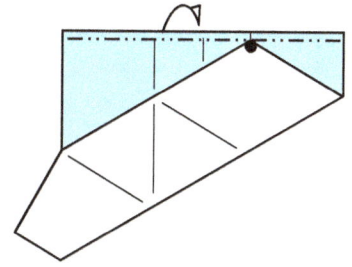

**9**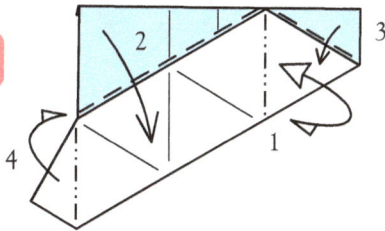

1. Fold and unfold along a hidden crease.
2-4. Fold in order.

**10**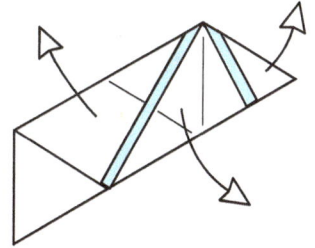

Unfold almost everything.

**11**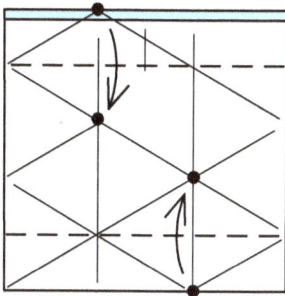

**12**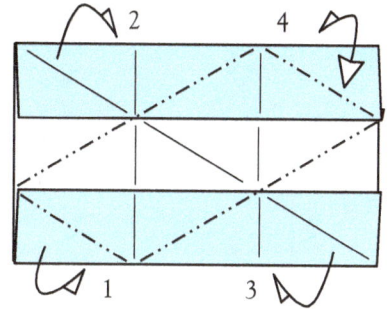

1-3. Fold behind in order.
4. Fold and unfold.

**13**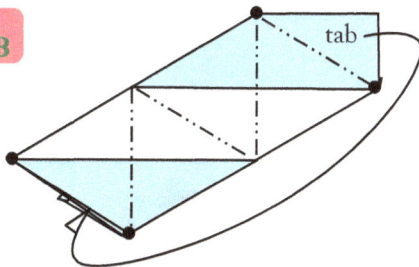

Tuck the tab into pocket.
The pairs of dots will meet.

**14**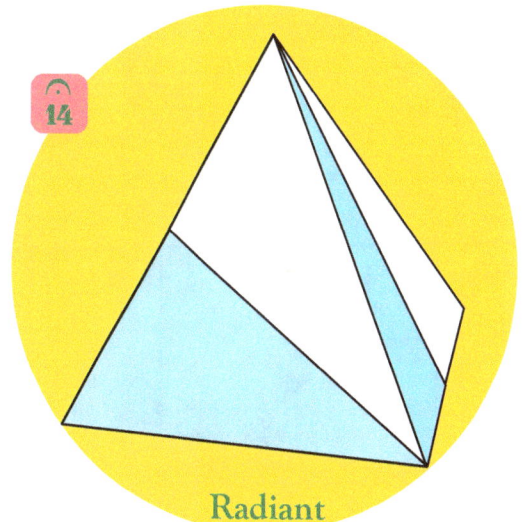

Radiant
Tetrahedron

# Tetrahedron of Diamonds

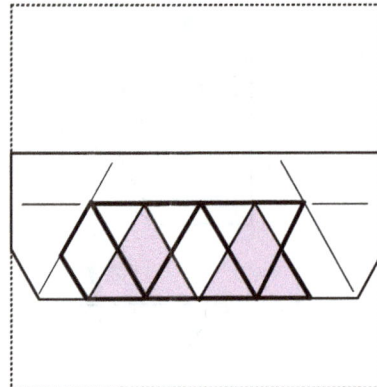

Each triangular face has a diamond and two triangles. The colors alternate on the faces.

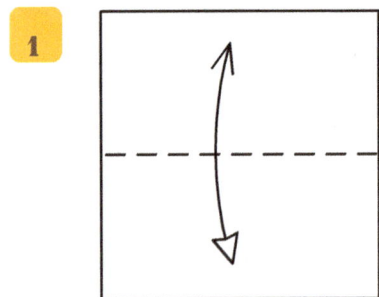

**1** Fold and unfold.

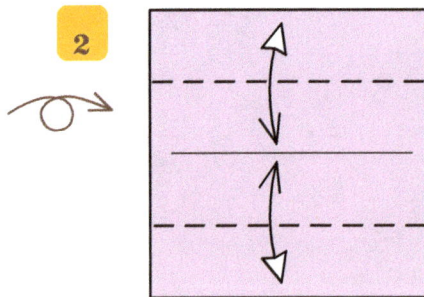

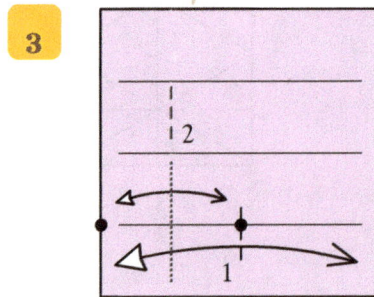

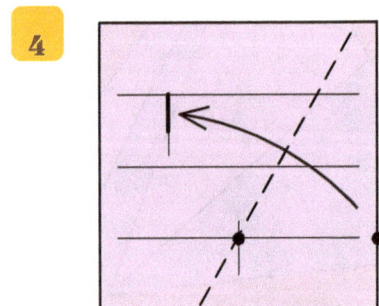

**2** Fold and unfold.

**3** Fold and unfold.

**4** Bring the dot to the line.

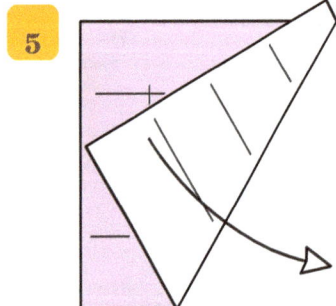

**5** Unfold.

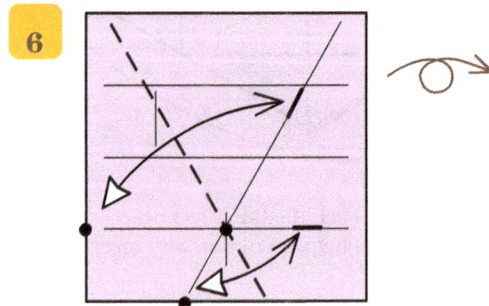

**6** Fold and unfold. Rotate 180°.

**7**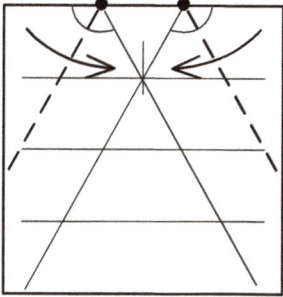

**8**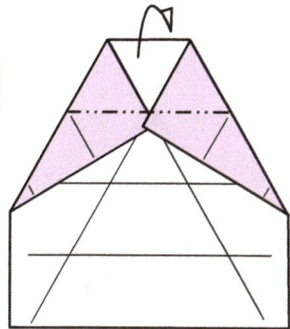

Fold along a hidden crease. Rotate 180°.

**9**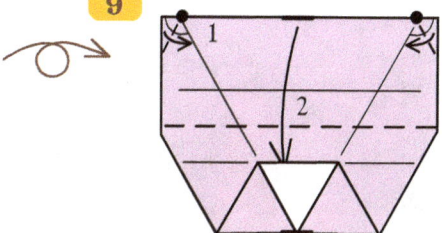

1. Fold on the left and right.
2. Fold in half between the layers.

**10**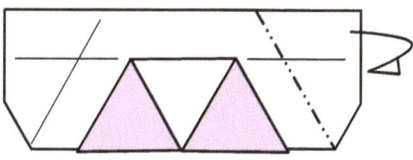

Fold along the crease.

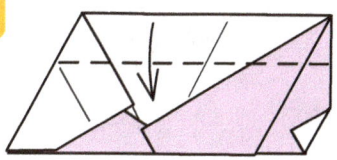

**11**

Fold along the crease.

**12**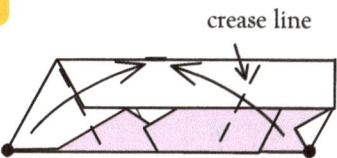

crease line

The two dots will meet on the top line.

**13**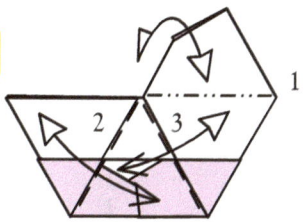

Fold and unfold at 1, 2, and 3.

**14**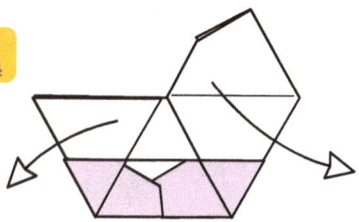

Unfold.

**15**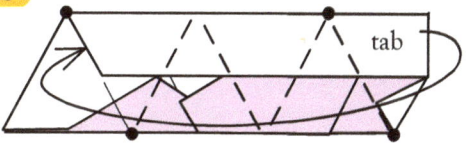

tab

Tuck the tab into the pocket. The pairs of dots will meet.

**16**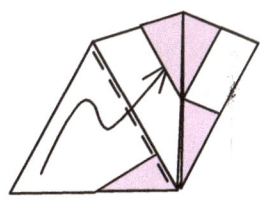

Tuck inside.

**17**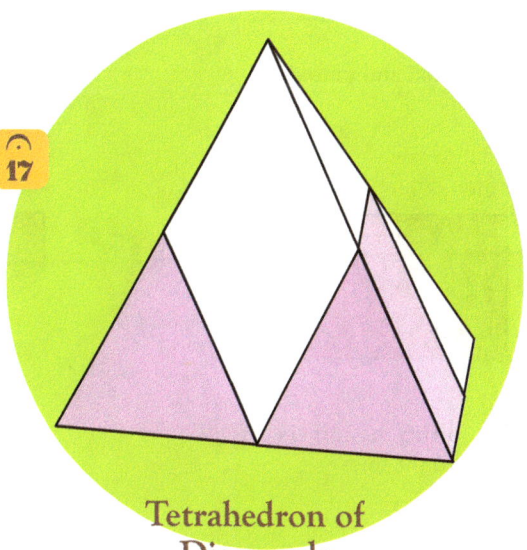

Tetrahedron of Diamonds

# Tetrahedron of Triangles

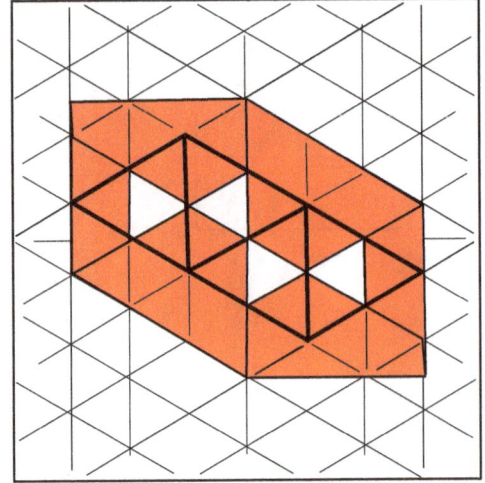

Each triangular face is composed of four triangles, with a color change for the central triangle. Odd symmetry is used.

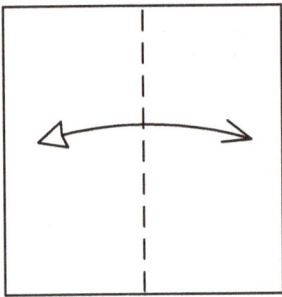

Fold and unfold.

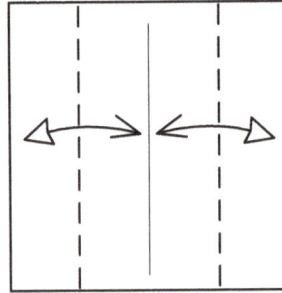

Fold and unfold.

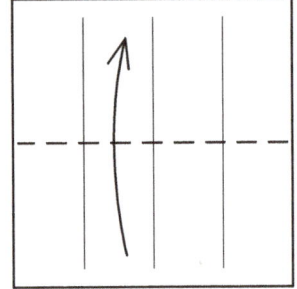

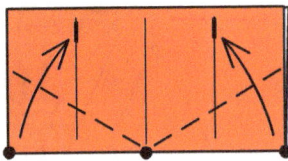

Bring the corners to the lines.

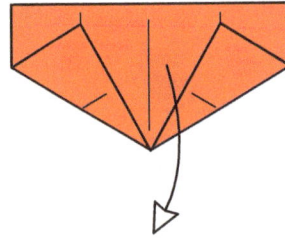

Unfold.

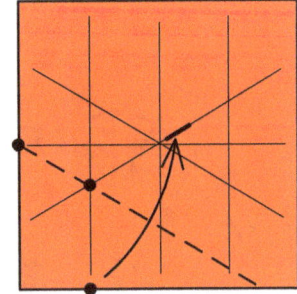

Bring the dot to the line.

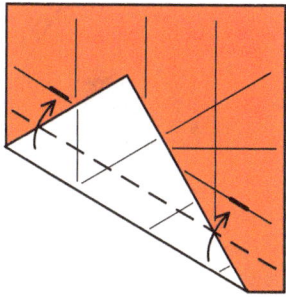

**7** Fold to the bold line.

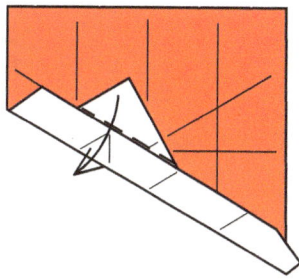

**8**

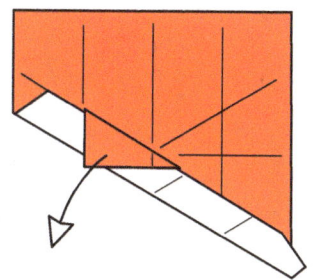

**9** Unfold.

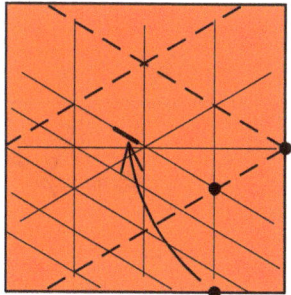

**10** Repeat steps 6–9 three times, on the right and above.

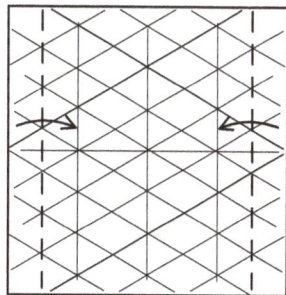

**11** Fold to the creases.

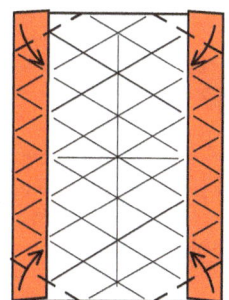

**12** Fold along the creases.

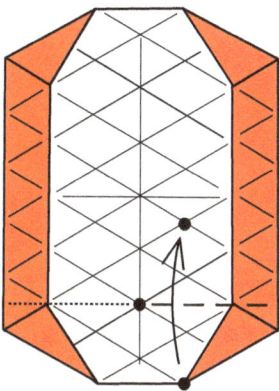

**13**

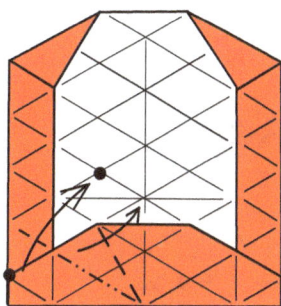

**14** Mountain-fold along the crease for this squash fold.

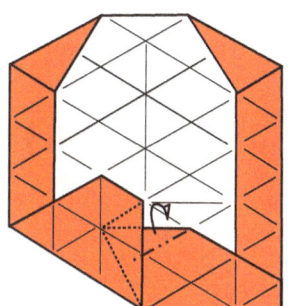

**15** Squash-fold.

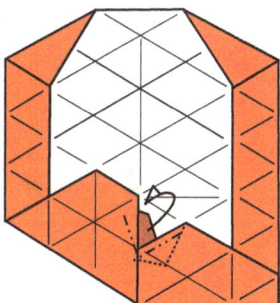

**16** Make a small, hidden squash fold, so the darker paper is hidden. Rotate 180°.

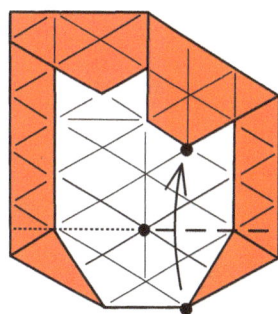

**17** Repeat steps 13–16. Rotate.

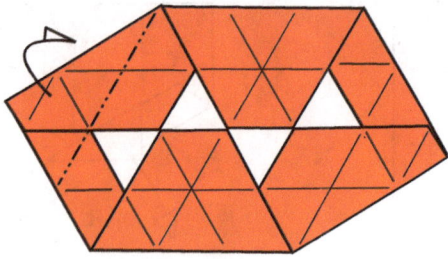

**18**

Fold along the crease.

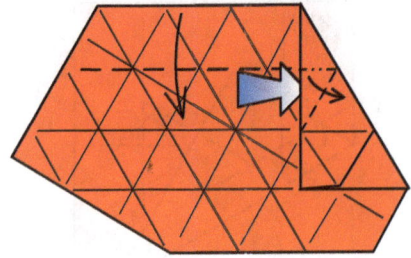

**19**

Squash-fold.

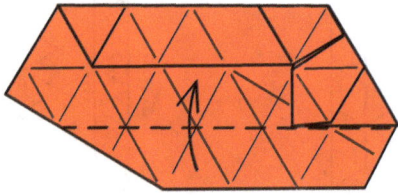

**20**

Fold along the crease.

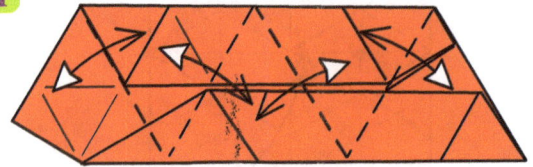

**21**

Fold and unfold
along the creases.

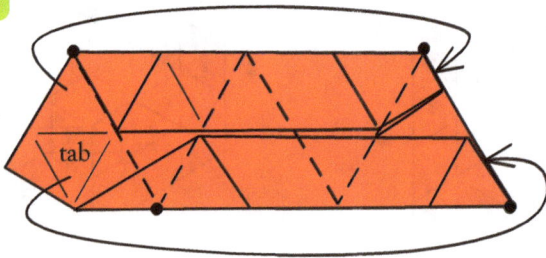

**22**

tab

Tuck the tab into the pockets.
The pairs of dots will meet.

**23**

**Tetrahedron of Triangles**

# Capped Tetrahedron

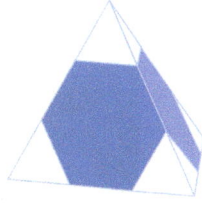

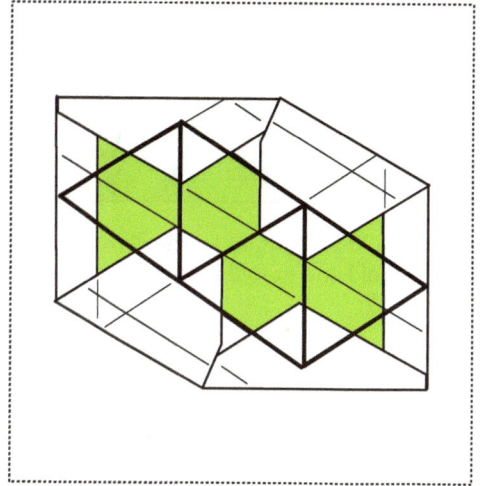

This tetrahedron has colored hexagons with white caps on each of the four faces.

The figure above shows step 28 embedded in the original square, showing how the colors are placed on the crease pattern. The paper is divided into 11ths and odd symmetry is used.

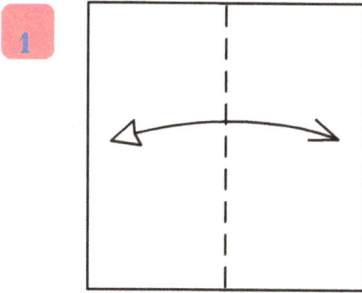

**1** Fold and unfold.

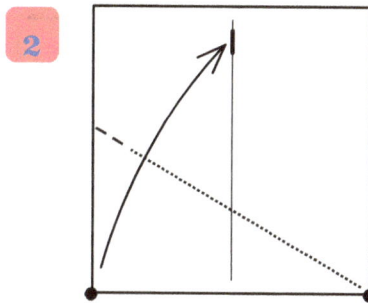

**2** Bring the left dot to the line. Crease on the left.

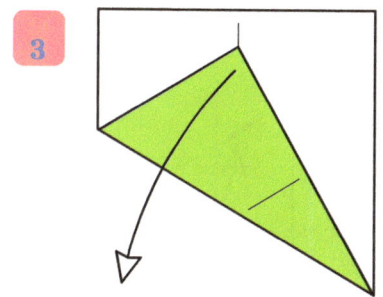

**3** Unfold and rotate 180°.

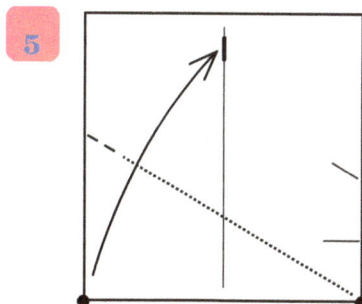

**4**

**5** Repeat steps 2–4.

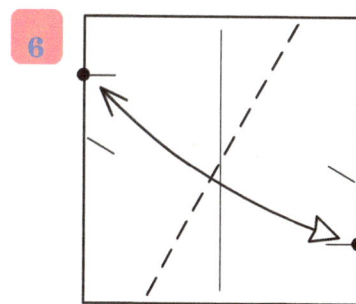

**6** Fold and unfold.

**7**

1. Fold and unfold on the diagonal.
2. Fold and unfold on the right.

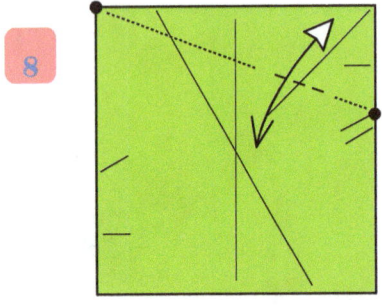

**8**

Fold and unfold at
the intersection.

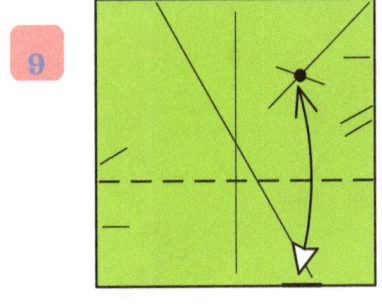

**9**

Fold and unfold.

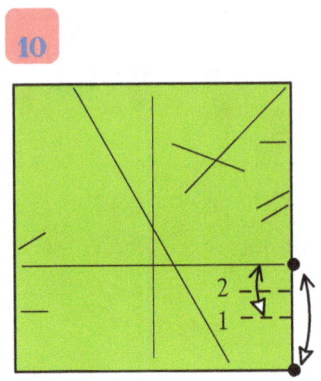

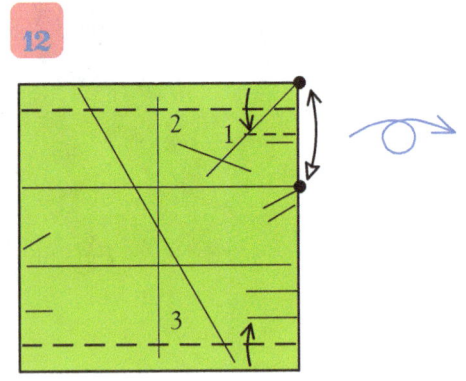

**10**

Fold and unfold twice.

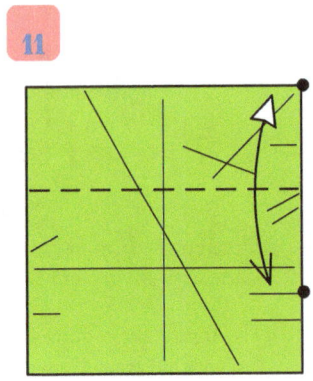

**11**

Fold and unfold.

**12**

1. Fold and unfold.
2, 3. Fold to the marks.
Rotate 90°.

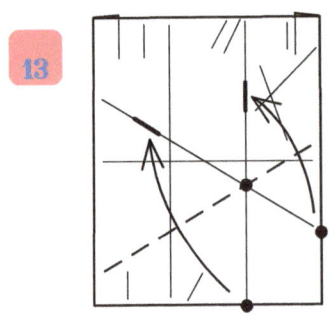

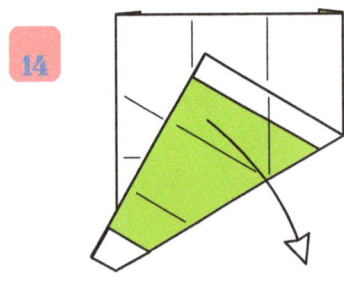

**13**

**14**

Unfold.

**15**

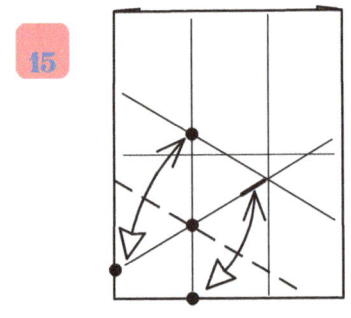

Fold and unfold.
Rotate 180°.

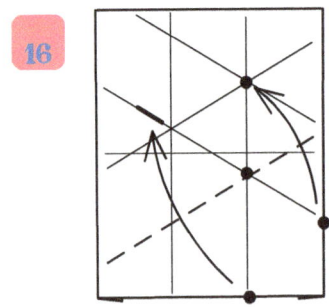

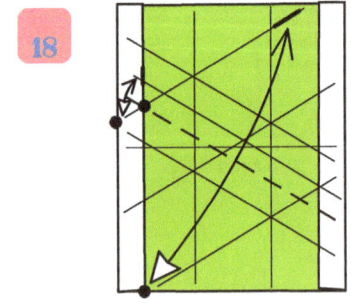

**16**

Repeat steps 13–15.

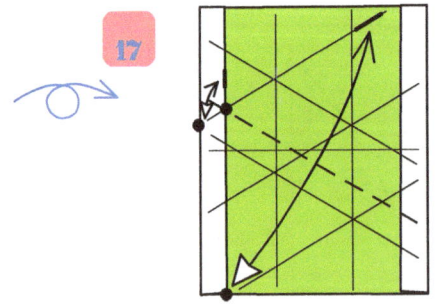

**17**

Fold and unfold.
Rotate 180°.

**18**

Repeat step 17.

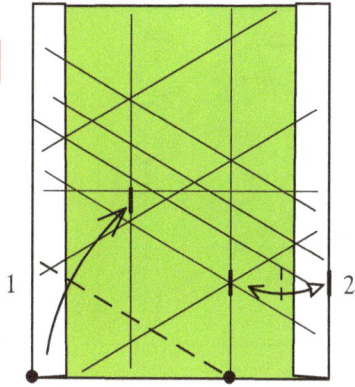

1. The dot will meet the line.
2. Fold and unfold.

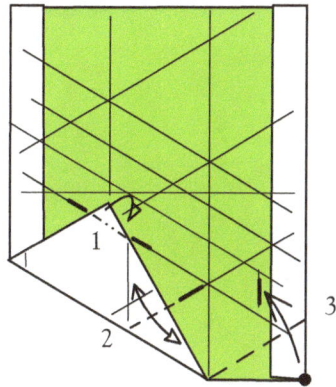

1. Fold behind along the bold line.
2. Fold and unfold along the bold line.
3. The dot will meet the line.

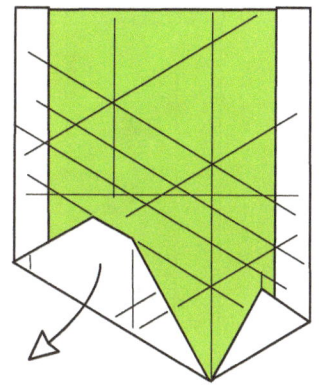

Unfold and rotate 180°.

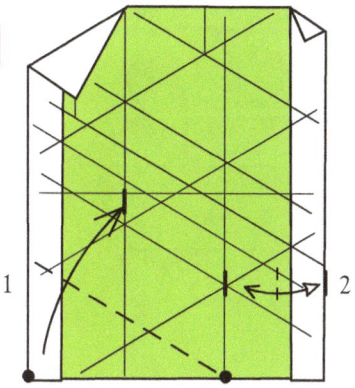

Repeat steps 19–21.

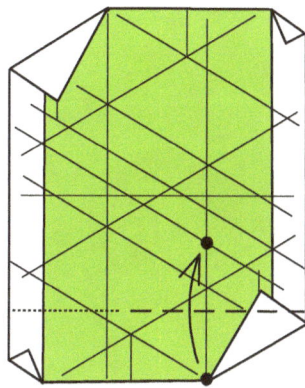

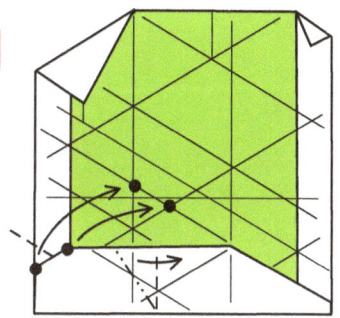

Squash-fold so the pair of dots meet. Valley-fold along the crease.

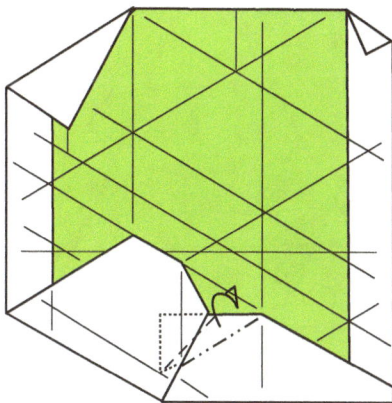

This is similar to a squash fold.

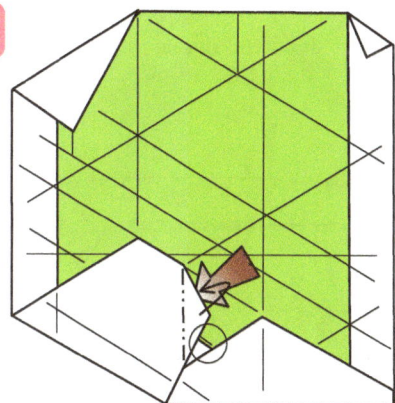

Note that inside the circle, the edge of the white paper is parallel to the crease slightly above it. Reverse-fold and rotate 180°.

**27**

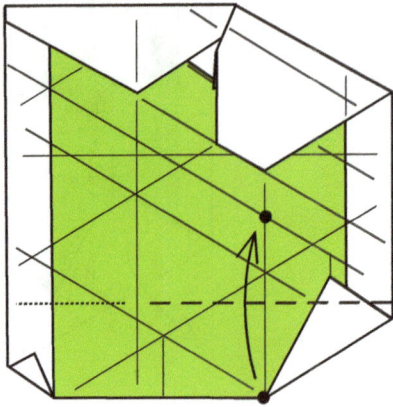

Repeat steps 23–26.

**28**

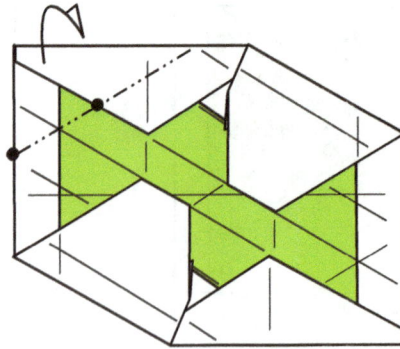

Fold along the crease between the dots. Rotate.

**29**

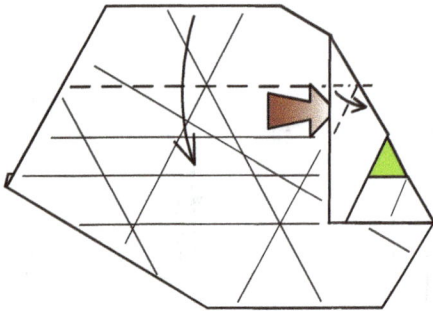

Squash-fold.

**30**

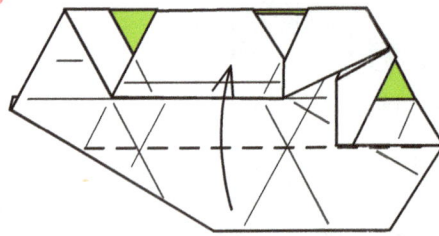

Fold along the crease.

**31**

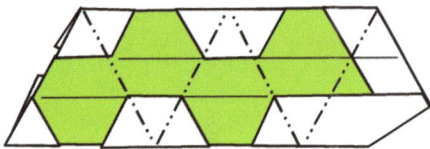

Fold and unfold along the creases.

**32**

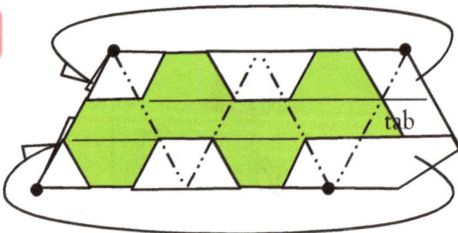

Tuck the tab into the pockets. The pairs of dots will meet.

**33**

Capped Tetrahedron

# Trio of Grand Pyramids

Here is a trio of pyramids where the base is a regular polygon and the sides are isosceles triangles. While the tetrahedron is a triangular pyramid, pyramids with more sides are found. A square, pentagonal, and hexagonal pyramid add grandeur to a desert scene. The models become progressively more complex.

# Great Pyramid

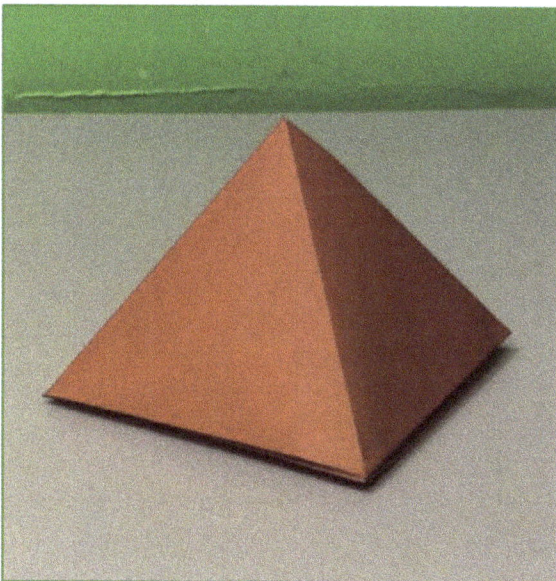

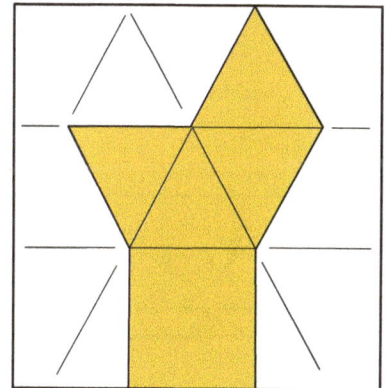

This classically proportioned pyamid is formed from a square base and four equilateral triangles and has an apex angle of 60°. The crease pattern shows a hexagon above a square. The line dividing the two shapes is formed in step 4.

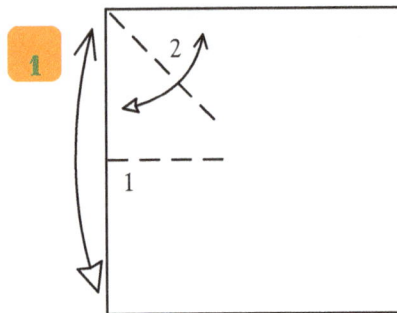

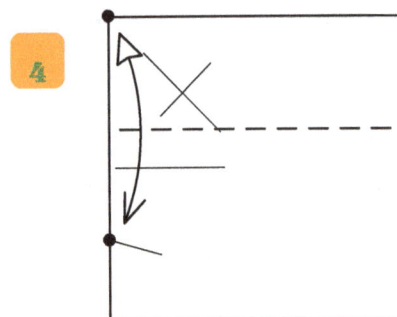

**1** Fold and unfold on the left at 1 and 2.

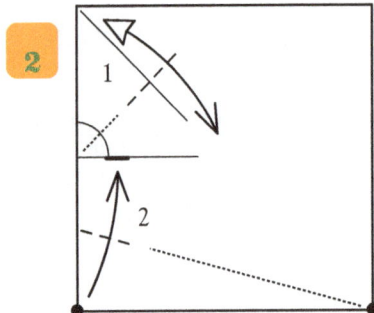

**2**
1. Fold and unfold at the intersection.
2. Bring the lower left corner to the center line.

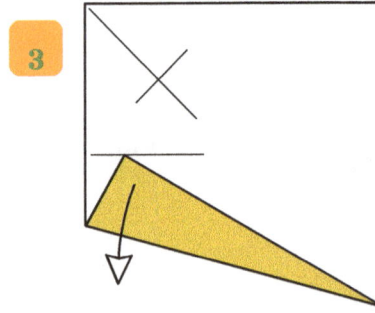

**3** Unfold.

**4** Fold and unfold.

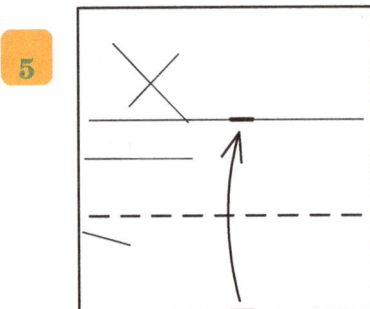

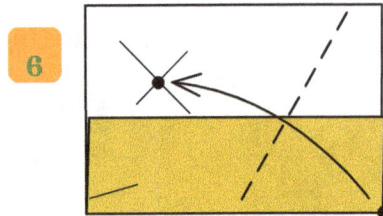

**5**

**6**

**7** Fold and unfold along a hidden crease.

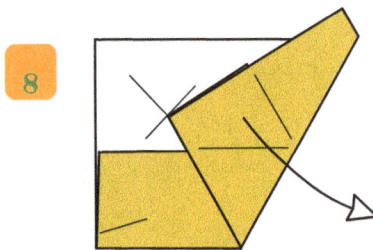

**8** Unfold.

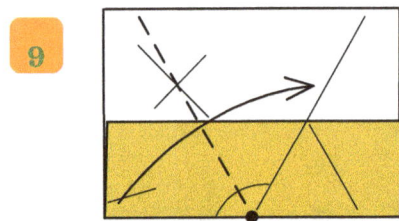

**9** Repeat steps 6–8 in the opposite direction.

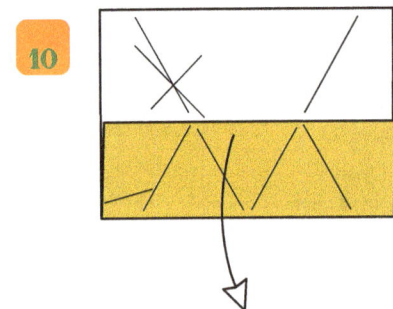

**10** Unfold.

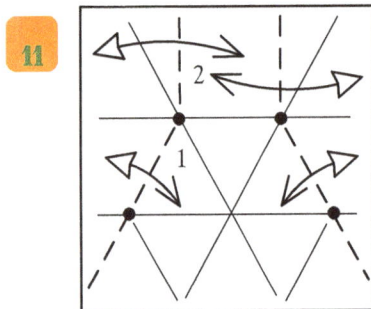

**11**
1. Fold and unfold along the creases between the dots and extend them.
2. Fold and unfold. Rotate 180°.

**12** Fold and unfold.

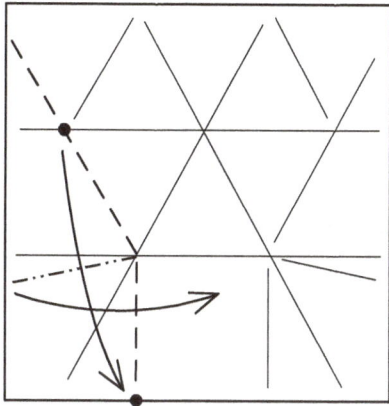

**13**

Fold along the creases. The model will become 3D.

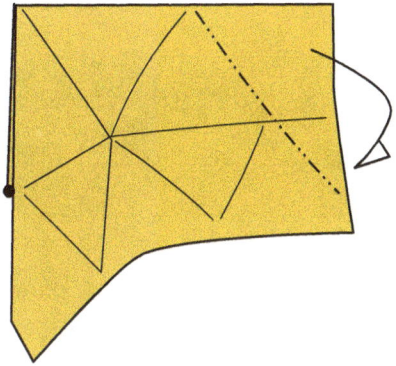

**14**

Repeat step 13 on the right.

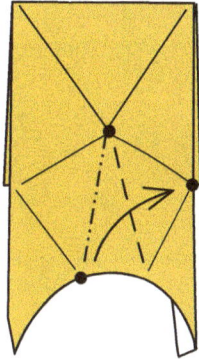

**15**

Puff out at the upper dot and flatten at the top. Fold along the creases.

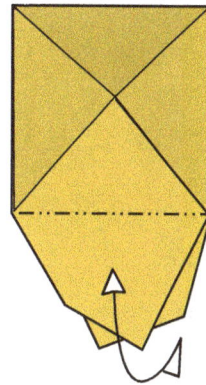

**16**

Fold and unfold.

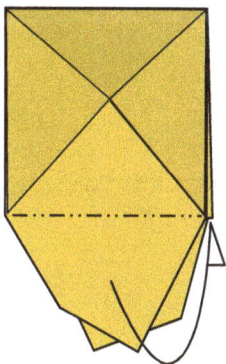

**17**

Tuck inside.

**18**

**Great Pyramid**

# Golden Pentagonal Pyramid

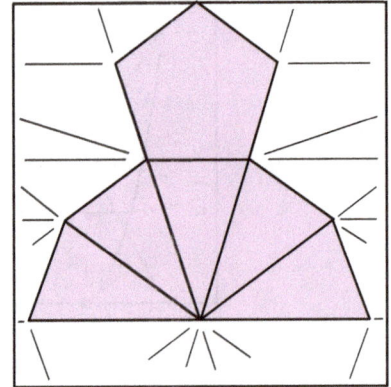

This pyramid is formed from a pentagonal base and five isosceles triangles, with an apex angle of 36°. The crease pattern shows even symmetry.

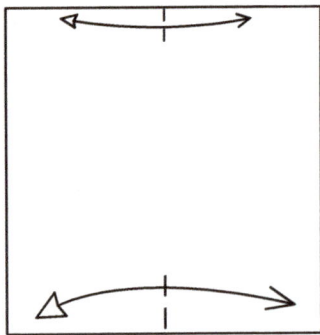

**1**

Fold and unfold. Make a small crease at the top and a slighty larger one at the bottom.

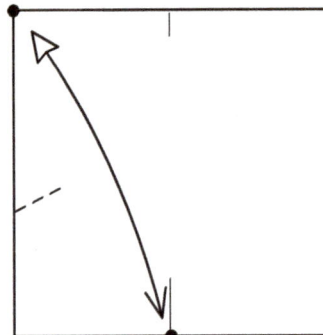

**2**

Fold and unfold on the left.

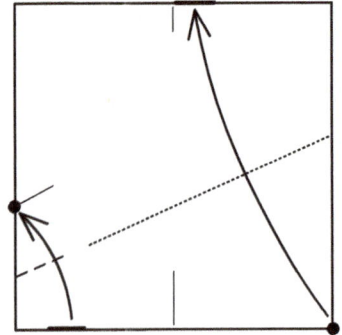

**3**

Bring the lower dot to the top edge and the bottom edge to the dot on the left. Crease on the left.

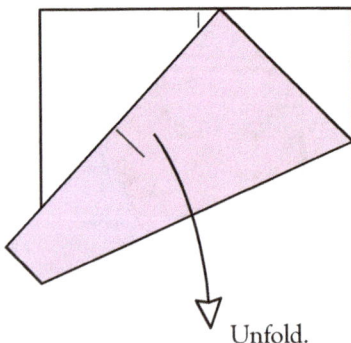

**4**

Unfold.

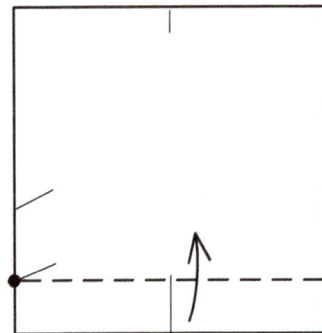

**5**

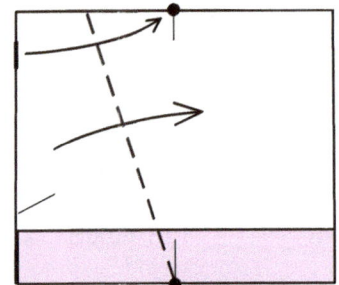

**6**

Fold the left edge to the upper dot.

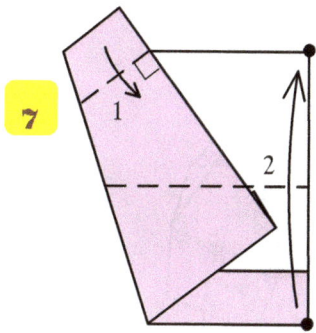

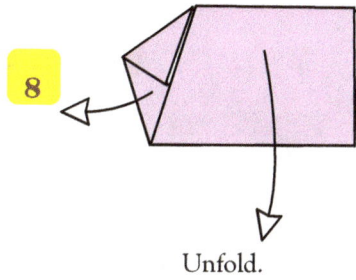

Unfold.

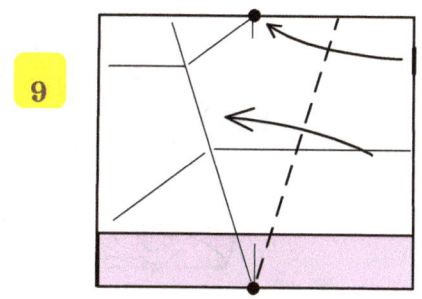

Repeat steps 6–8
on the right.

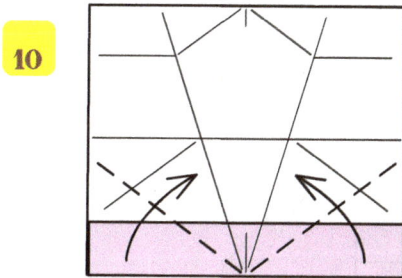

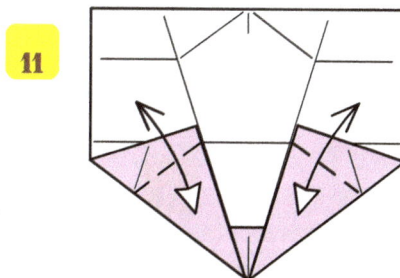

Fold and unfold all the
layers along hidden creases.

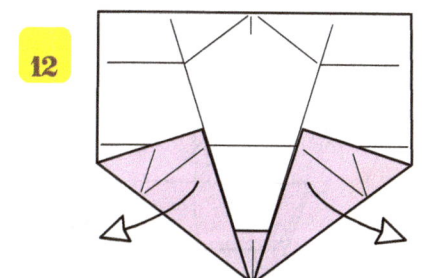

Unfold.

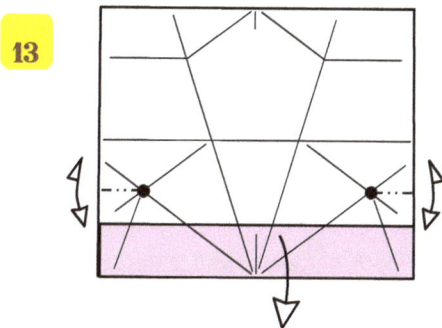

Fold and unfold at the sides
and unfold at the bottom.

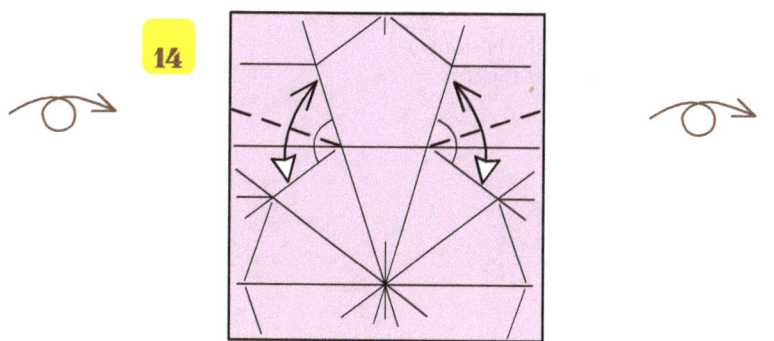

Fold and unfold to bisect
the angles. Rotate 180°.

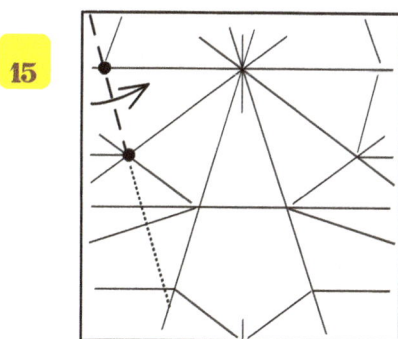

Fold along the crease
between the dots.

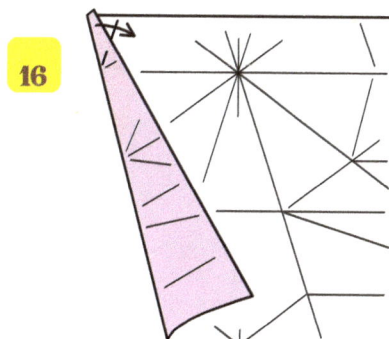

Fold along the crease.

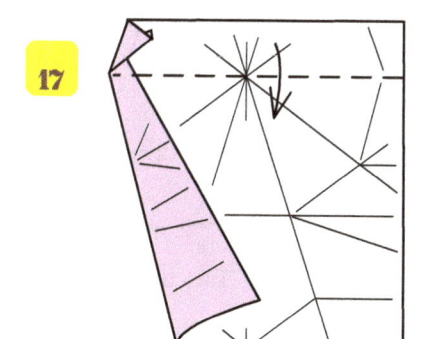

*Golden Pentagonal Pyramid*  **93**

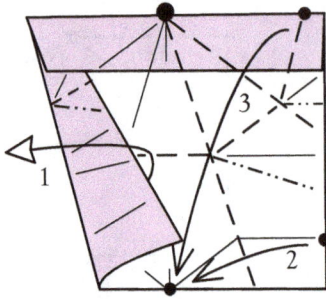

**18**

The model will become 3D. Unfold on the lower left, bring the dots on the right to the lower dot. The large dot will be at the top of the pyramid.

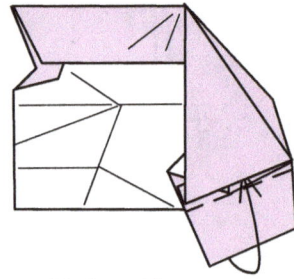

**19**

Tuck inside.

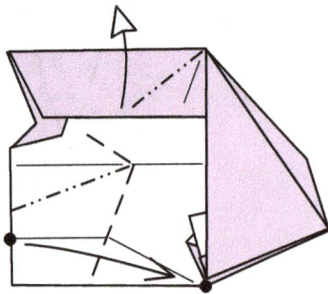

**20**

Fold at the bottom and unfold at the top.

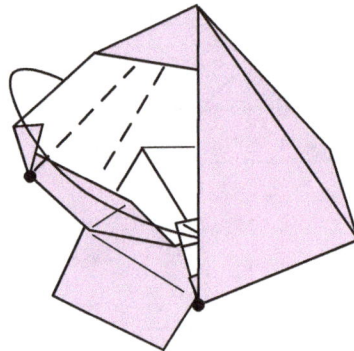

**21**

Wrap around and tuck inside. The dots will meet.

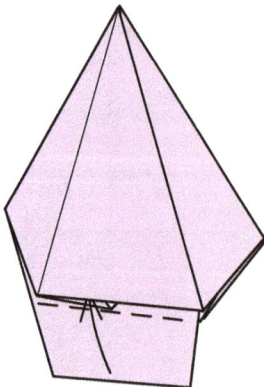

**22**

Tuck inside.

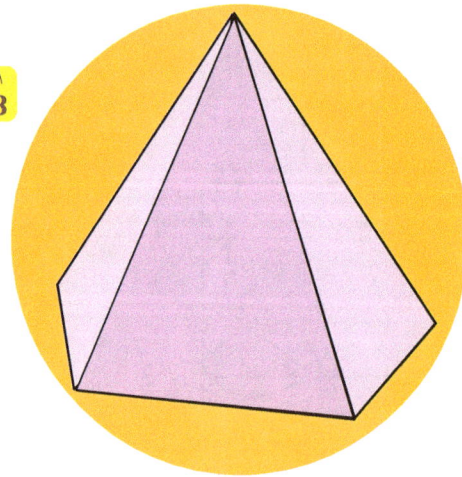

**23**

**Golden Pentagonal Pyramid**

# Hexagonal Pyramid

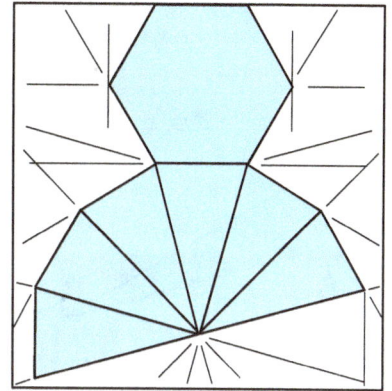

This pyramid is formed from a hexagonal base and six isosceles triangles, with an apex angle of 30°. The crease pattern shows mainly even symmetry.

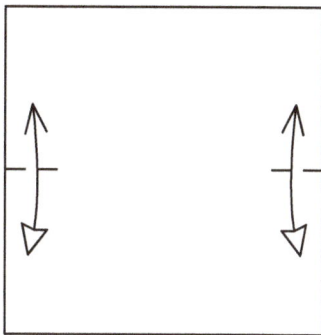

**1**

Fold and unfold on the left and right.

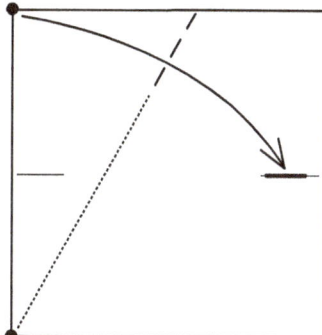

**2**

Bring the corner to the line and crease at the top.

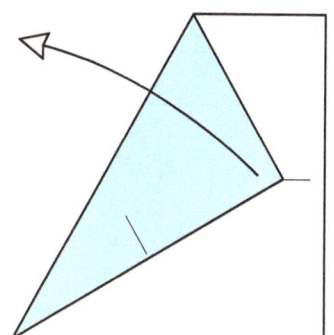

**3**

Unfold.

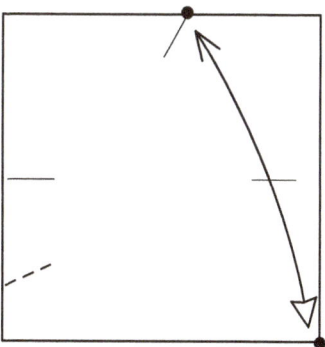

**4**

Fold and unfold on the left.

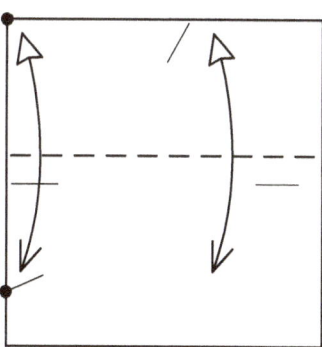

**5**

Fold and unfold.

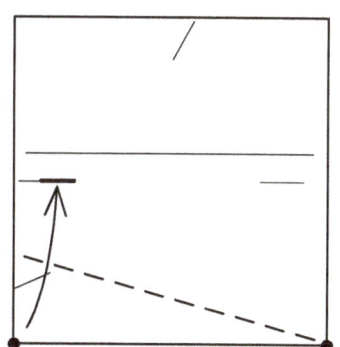

**6**

Bring the corner to the line.

**7**

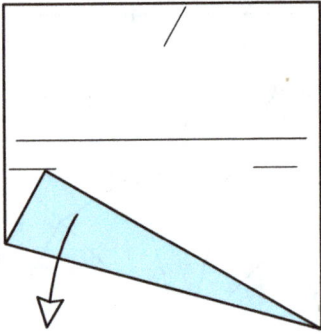

Unfold.

**8**

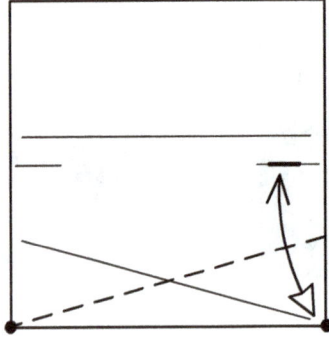

Fold and unfold.

**9**

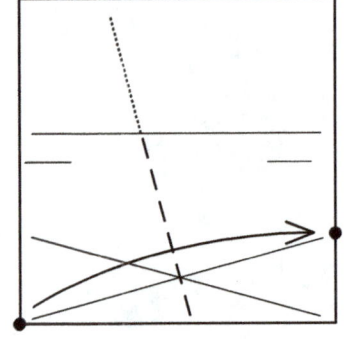

**10**

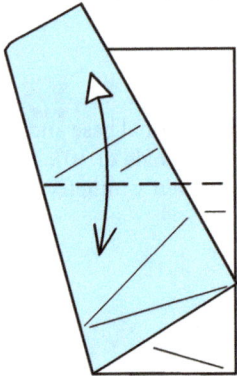

Fold and unfold along
a hidden crease.

**11**

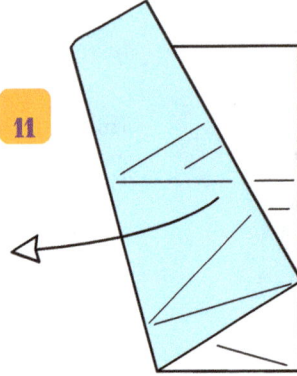

Unfold.

**12**

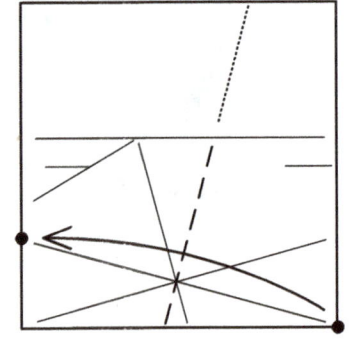

Repeat steps 9–11
on the right.

**13**

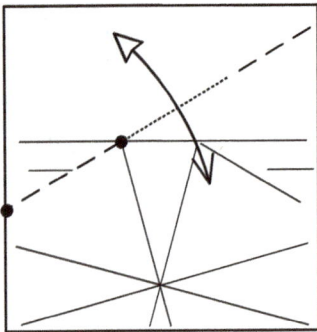

Fold and unfold on the left
and right. Fold along the
crease between the dots.

**14**

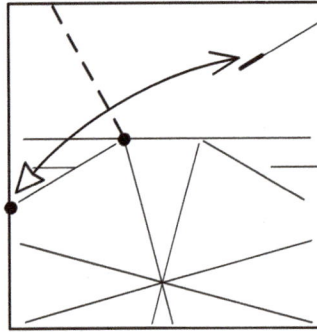

Fold and unfold.

**15**

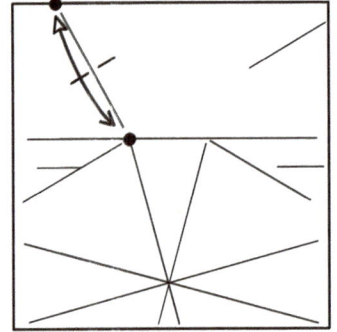

Fold and unfold.

**16**

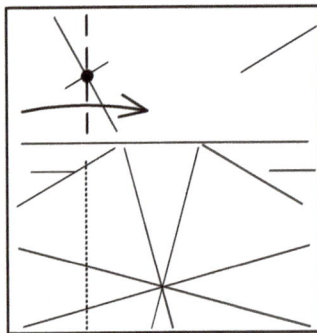

**17**

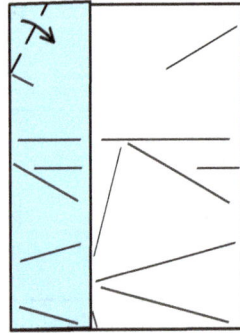

Fold along the crease.

**18**

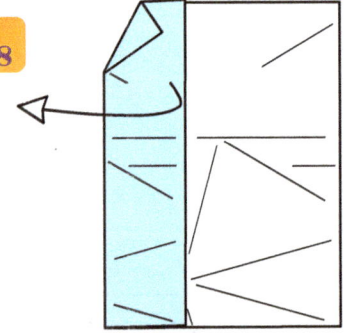

Unfold.

**19**

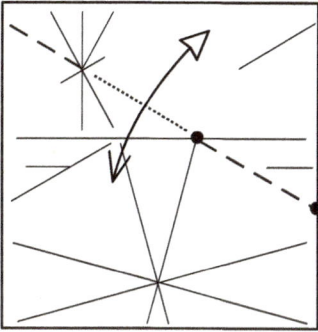

Repeat steps 13–18
on the right.

**20**

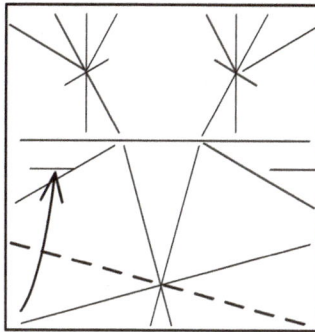

**21**

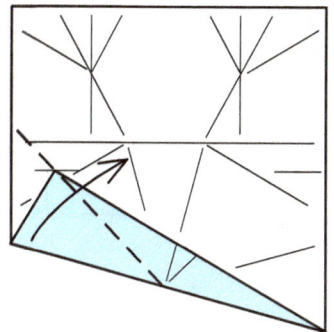

**22**

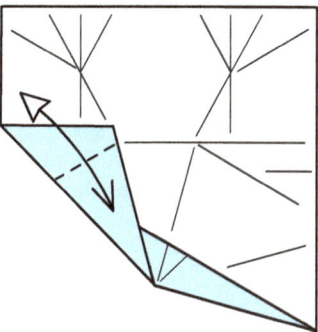

Fold and unfold along
a hidden crease.

**23**

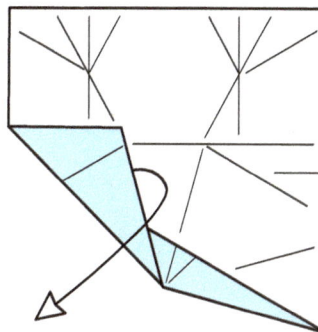

Unfold.

**24**

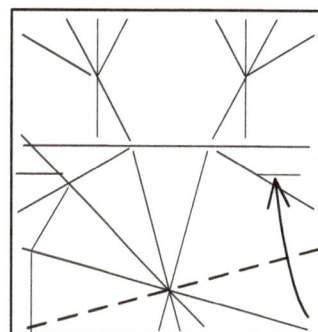

Repeat steps 20–23
on the right.

**25**

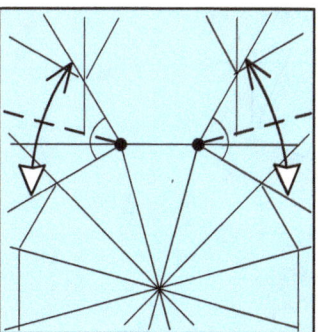

Fold and unfold to bisect
the angles. Rotate 180°.

**26**

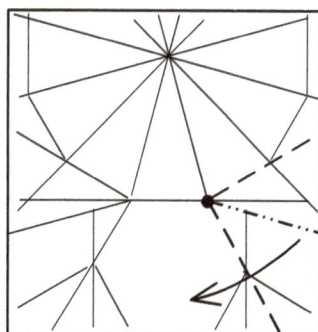

Push in at the dot.

**27**

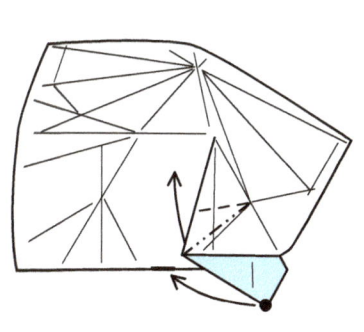

**28**

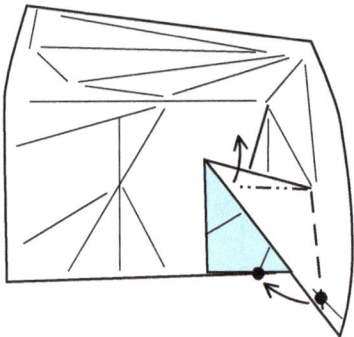

**29**

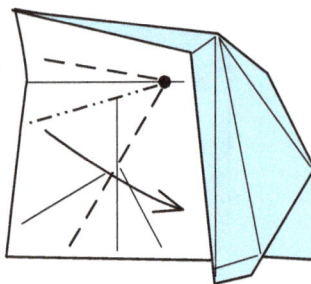

Repeat steps 26–28
on the left.

**30**

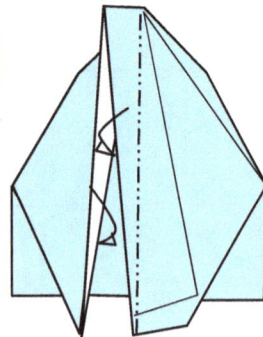

**31**

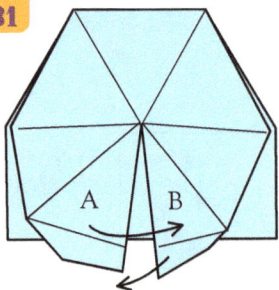

Region A will
cover region B.

**32**

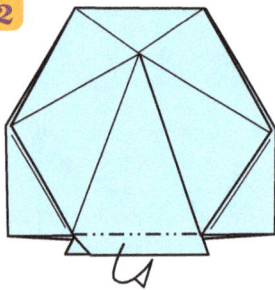

Tuck inside.

**33**

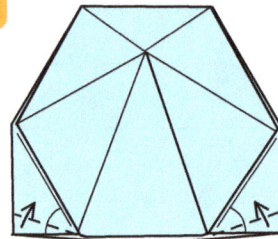

Fold at one-third
of the angle.

**34**

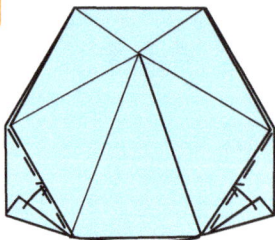

Tuck inside.

**35**

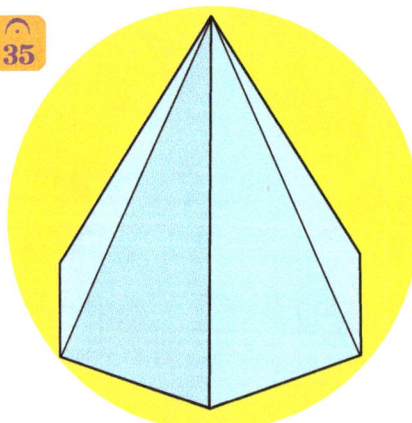

**Hexagonal Pyramid**

# Fourth Movement

## Allegro: Deep in the Desert

𝄢 The desert is teaming with interesting life. A Veiled Chameleon and Green Iguana run around a Saguaro Cactus. A Roadrunner leads the way to an Armadillo while a ride on a Dromedary or Camel lets you explore deep in the desert. Watch out for the Scorpion and don't forget to include a snake for a desert scene. A wide range of folding techniques add enjoyment to desert life.

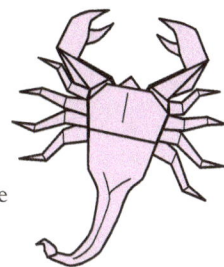

## Saguaro Cactus

Often used as the definitive symbol for Cacti in general, the Saguaro Cactus is the one that stands tall with what looks like raised arms. Saguaros are native to the Sonoran Desert in Arizona and Sonora, Mexico.

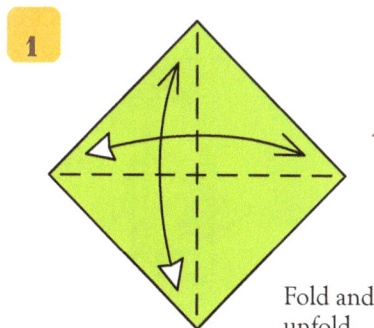

**1** Fold and unfold.

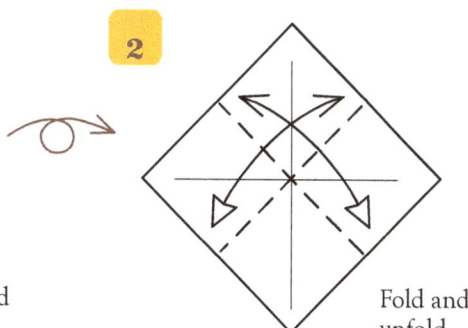

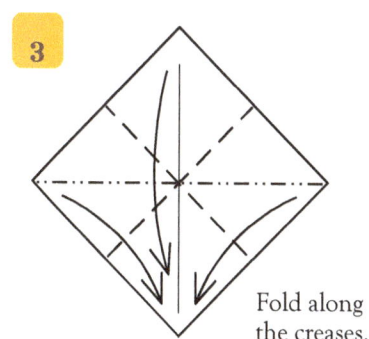

**2** Fold and unfold.

**3** Fold along the creases.

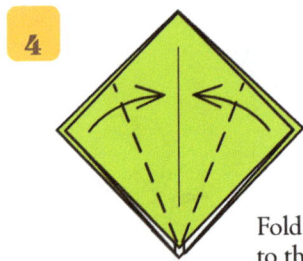

**4** Fold the top layers to the center.

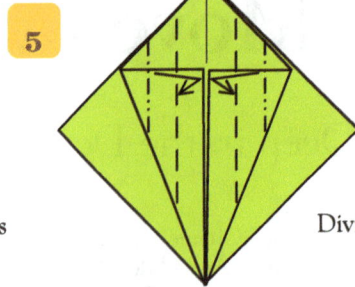

**5** Divide in thirds.

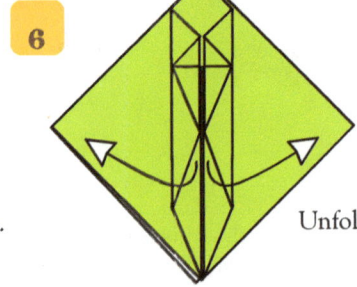

**6** Unfold.

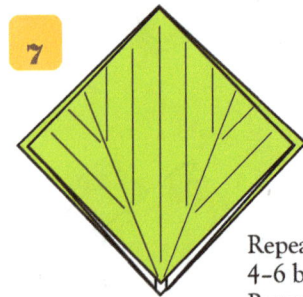

**7** Repeat steps 4–6 behind. Rotate 180°.

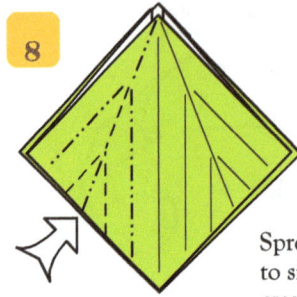

**8** Spread the paper to sink along the creases.

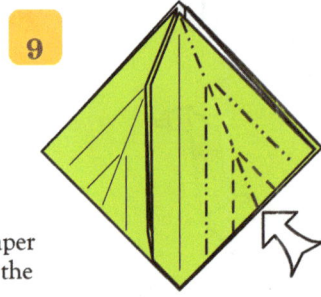

**9** Repeat step 8 three times, on the right and behind.

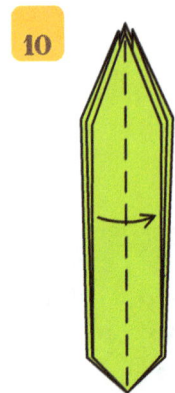

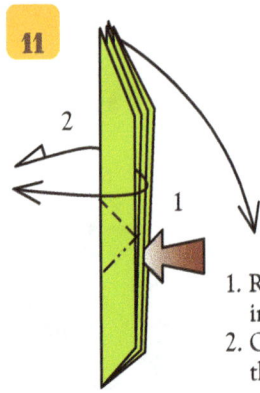

**10**

**11**
1. Reverse-fold the inner flap.
2. Outside-reverse-fold the outer flap.

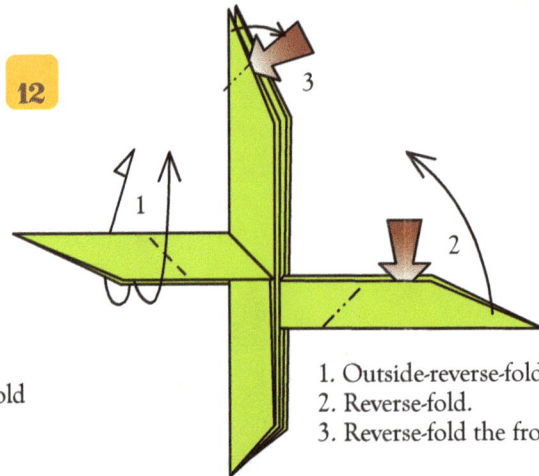

**12**
1. Outside-reverse-fold.
2. Reverse-fold.
3. Reverse-fold the front flap.

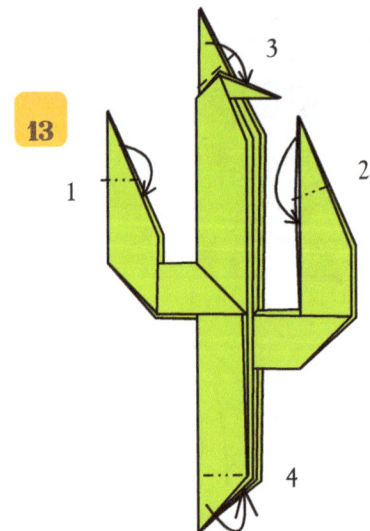

**13**
1. Reverse-fold.
2. Reverse-fold.
3. Fold between the layers.
4. Reverse-fold.

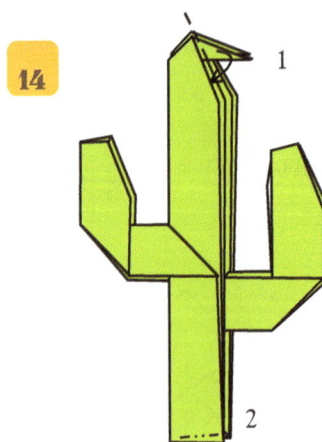

**14**
1. Fold the layers inside to lock the top.
2. Make soft folds so the Cactus can stand.

**15**

**Saguaro Cactus**

# Roadrunner

While the Roadrunner can fly, it flies poorly and is better known for its speedy running ability on land. Due to its high speed, it is one of the few birds that preys on rattlesnakes.

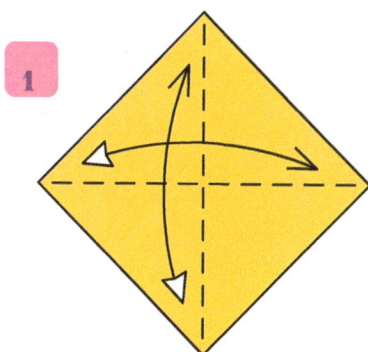

**1** Fold and unfold.

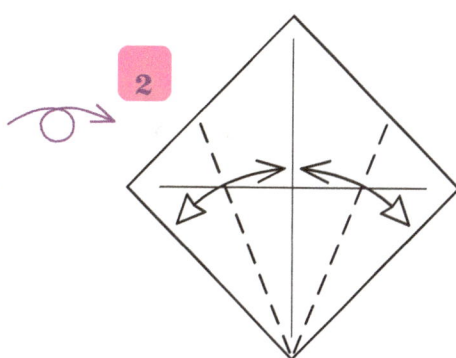

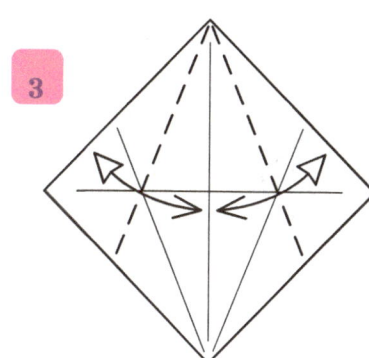

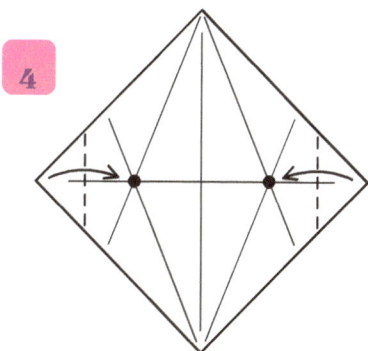

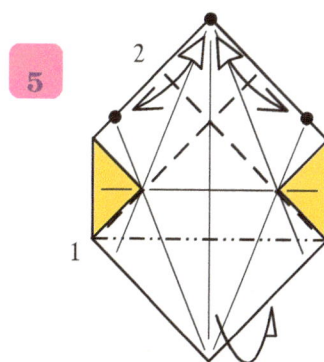

**2** Fold and unfold.

**3** Fold and unfold.

**4**

**5**
1. Fold behind.
2. Fold and unfold.

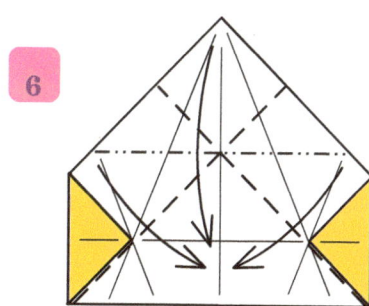

**6** Fold along the creases.

**7**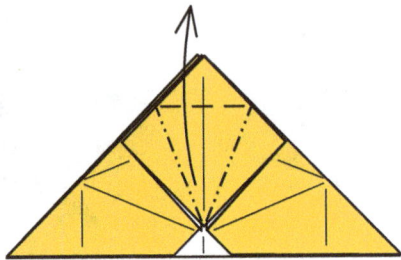

Petal-fold.

**8**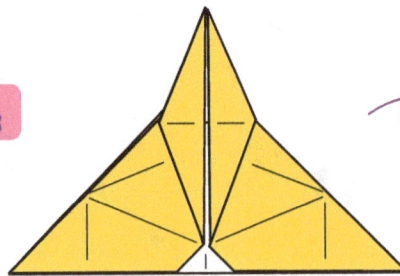

**9**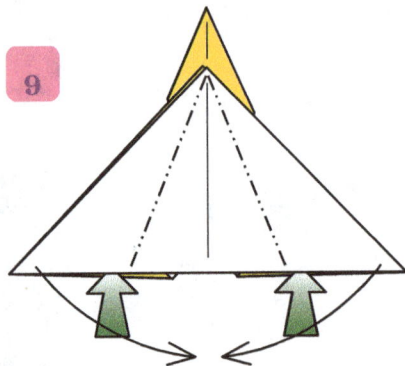

Make reverse folds.

**10**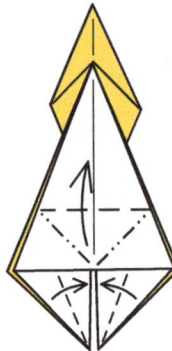

Petal-fold.

**11**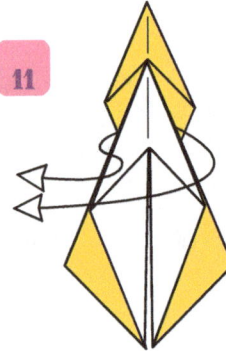

Double-unwrap-fold.

**12**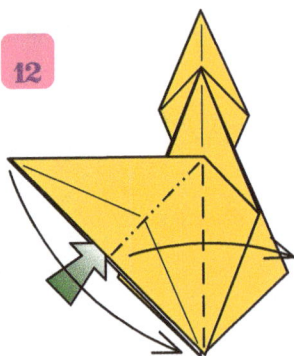

Squash-fold.

**13**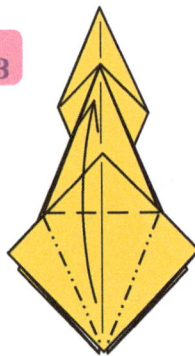

Petal-fold.

**14**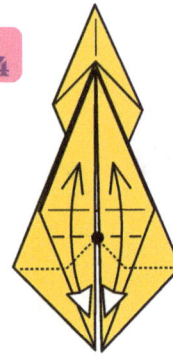

Fold and unfold
the top layers.

**15**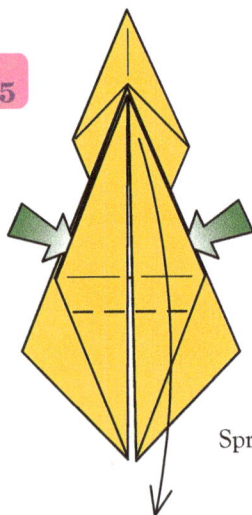

Spread-squash-fold.

**16**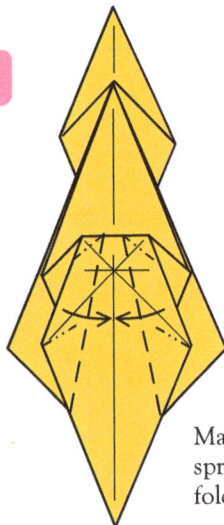

Make small
spread-squash
folds.

**17**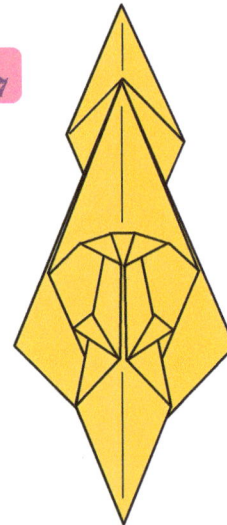

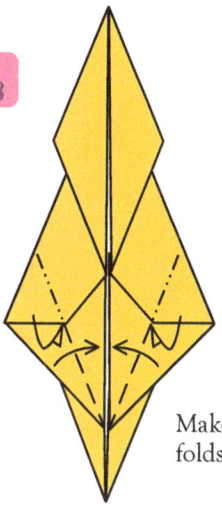

**18**

Make reverse folds.

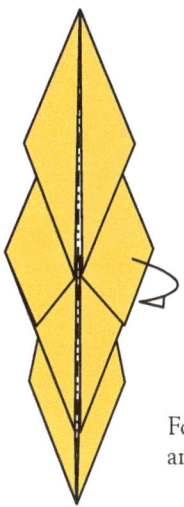

**19**

Fold in half and rotate.

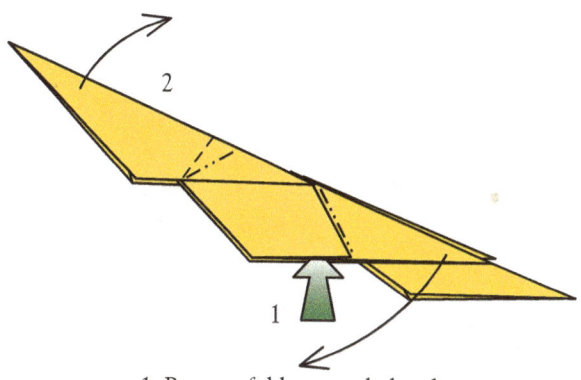

**20**

1. Reverse-fold, repeat behind.
2. Crimp-fold.

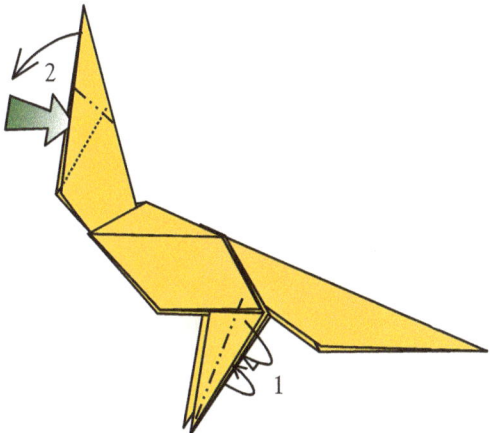

**21**

1. Fold inside on both sides, repeat behind.
2. Reverse-fold.

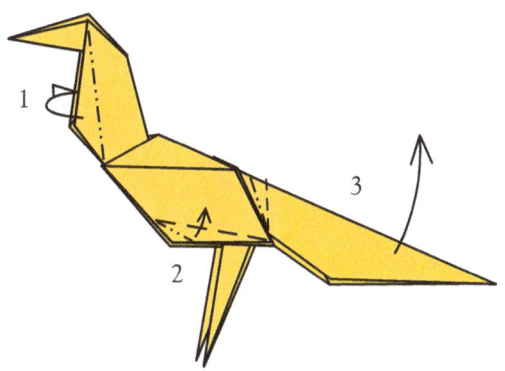

**22**

1. Fold inside, repeat behind.
2. Spread-squash-fold, repeat behind.
3. Crimp-fold.

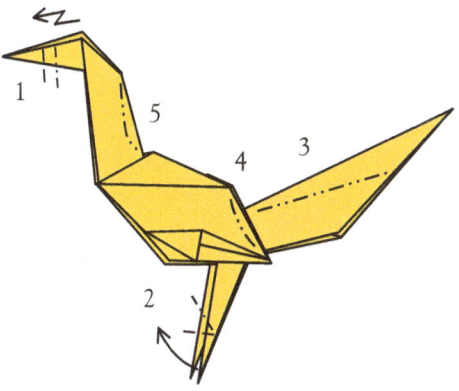

**23**

1. Crimp-fold.
2. Crimp-fold, repeat behind.
3. Shape the tail.
4. Shape the wings, repeat behind.
5. Shape the neck.
The Roadrunner can stand.

**24**

**Roadrunner**

# Veiled Chameleon

This is the famous reptile that has the ability to change its color in order to blend in with its surroundings. Its eyes also have an interesting feature, the ability to rotate separately and look at two different things at once.

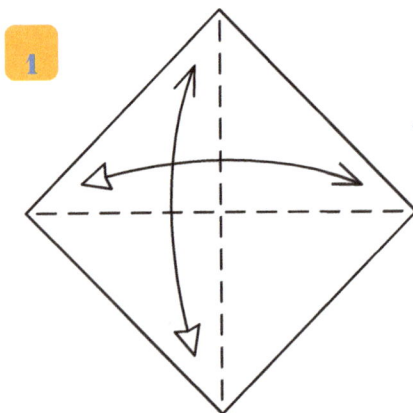

**1**

Fold and unfold.

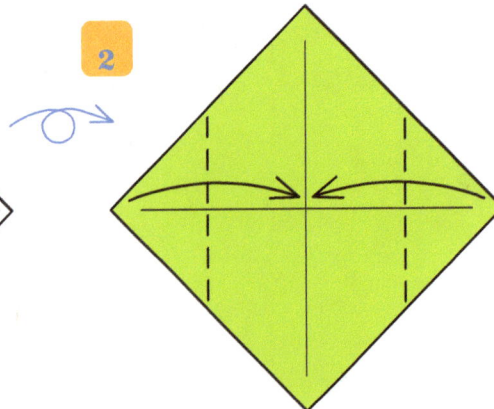

**2**

Fold the corners to the center.

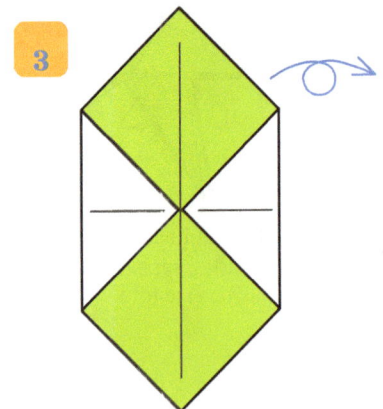

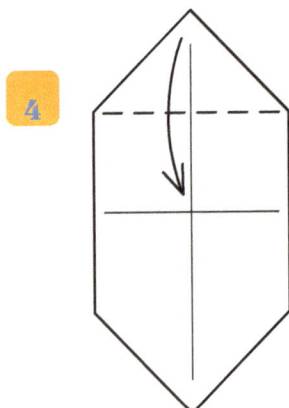

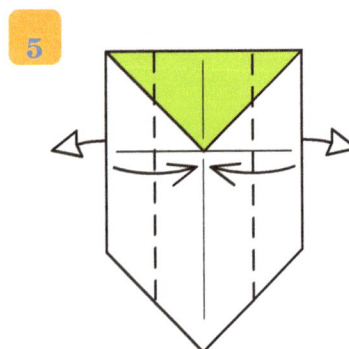

**3**

**4**

**5**

Fold to the center and swing out from behind.

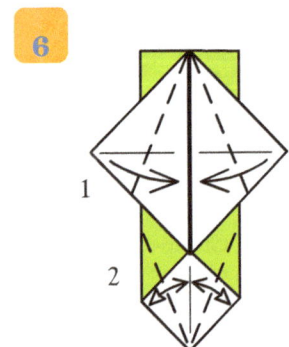

**6**

1. Fold to the center.
2. Fold to the center and unfold.

**7**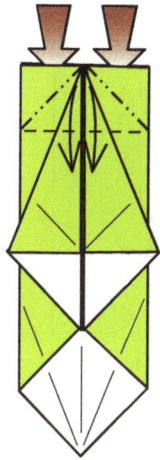

Make squash folds.

**8**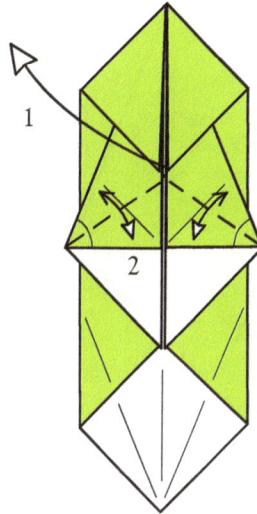

1. Pull out the hidden paper.
2. Fold and unfold the top layer.

**9**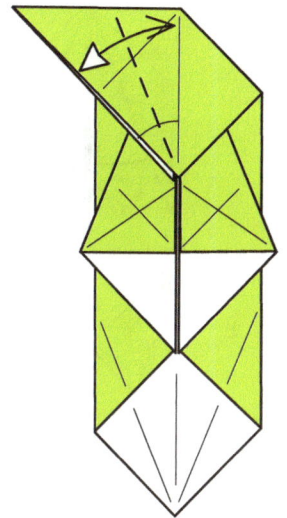

Fold and unfold.

**10**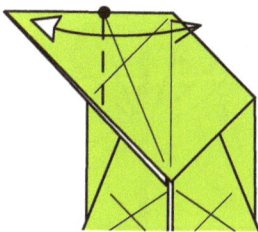

Only the top is drawn.
Fold and unfold.

**11**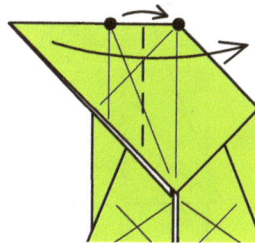

**12**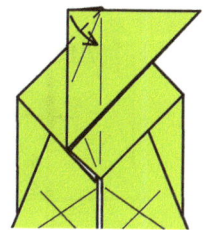

**13**

Unfold back
to step 11.

**14**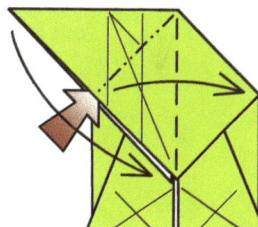

Squash-fold.

**15**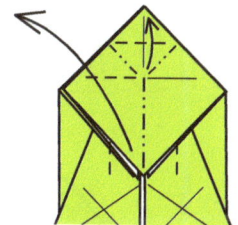

This is similar to
a squash fold.

**16**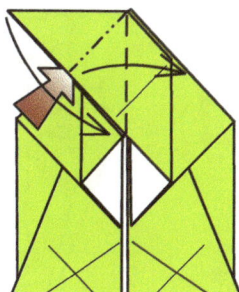

Squash-fold.

**17**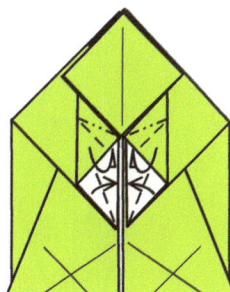

**18**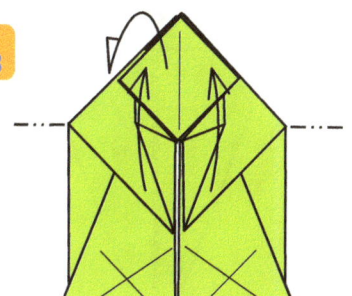

Pivot along the line.

**19**

Unfold.

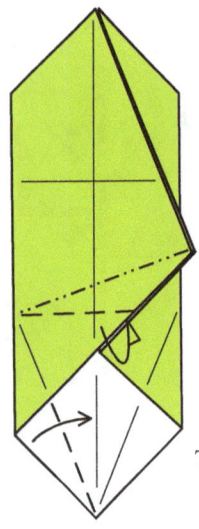

**20**

Tuck inside.

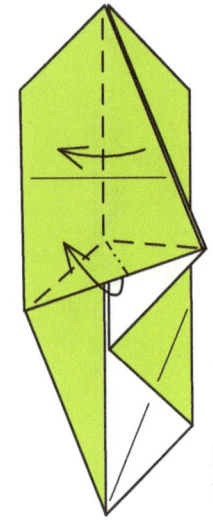

**21**

Lift up up the bottom.

**22**

Repeat steps 19–21 on the right.

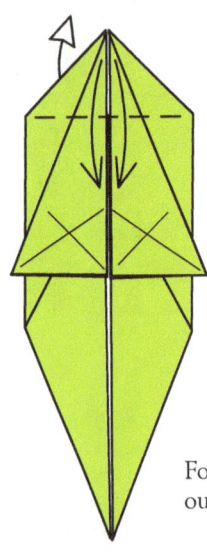

**23**

Fold down and swing out from behind.

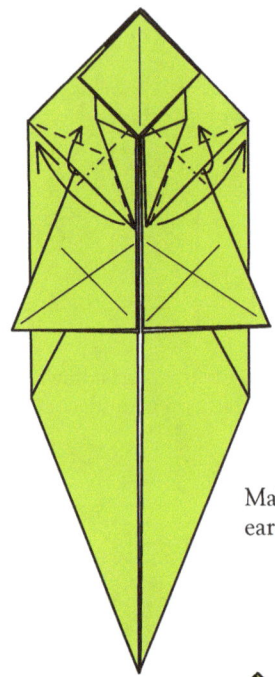

**24**

Make rabbit ears.

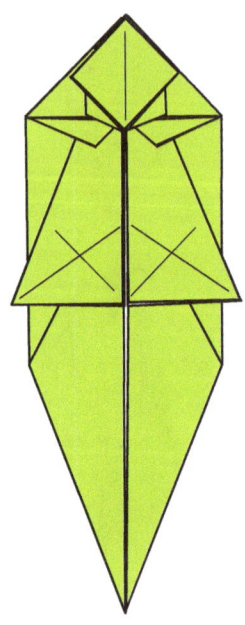

**25**

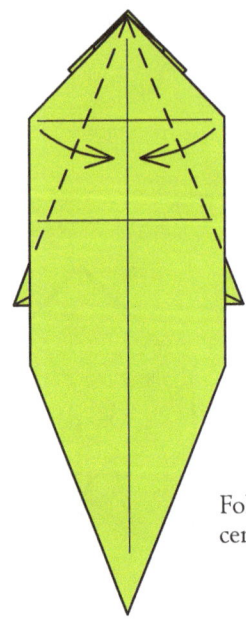

**26**

Fold to the center.

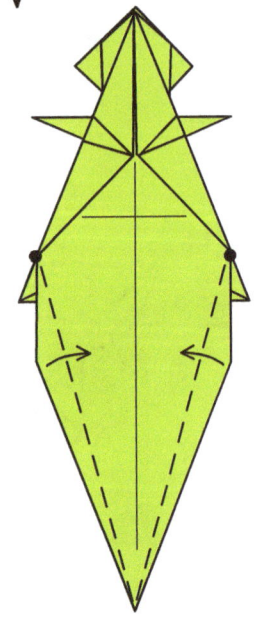

**27**

**28**

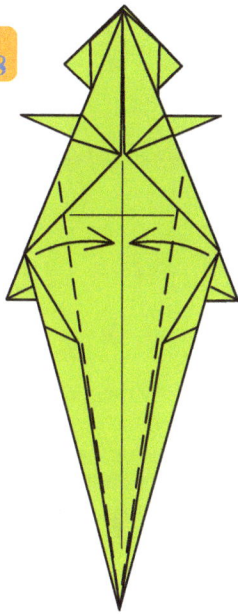

**29**

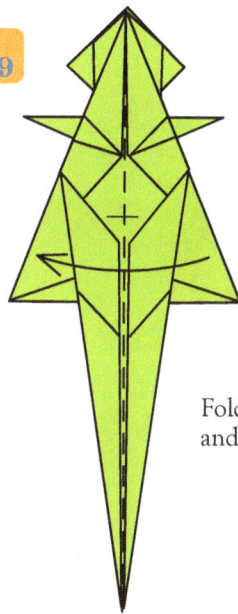

**30**

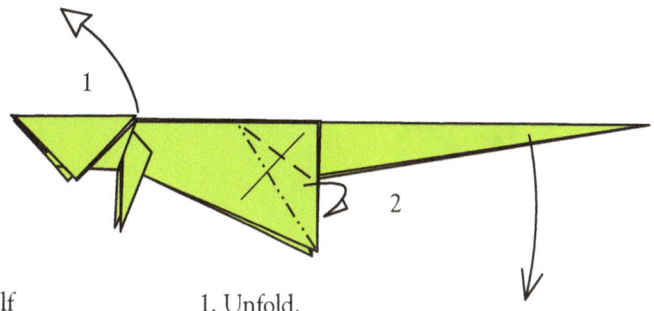

Fold in half
and rotate 90°.

1. Unfold.
2. Crimp-fold.

**31**

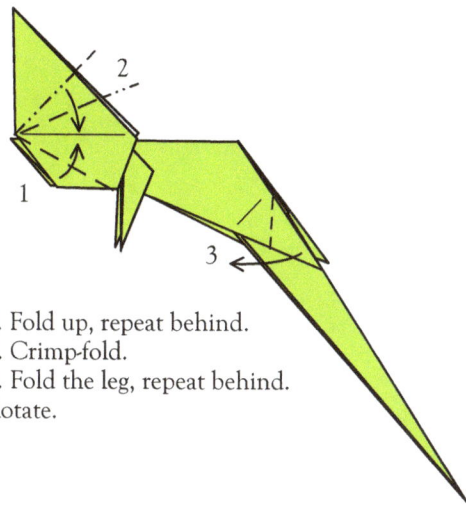

1. Fold up, repeat behind.
2. Crimp-fold.
3. Fold the leg, repeat behind.
Rotate.

**32**

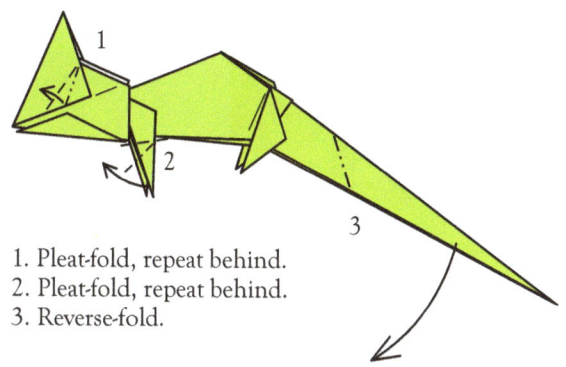

1. Pleat-fold, repeat behind.
2. Pleat-fold, repeat behind.
3. Reverse-fold.

**33**

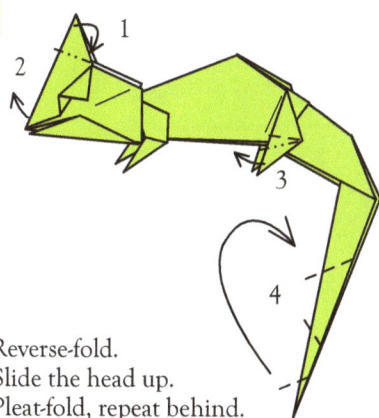

1. Reverse-fold.
2. Slide the head up.
3. Pleat-fold, repeat behind.
4. Shape the tail with inside
   and outside reverse folds.

**34**

Veiled Chameleon

# Green Iguana

These large lizards have become popular as pets, though keeping them can be challenging. They can grow very large and can become aggressive but many owners find joy in raising them from small babies. Iguanas are officially classified as carnivores but tend to follow a mainly herbivorous diet.

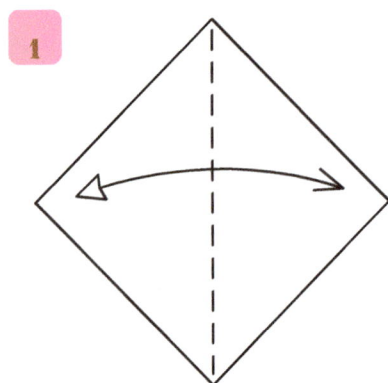

**1**

Fold and unfold.

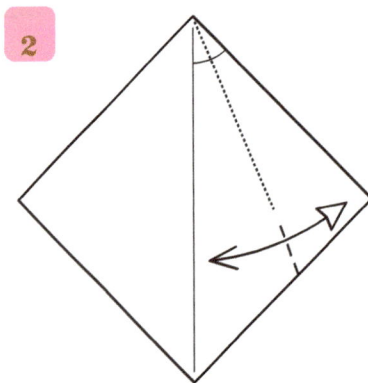

**2**

Fold and unfold on the edge.

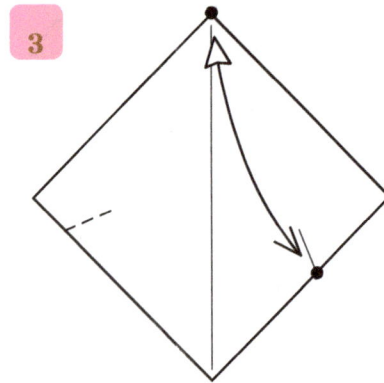

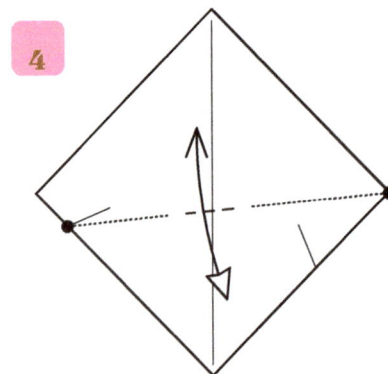

**3**

Fold and unfold on the edge.

**4**

Fold and unfold on the diagonal.

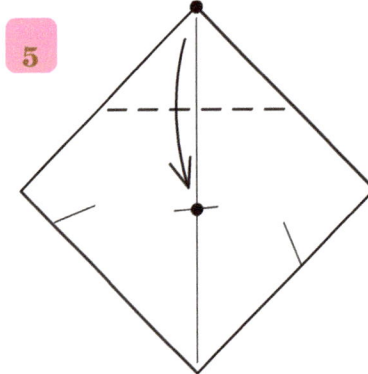

**5**

The dots will meet.

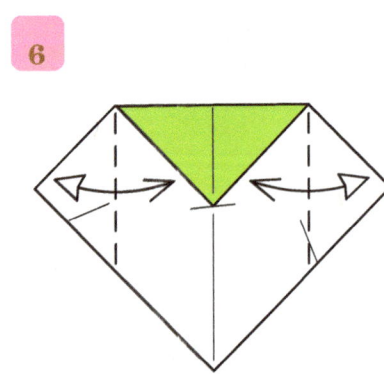

**6**

Fold and unfold.

**7**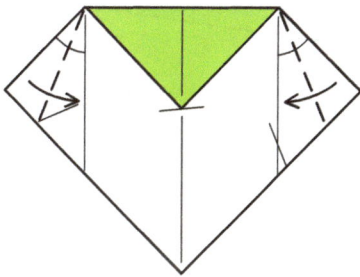

**8**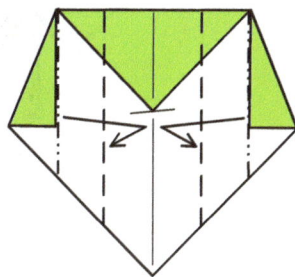

Pleat-fold to the center.

**9**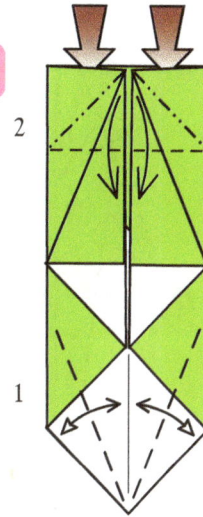

1. Fold to the center and unfold.
2. Continue with steps 7–18 of the Veiled Chameleon. (Skip step 8.2)

**10**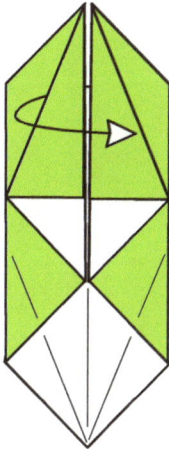

Unfold.

**11**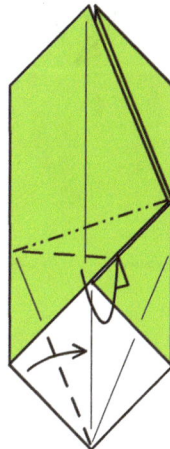

Tuck inside.

**12**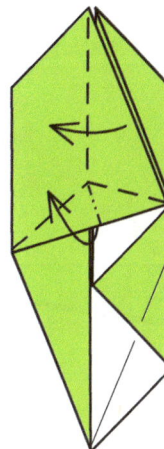

Lift up up the bottom.

**13**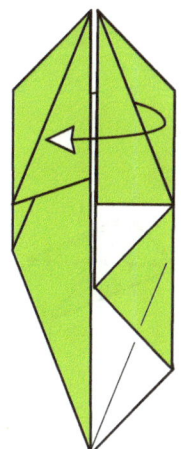

Repeat steps 10–12 on the right.

**14**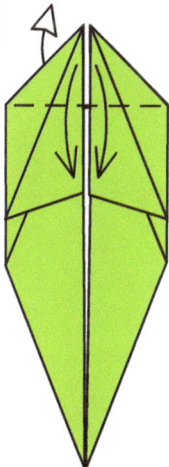

Fold down and swing out from behind.

**15**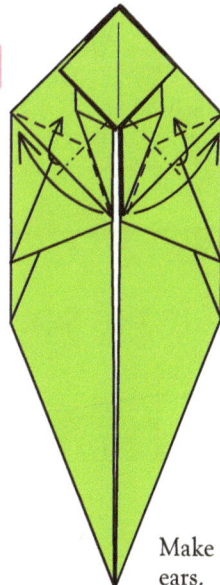

Make rabbit ears.

**16**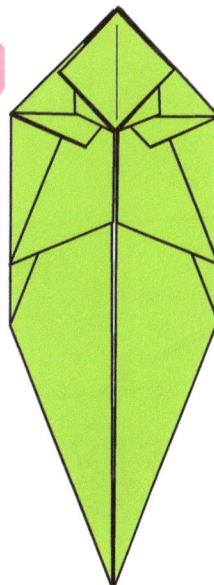

**17**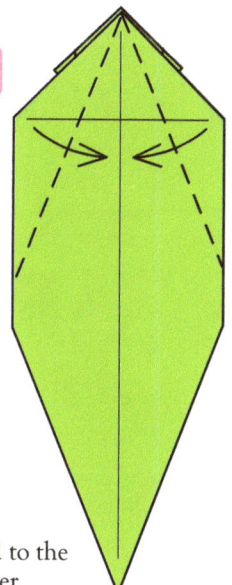

Fold to the center.

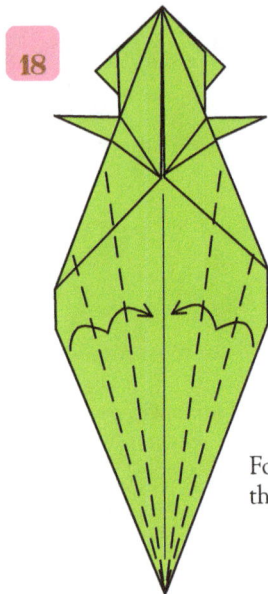

**18**

Fold in thirds.

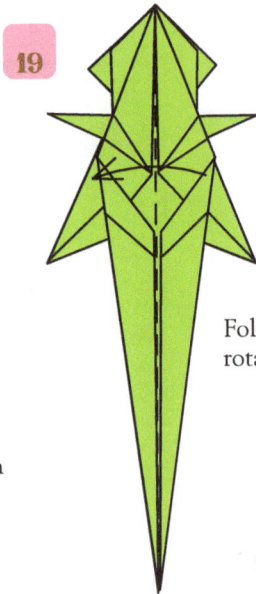

**19**

Fold in half and rotate 90°.

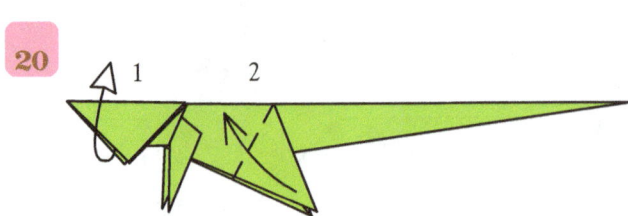

**20**

1. Lift up.
2. Fold the leg.
Repeat behind.

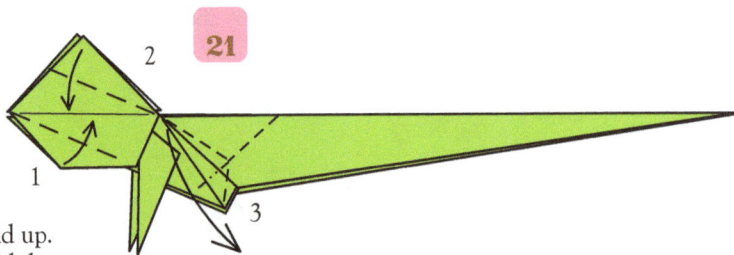

**21**

1. Fold up.
2. Fold down.
3. Rabbit-ear.
Repeat behind.

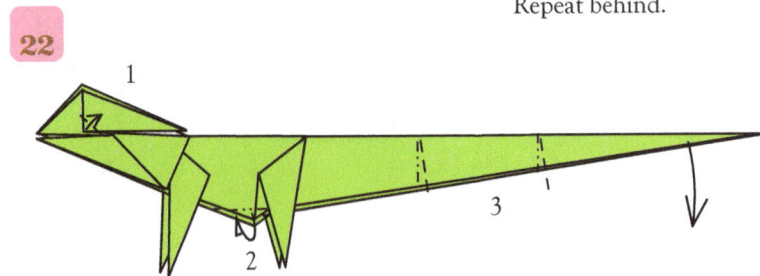

**22**

1. Fold the eye, repeat behind.
2. Fold inside, repeat behind.
3. Make crimp folds.

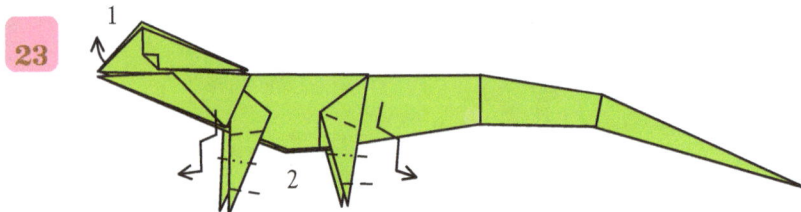

**23**

1. Slide the head up.
2. Bend the legs, repeat behind.

**24**

**Green Iguana**

# Armadillo

Carrying their own suit of armor, Armadillos are found in Central, South and North America. When frightened, Armadillos will roll up into a ball; this action is known as "volvation" and leaves only their protective armored shell facing their predators.

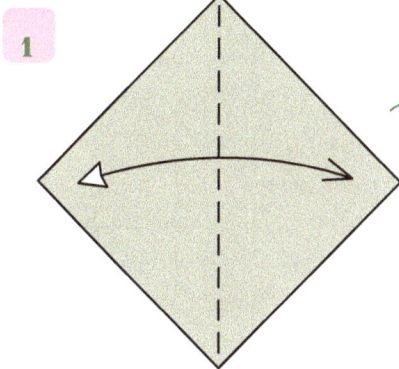

**1**
Fold and unfold.

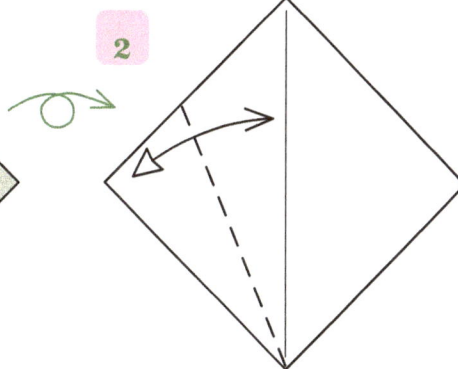

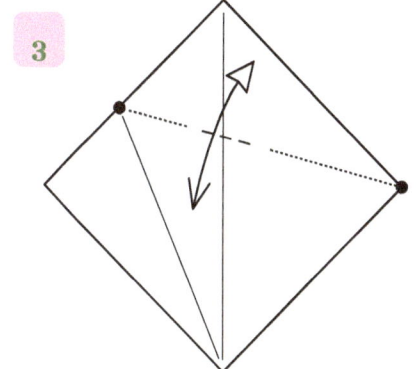

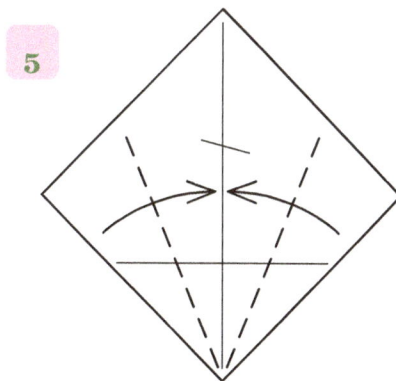

**2**
Fold and unfold.

**3**
Fold and unfold on the diagonal.

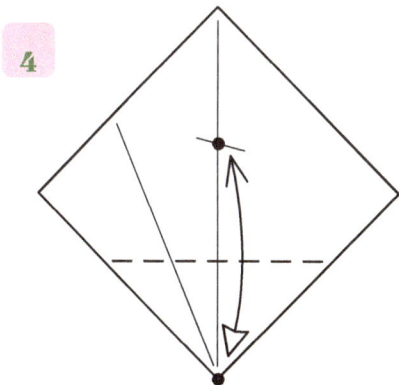

**4**
Fold and unfold.

**5**
Fold to the center.

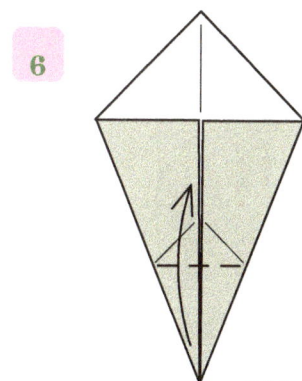

**6**
Fold along the hidden crease.

**7**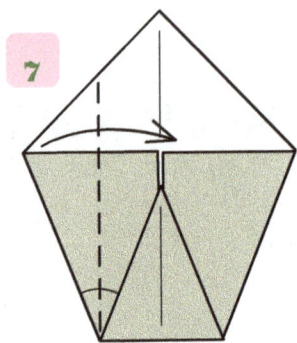

**8**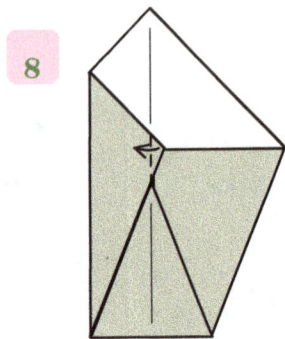

**9**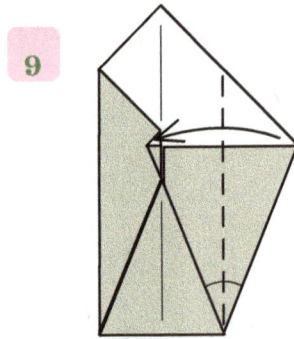

Repeat steps 7–8 on the right.

**10**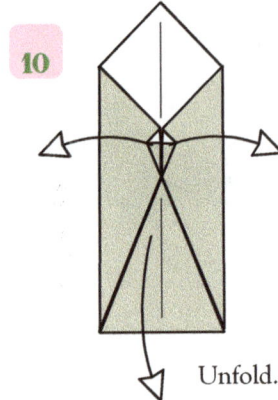

Unfold.

**11**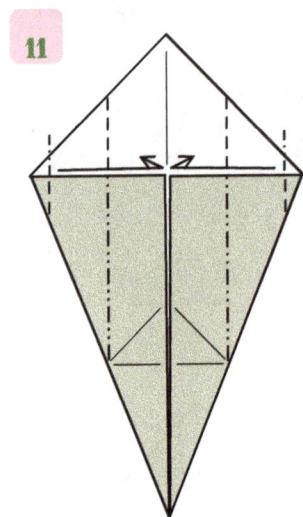

Make reverse folds along the creases.

**12**

Make reverse folds.

**13**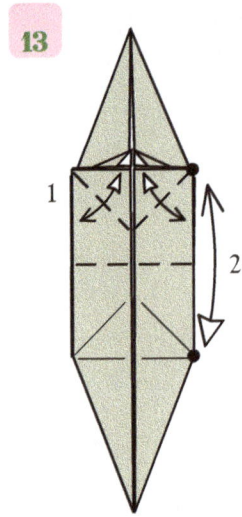

1. Fold and unfold the top layer.
2. Fold and unfold.

**14**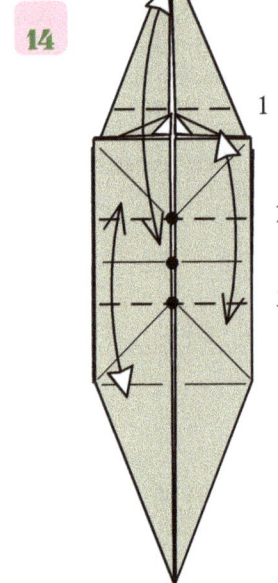

Fold and unfold.

**15**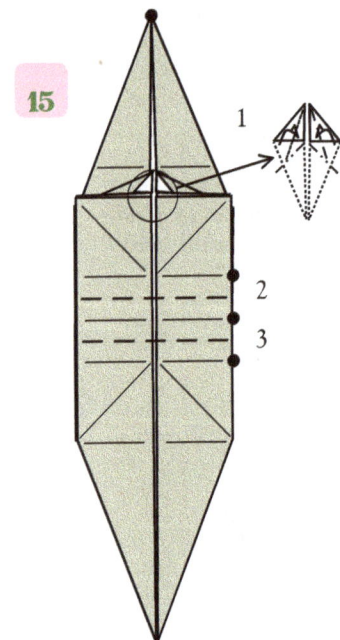

1. Make reverse folds.
2, 3. Fold and unfold between the dots.

**16**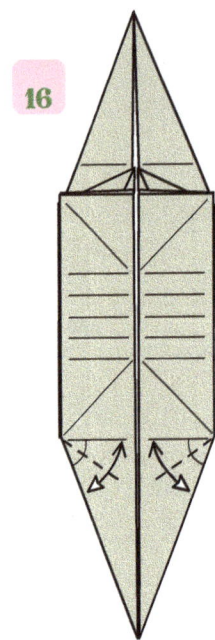

Fold and unfold.

**17**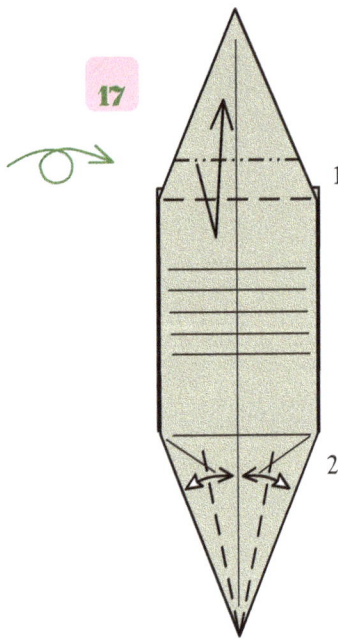

1. Mountain-fold along the crease for this pleat fold.
2. Fold and unfold.

**18**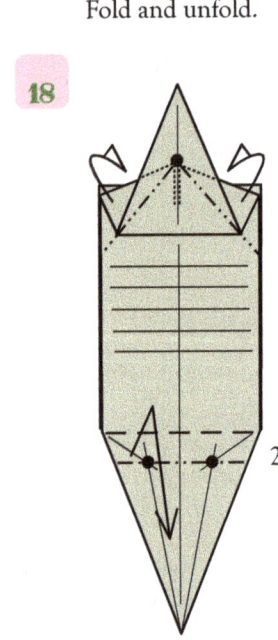

1. Fold behind.
2. Pleat-fold.

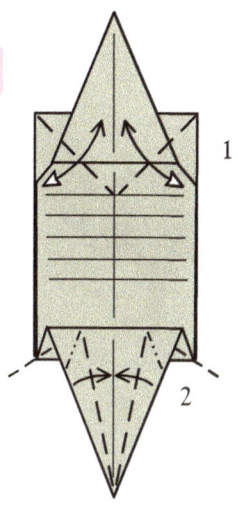

**19**

1. Fold and unfold.
2. Make squash folds.

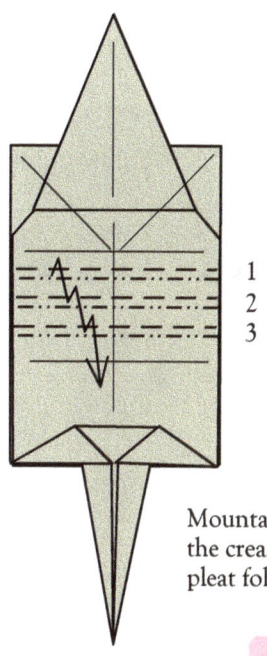

**20**

Mountain-fold along the creases for these pleat folds.

1
2
3

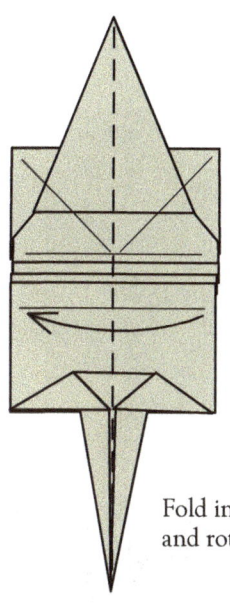

**21**

Fold in half and rotate 90°.

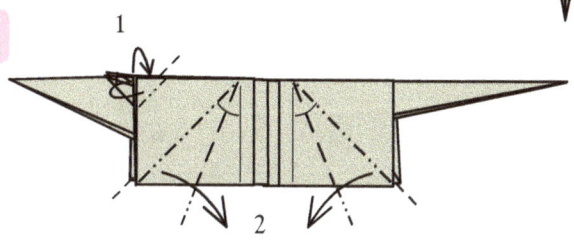

**22**

1
2

1. Mountain-fold the top layer, valley-fold the white layer, repeat behind.
2. Make crimp folds.

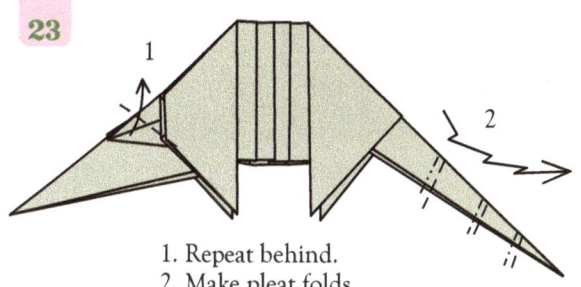

**23**

1
2

1. Repeat behind.
2. Make pleat folds.

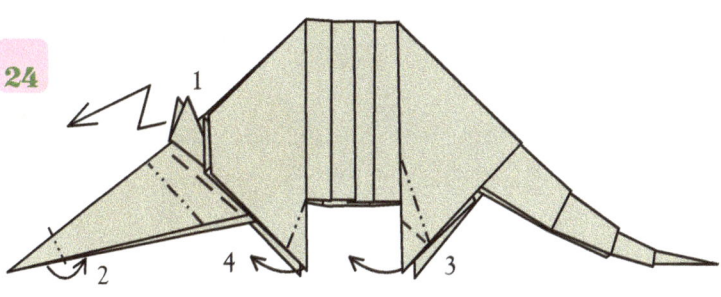

**24**

1
2
4
3

1. Crimp-fold.
2. Reverse-fold.
3. Crimp-fold, repeat behind.
4. Reverse-fold, repeat behind.

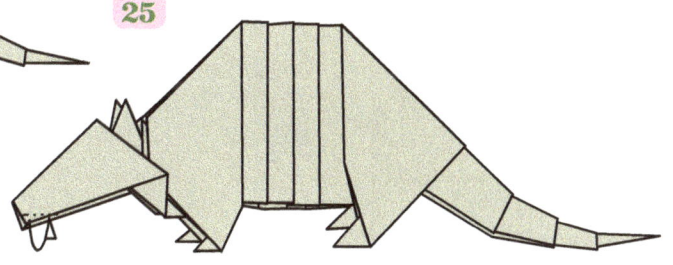

**25**

Repeat behind.

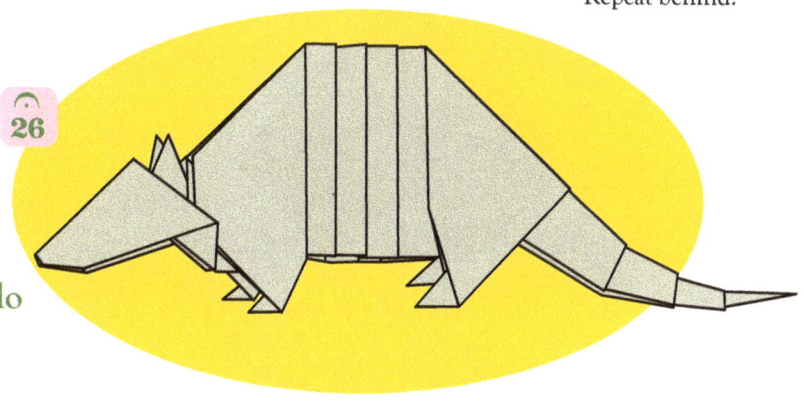

**26**

**Armadillo**

# Dromedary

This single-hump camel is known for its swiftness and has short hair and a slim body and limbs. Dromedaries are also known as Arabian Camels and are prized for their running abilities.

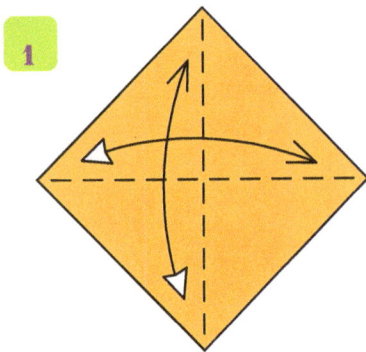

**1**

Fold and unfold.

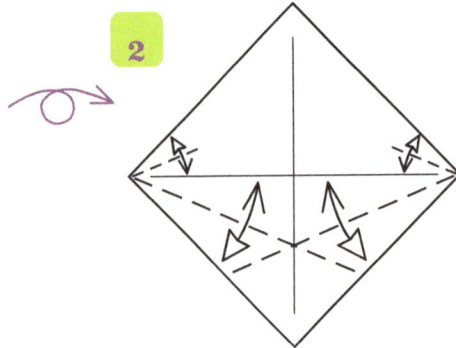

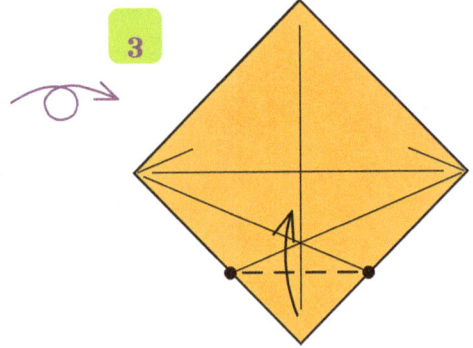

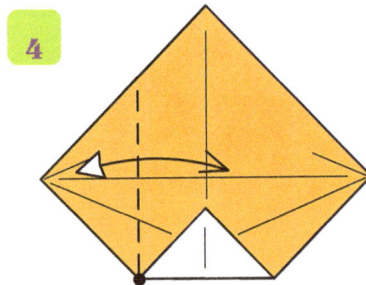

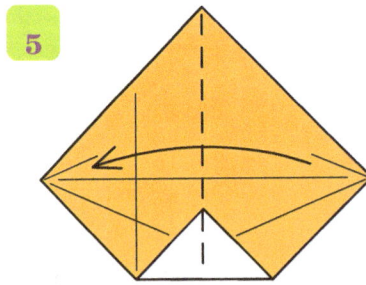

**2**

Fold and unfold.

**3**

**4**

Fold and unfold.

**5**

Fold in half and rotate 90°.

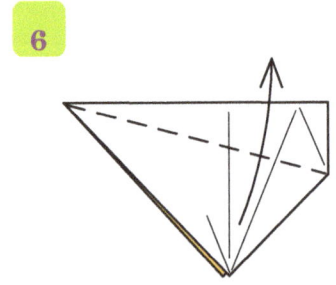

**6**

Fold the top layer.

**7**

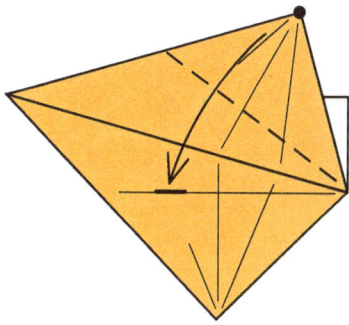

**8**

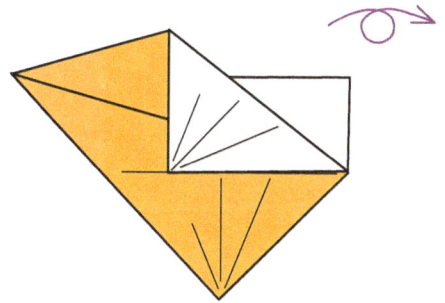

**9**

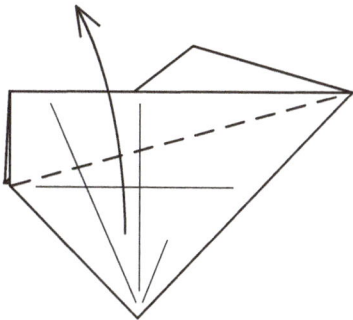

**10**

**11**

Squash-fold.
Repeat behind.

**12**

Fold along the partially
hidden edge. Repeat behind.

**13**

Repeat behind.

**14**

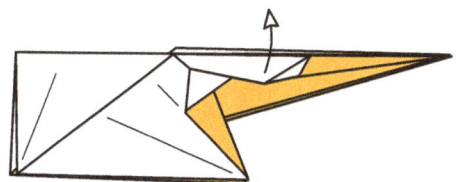

Unfold and repeat behind.

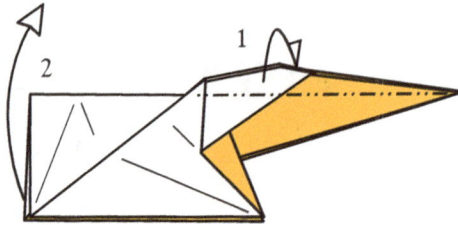

**15**

1. Fold inside, repeat behind.
2. Unfold.

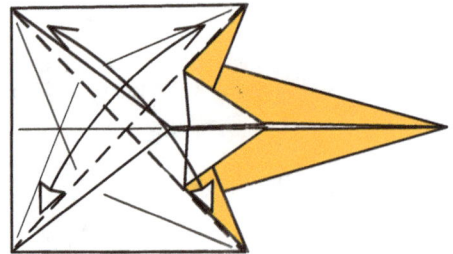

**16**

Fold and unfold.

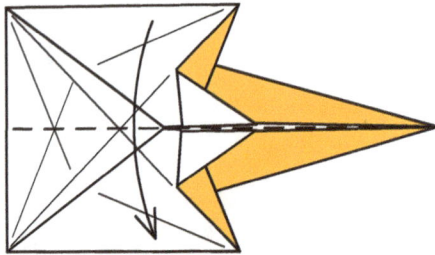

**17**

Fold in half.

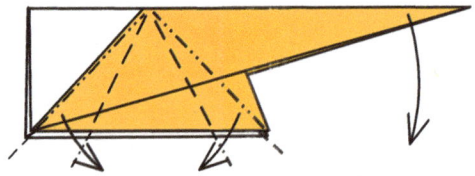

**18**

Make crimp folds.

**19**

View of inside: Petal-fold and repeat behind.

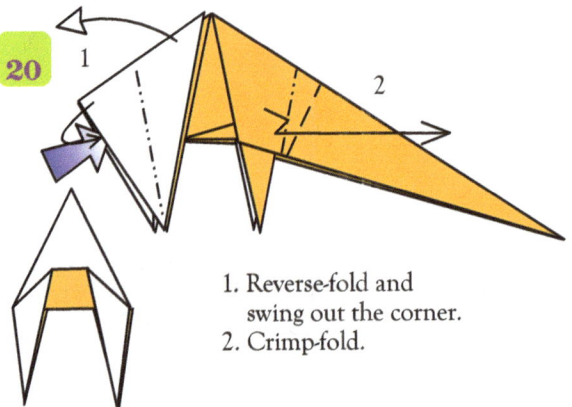

**20**

View of inside.

1. Reverse-fold and swing out the corner.
2. Crimp-fold.

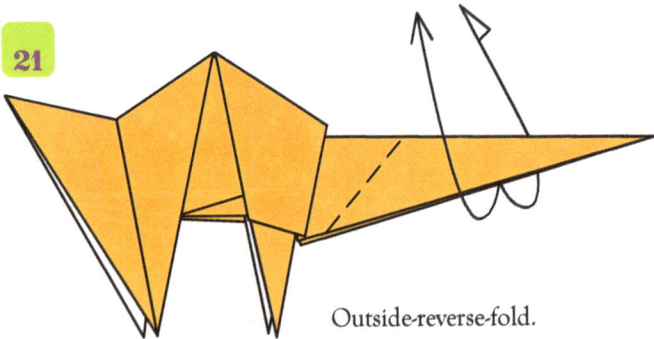

**21**

Outside-reverse-fold.

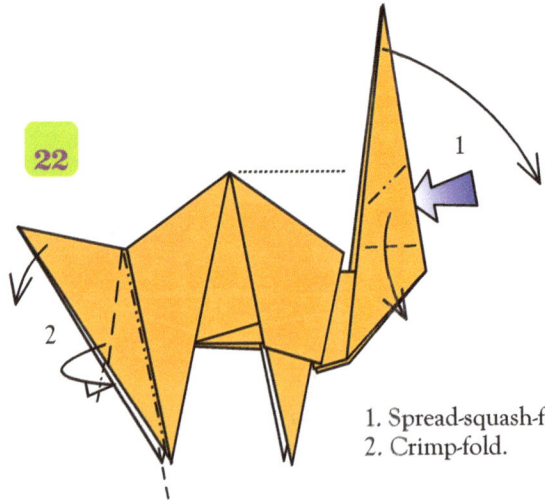

**22**

1. Spread-squash-fold.
2. Crimp-fold.

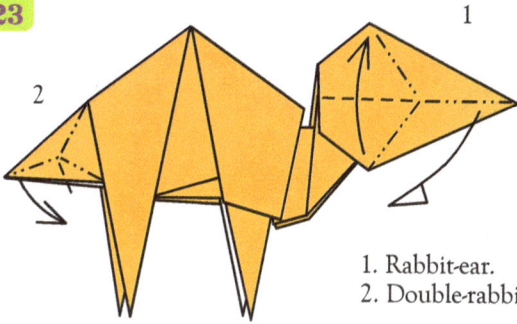

**23**

1. Rabbit-ear.
2. Double-rabbit-ear.

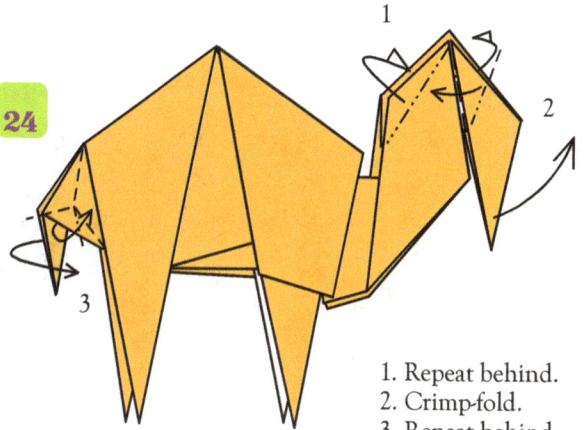

**24**

1. Repeat behind.
2. Crimp-fold.
3. Repeat behind.

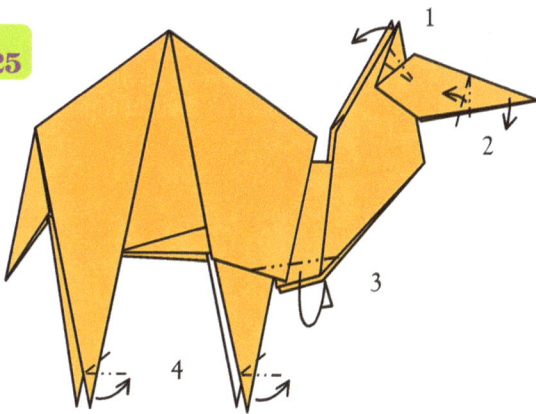

**25**

1. Squash-fold, repeat behind.
2. Crimp-fold.
3. Fold inside, repeat behind.
4. Spread to form the hooves, repeat behind.

**26**

1. Reverse-fold.
2. Thin and shape the legs, repeat behind.
3. Shape the back.

**27**

**Dromedary**

# Camel

Also known as Bactrian Camels, these two-humped have served as domesticated beasts of burden for millennia. Heavier and with thicker fur than Dromedaries, these Camels can go without water for a week, living off the fat stored in their humps.

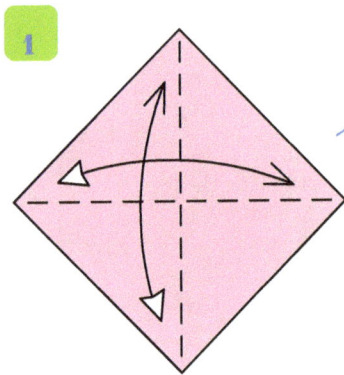

**1**

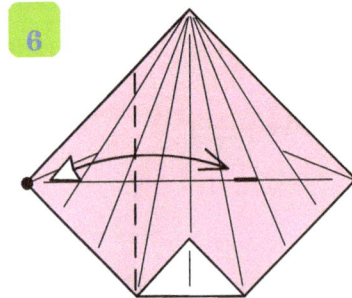

Fold and unfold.

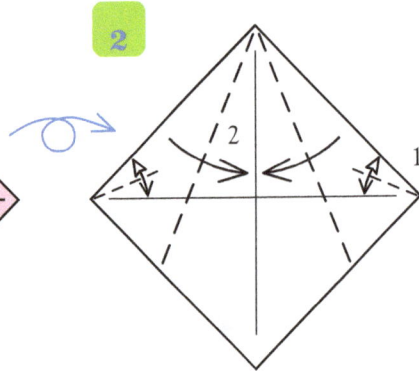

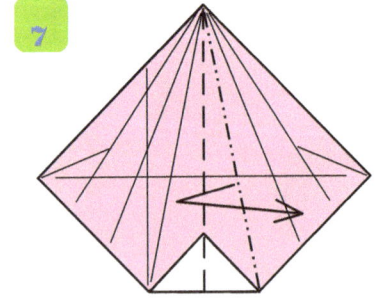

**2**

1. Fold and unfold.
2. Fold to the center.

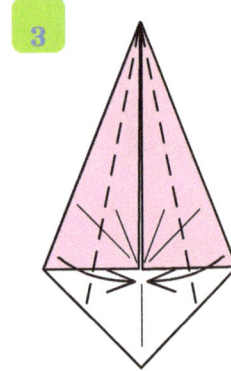

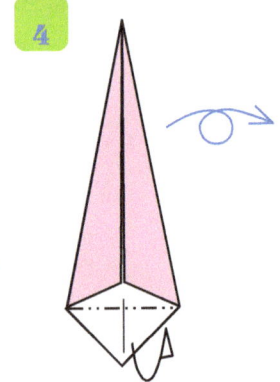

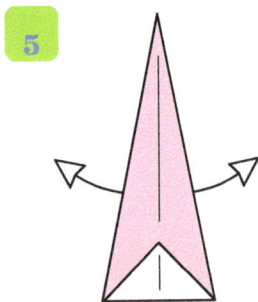

**3**

**4**

**5**

Unfold.

**6**

Fold and unfold.

**7**

Pleat-fold along the creases. Rotate 90°.

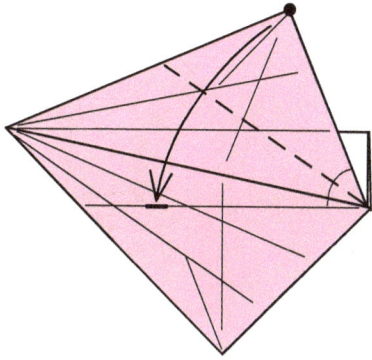

**8**

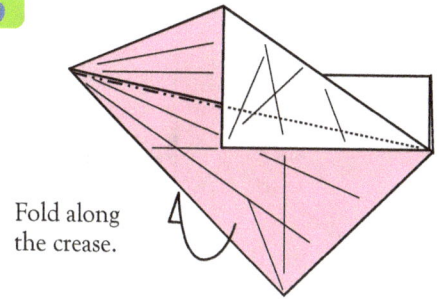

**9**

Fold along
the crease.

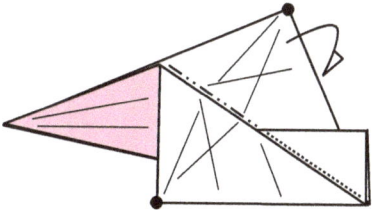

**10**

The dots will meet.

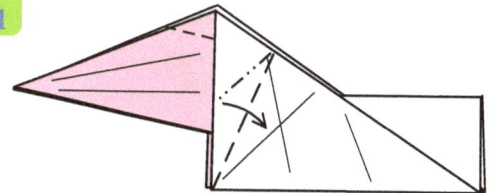

**11**

Valley-fold along the crease for
this squash fold. Repeat behind.

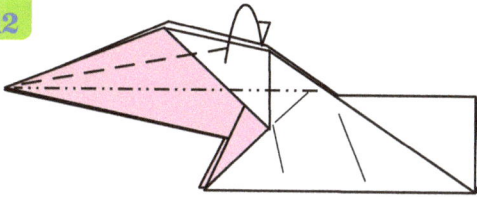

**12**

Pleat-fold along the
creases. Repeat behind.

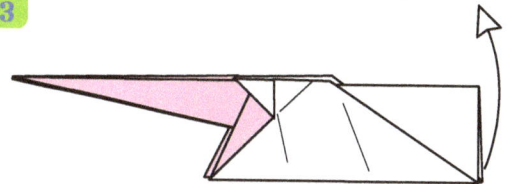

**13**

Unfold.

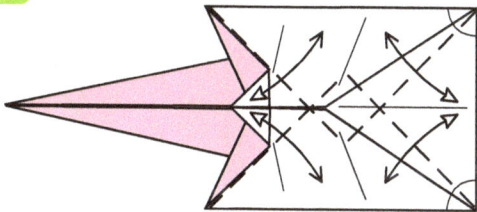

**14**

Fold and unfold.

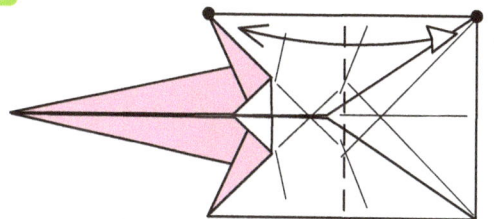

**15**

Fold and unfold.

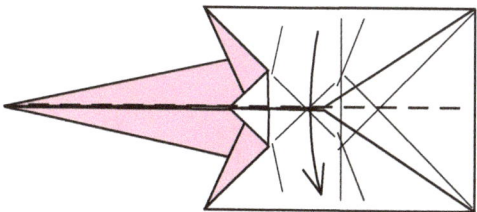

**16**

Fold in half.

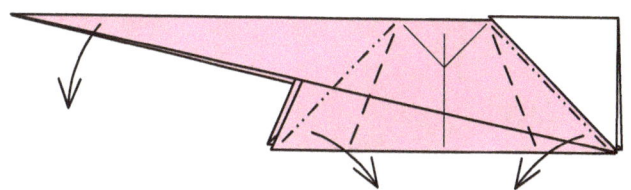

**17**

Mountain-fold along the
creases for these crimp folds.

*Camel* **119**

**18**

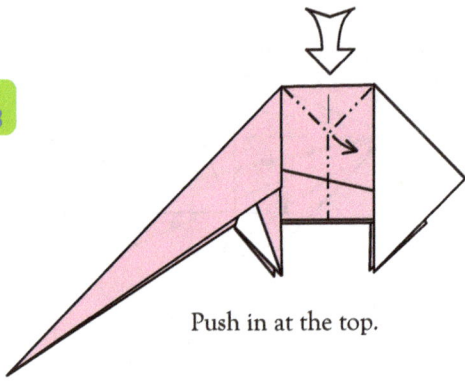

Push in at the top.

**19**

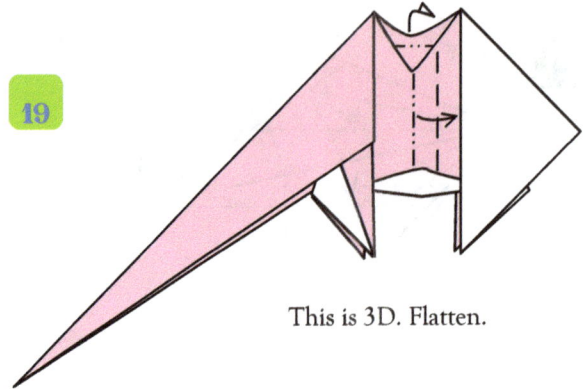

This is 3D. Flatten.

**20**

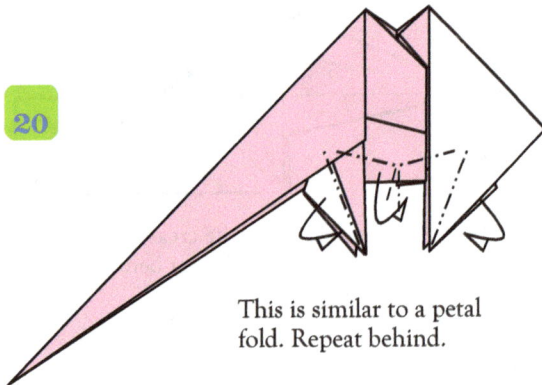

This is similar to a petal fold. Repeat behind.

**21**

2

1

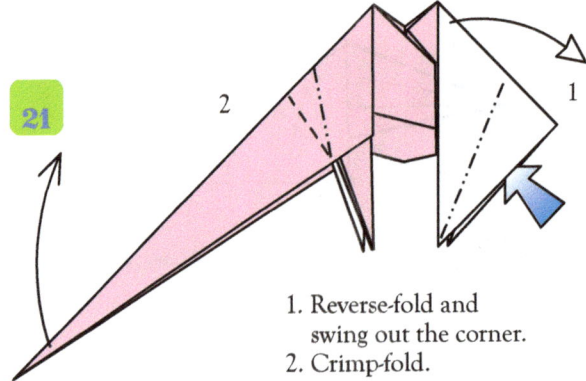

1. Reverse-fold and swing out the corner.
2. Crimp-fold.

**22**

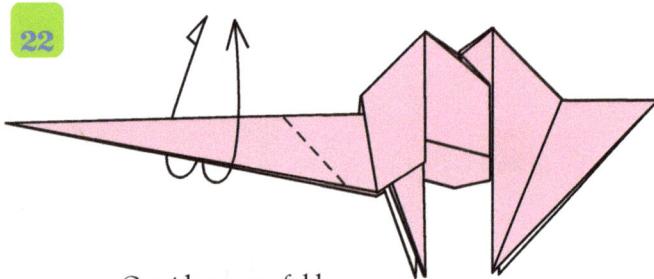

Outside-reverse-fold.

**23**

1

2

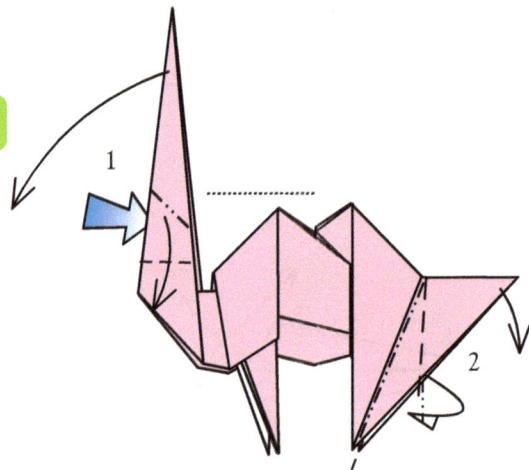

1. Spread-squash-fold.
2. Crimp-fold.

**24**

1

2

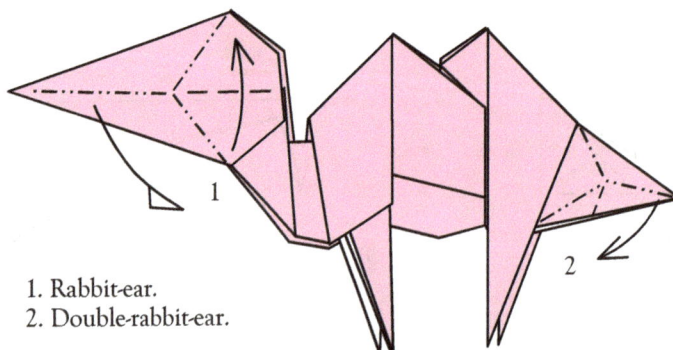

1. Rabbit-ear.
2. Double-rabbit-ear.

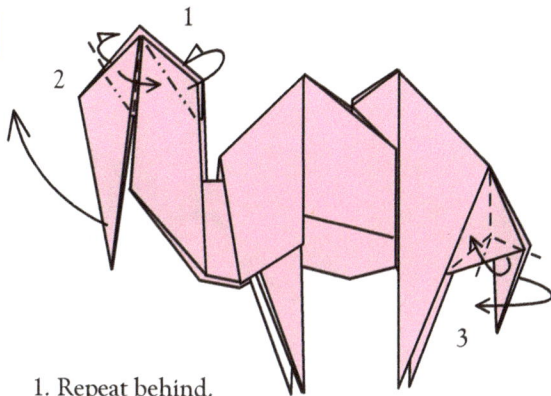

**25**

1. Repeat behind.
2. Crimp-fold.
3. Repeat behind.

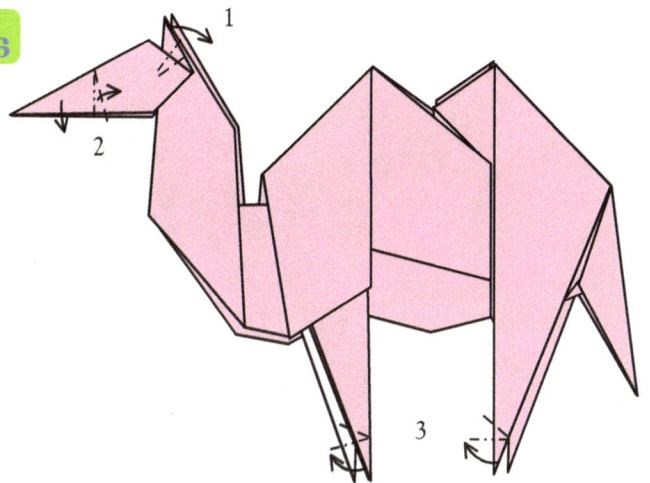

**26**

1. Squash-fold, repeat behind.
2. Crimp-fold.
3. Spread to form the hooves, repeat behind.

**27**

1. Reverse-fold.
2. Thin and shape the legs, repeat behind.
3. Shape the back.

**28**

Camel

*Camel* **121**

# Scorpion

Scorpions, like spiders, are Arachnids. Their most famous feature is the sharp stinger at the end of their tail, and they also have large pincers. Though all scorpions are venomous to varying degrees, very few varieties are poisonous to humans.

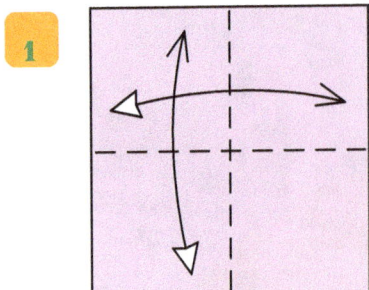

**1** Fold and unfold.

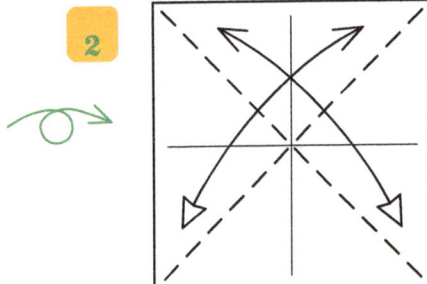

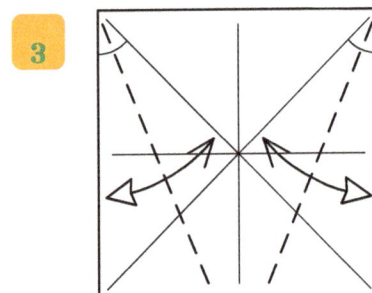

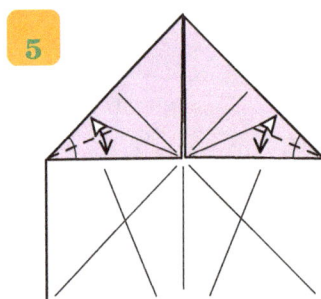

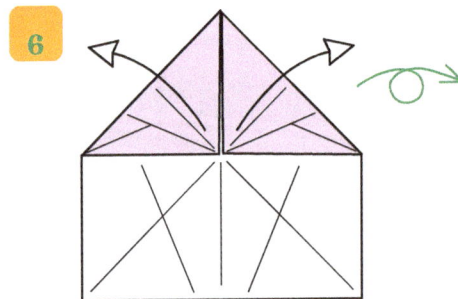

**2** Fold and unfold.

**3** Fold and unfold.

**4** Fold and unfold.

**5** Fold and unfold.

**6** Unfold.

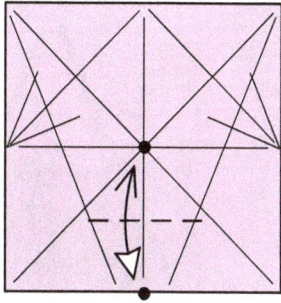

**7**

Fold and unfold.

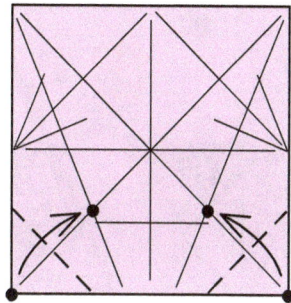

**8**

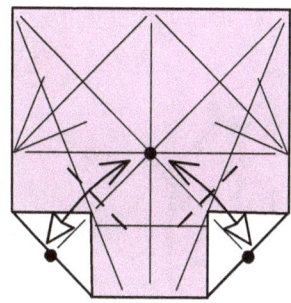

**9**

Fold and unfold.

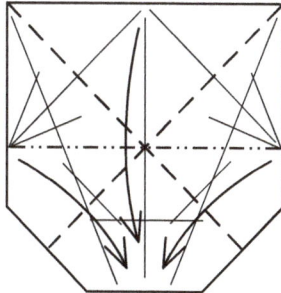

**10**

Fold along the creases.

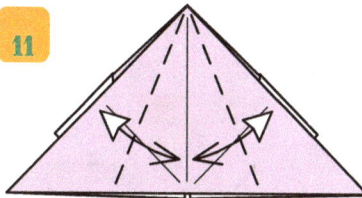

**11**

Fold and unfold.
Repeat behind.

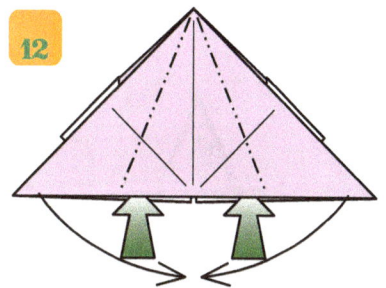

**12**

Make reverse folds.

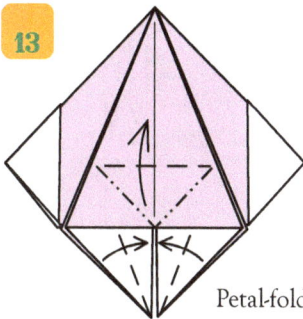

**13**

Petal-fold.

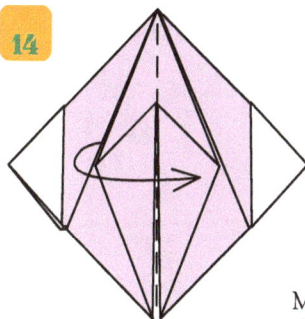

**14**

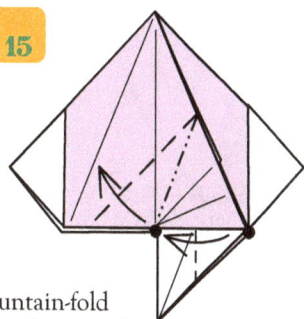

**15**

Mountain-fold
along the crease for
this squash fold.

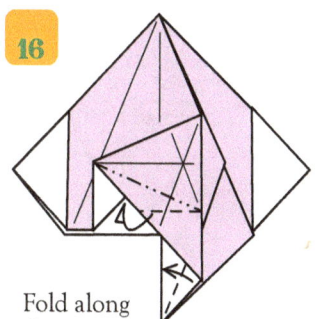

**16**

Fold along
the creases.

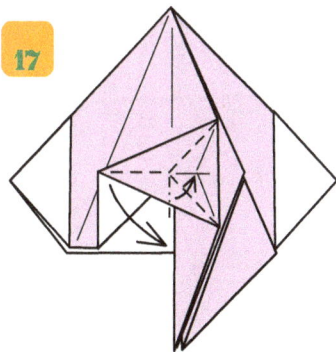

**17**

This is similar
to a rabbit ear.

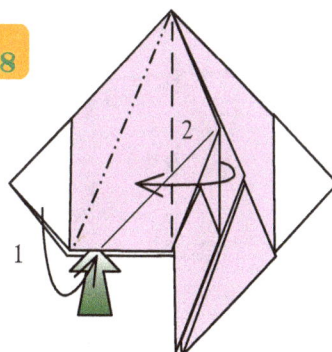

**18**

1. Reverse-fold.
2. Fold the top flap.

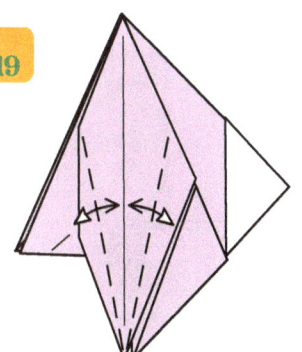

**19**

Fold and unfold.

**20**

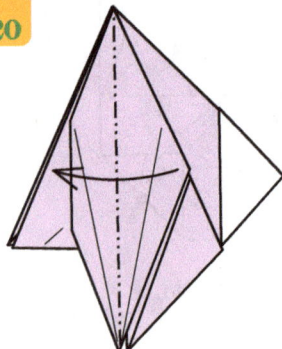

**21**

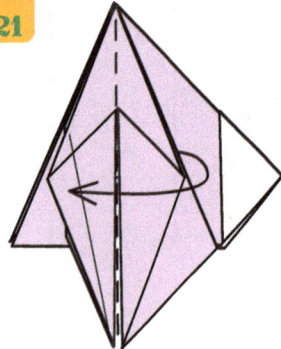

Repeat steps 14–20 on the right.

**22**

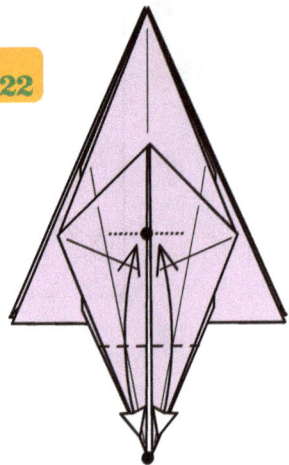

Fold and unfold.

**23**

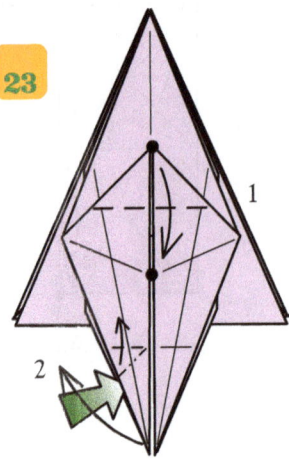

Squash-fold.

**24**

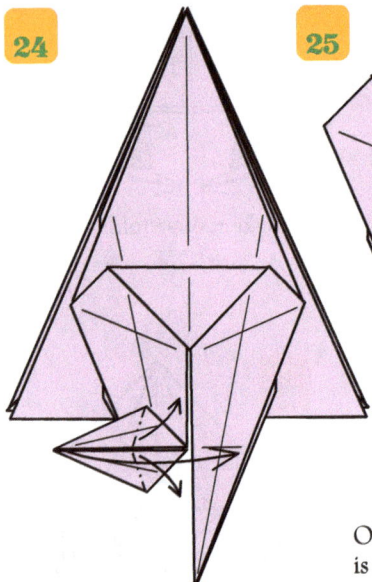

Spread the layers.

**25**

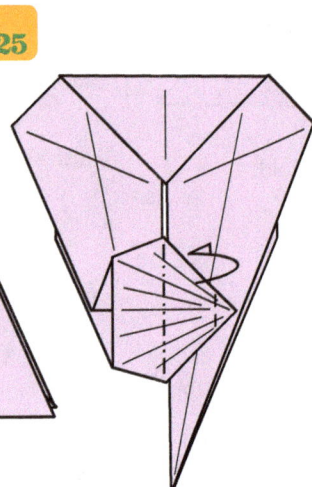

Only part of the model is drawn. Tuck inside.

**26**

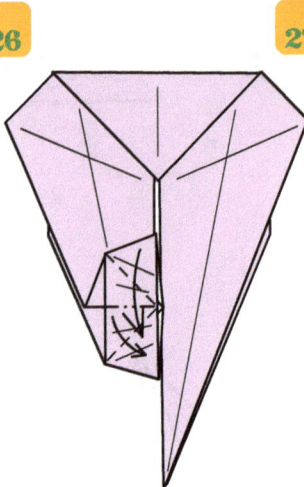

**27**

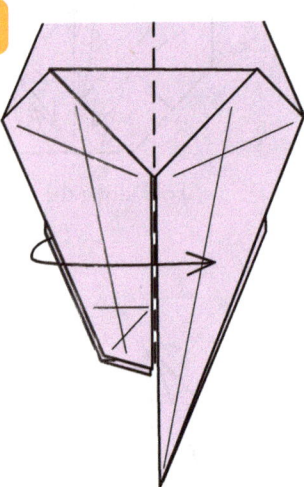

**28**

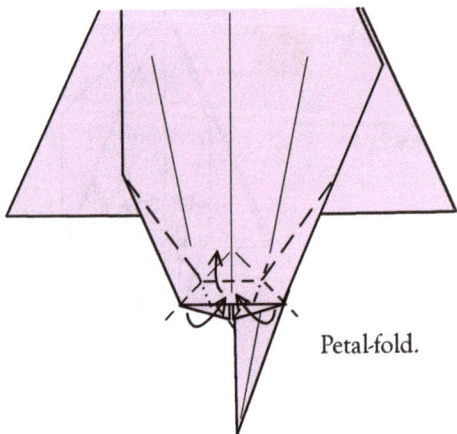

Petal-fold.

**29**

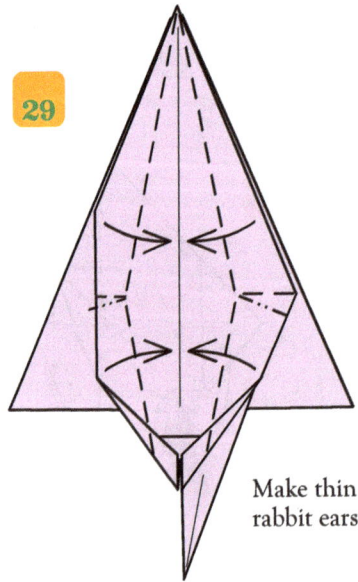

Make thin rabbit ears.

**30**

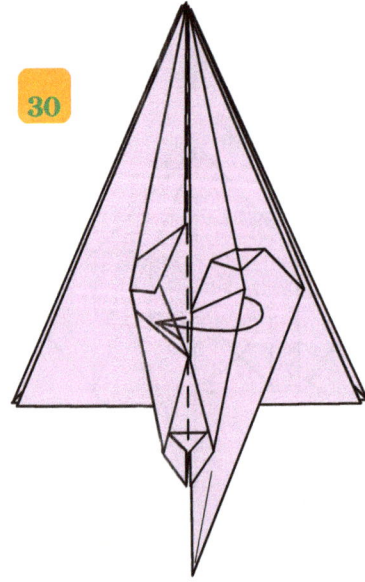

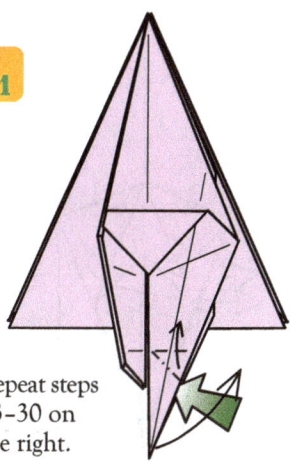

**31**

Repeat steps
23–30 on
the right.

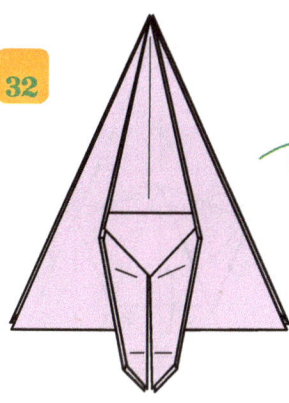

**32**

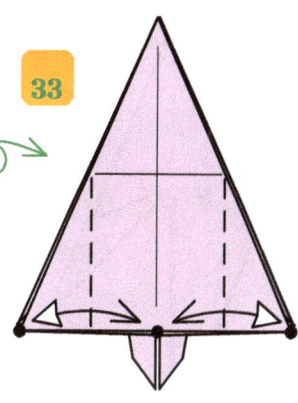

**33**

Fold and unfold
the top layers.

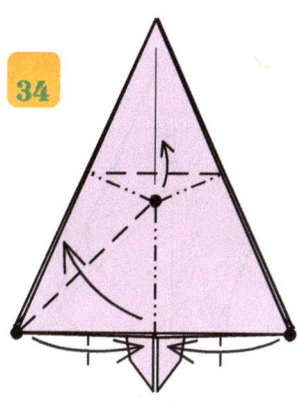

**34**

Lift up at the dot in the
center. The bottom dots
will meet.

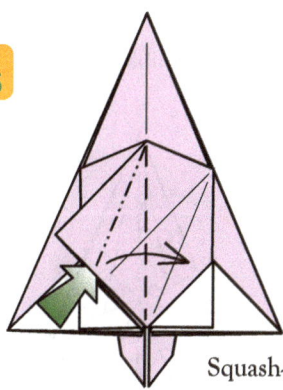

**35**

Squash-fold.

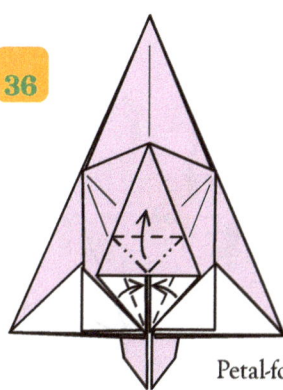

**36**

Petal-fold.

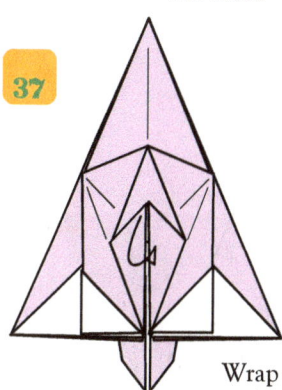

**37**

Wrap around
and tuck inside.

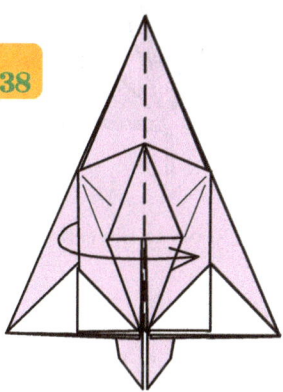

**38**

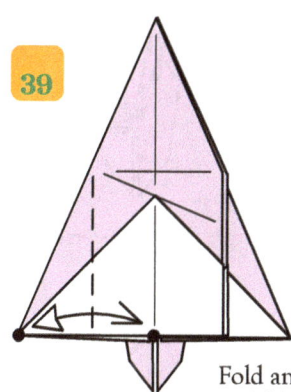

**39**

Fold and
unfold.

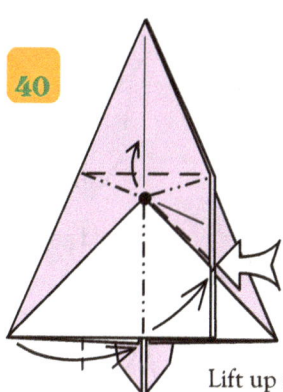

**40**

Lift up at
the dot.

**41**

Fold and
unfold.

**42**

Fold and unfold.

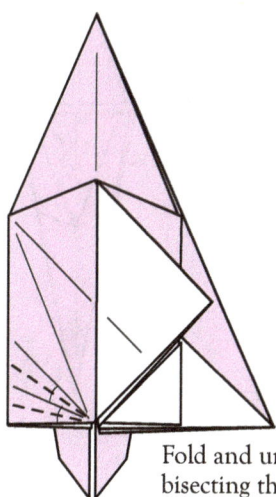

**43**

Fold and unfold,
bisecting the angles.

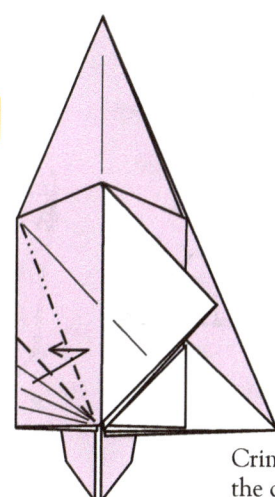

**44**

Crimp-fold along
the creases.

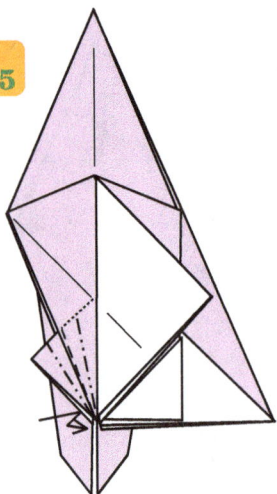

**45**

Make three reverse folds along the creases.

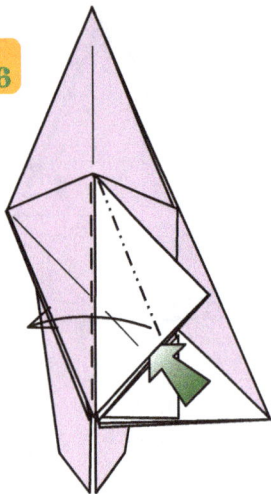

**46**

Squash-fold.

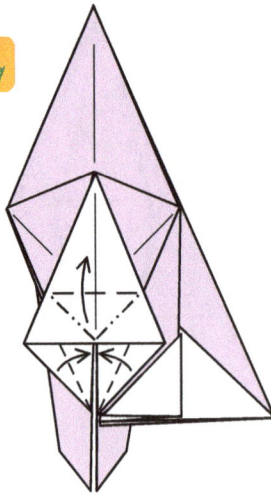

**47**

Petal-fold.

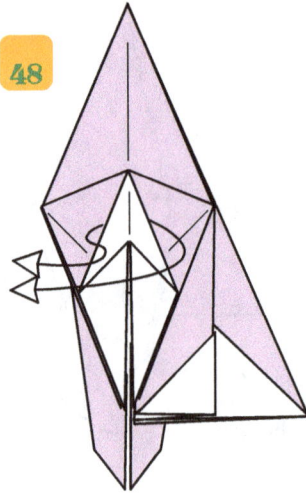

**48**

Double-unwrap-fold.

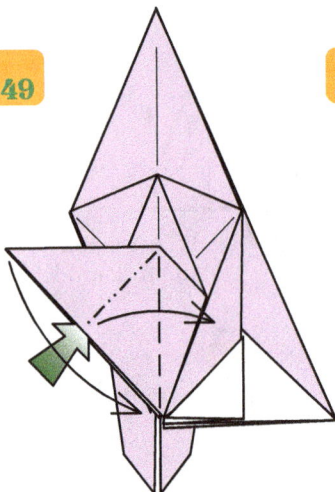

**49**

Squash-fold.

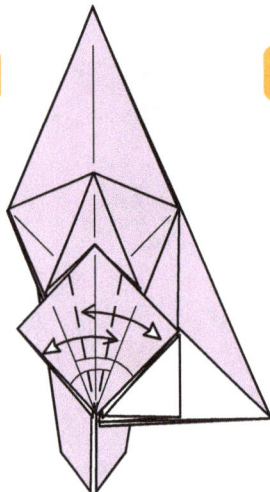

**50**

Fold and unfold.

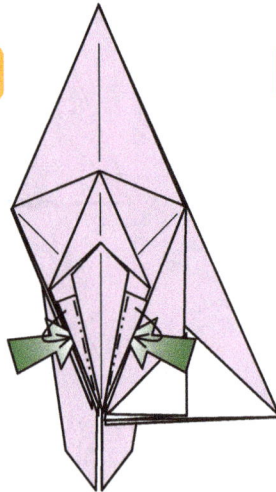

**51**

Make reverse folds.

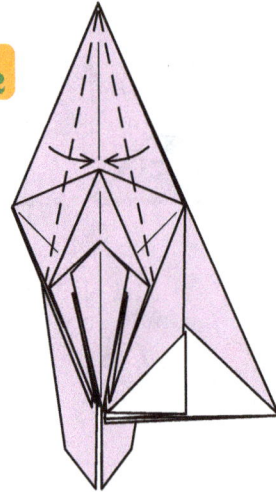

**52**

Fold to the center.

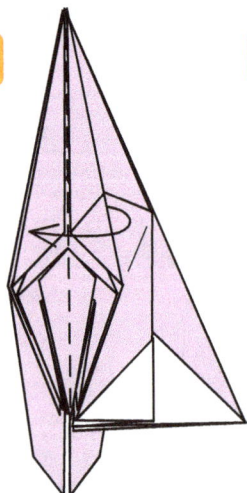

**53**

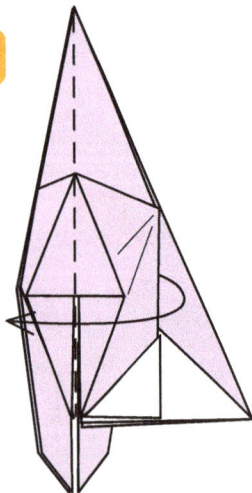

**54**

Repeat steps 38–53 on the right. Rotate 180°.

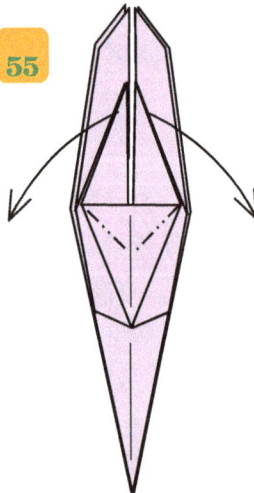

**55**

Reverse-fold all the flaps together. Make small squash folds at the top.

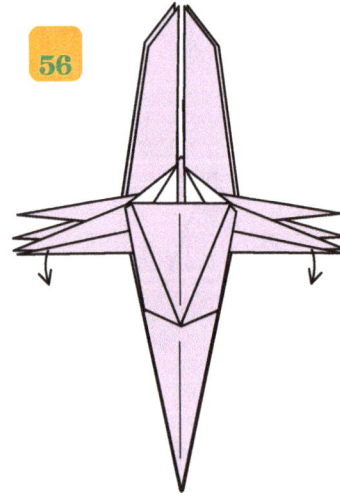

**56**

Slide the thin flaps down.

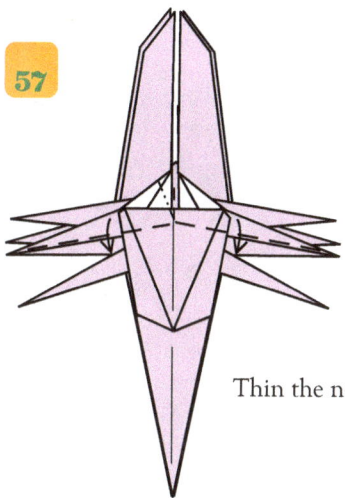

**57**

Thin the next flaps.

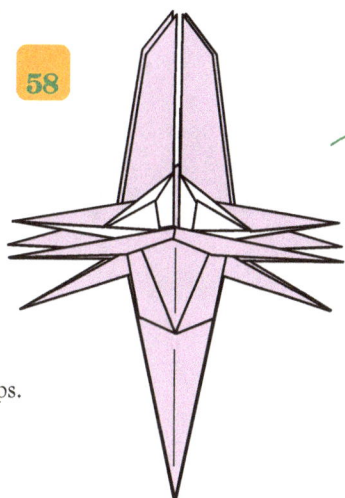

**58**

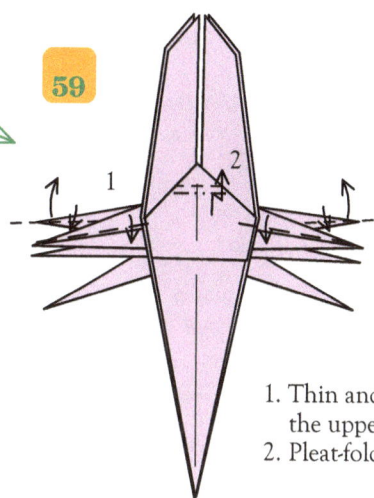

**59**

1. Thin and spread the upper legs.
2. Pleat-fold.

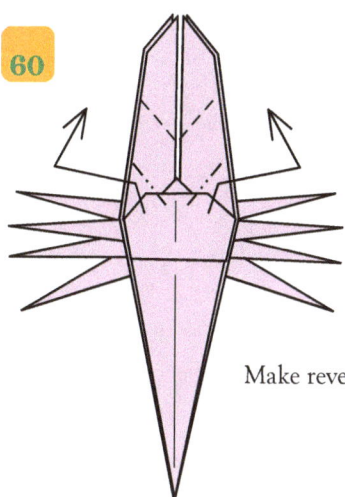

**60**

Make reverse folds.

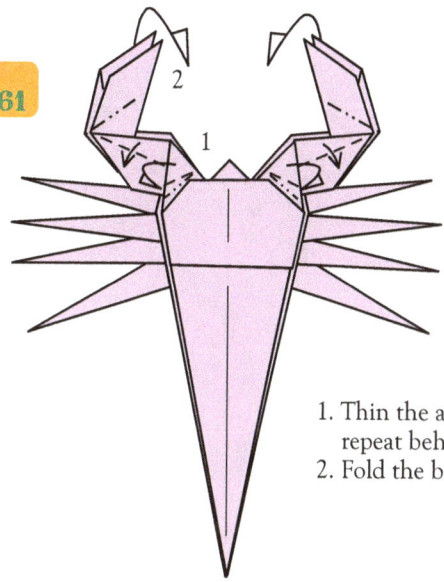

**61**

1. Thin the arms, repeat behind.
2. Fold the bottom layer.

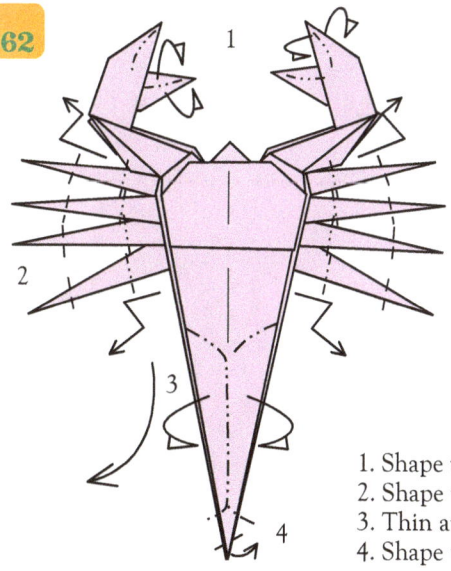

**62**

1. Shape the pinchers.
2. Shape the legs.
3. Thin and curl the tail.
4. Shape the tip of the tail.

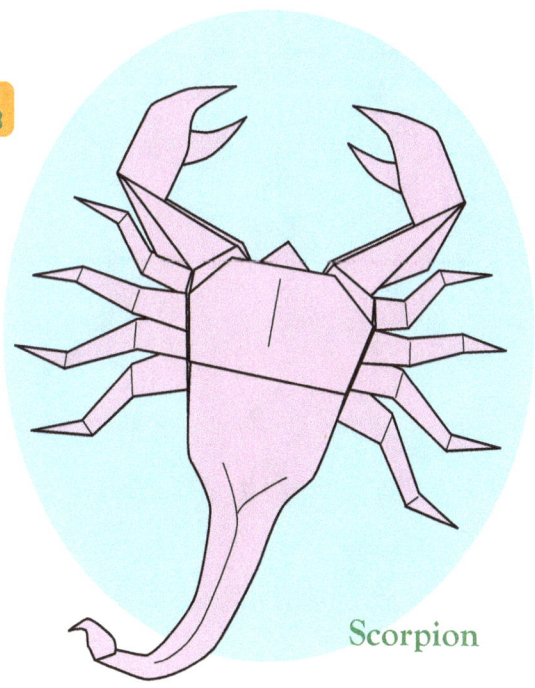

**63**

*Scorpion*

*Scorpion* **127**

www.ingramcontent.com/pod-product-compliance
Lightning Source LLC
Chambersburg PA
CBHW080625030426
42336CB00018B/3084